MANAGING EXTERNAL RELATIONS IN SCHOOLS
AND COLLEGES

MANAGING EXTERNAL RELATIONS IN SCHOOLS AND COLLEGES

Edited by

Jacky Lumby and Nick Foskett

P·C·P
Paul Chapman
Publishing Ltd

First published 1999

 Paul Chapman Publishing Ltd
A SAGE Publications Company
6 Bonhill Street
London EC2A 4PU

SAGE Publications Inc
2455 Teller Road
Thousand Oaks, California 91320

SAGE Publications India Pvt Ltd
32, M-Block Market
Greater Kailash-I
New Delhi 110 948

British Library Cataloguing in Publication data
A catalogue record for this book is available from the British Library

ISBN 1 85396 460 3
ISBN 1 85396 461 1 (pbk)

Library of Congress catalog card number available

Typeset by Anneset Ltd, Weston-super-Mare, Somerset
Printed and bound by Athenaeum Press, Tyne and Wear

A B C D E F 4 3 2 1 0 9

CONTENTS

SERIES EDITOR'S FOREWORD

The emergence of self-governing schools and colleges in many countries in the 1990s has served to enhance the significance of all aspects of management. This is particularly true of external relations because of the importance of developing and sustaining effective links with partners and clients. The vitality, and perhaps the survival, of schools depends on satisfying the demands of students and surrogate students such as parents and funding bodies. As a result, the management of relationships with a wide range of external groups has taken centre stage instead of being a peripheral issue.

The legislation which established self-managing educational institutions has been accompanied by heightened accountability requirements. As well as the disciplines of the market place, schools and colleges have to cope with increased demands for public accountability. These are manifested through regular inspections, the publication of performance data and, for some, the prospect of being 'named and shamed' for poor performance. The twin demands of public and market accountability represent a potentially devastating pincer movement for schools and colleges. Unpopular institutions do not recruit well, particularly amongst the discriminating middle classes, and this has a direct impact on their funding and on their ability to resource improvement. If this produces poor results, it is likely to be accompanied by negative publicity which inevitably leads to a further downturn in recruitment and the prospect of decline leading to closure.

Effective management of external relations is insufficient to reverse such a damaging spiral and will be ineffective if the fundamentals of sound teaching and learning are missing. However, it has a vital role to play as part of a strategy to enhance quality. As the boundary between schools and their communities and stakeholders becomes more permeable, proactive management of relationships with these potential clients and supporters is an essential element in ensuring that perceptions of the institution become, or remain, positive.

The development of effective managers in education requires the support of literature which presents the major issues in clear, intelligible language while drawing on the best of theory and research. The purpose of this series is to examine the management of schools and colleges, drawing on empirical evidence. The approach is analytical rather than descriptive and generates conclusions about the most appropriate ways of managing schools and colleges on the basis of research evidence.

The aim of this series, and of this volume, is to develop a body of literature with the following characteristics:

- Directly relevant to school and college management.
- Prepared by authors with national and international reputations.
- An analytical approach based on empirical evidence but couched in intelligible language.
- Integrating the best of theory, research and practice.

Managing External Relations in Schools and Colleges is the third volume in the series and its underlying rationale is that organisational 'health' depends to a significant extent on the ways in which leaders both represent the school to the community and respond to the requirements of the institution's stakeholders or partners. An inclusive approach to management, involving all with a legitimate interest in the organisation, is an essential part of the process of building a successful school or college. The purpose of this book is to provide insights into the nature of effective external relations as a central dimension of management in education.

Tony Bush
University of Leicester
September 1998

PREFACE

The community of any school or college is at the centre of a web of relationships with individuals and groups, some of which are experienced as personal and frequent while some are formal and periodic. The range of relationships may ripple outwards from parents who visit the infant classroom on a daily basis to the infrequent video conferencing link with a school on another continent. The increase in numbers of those to whom educational organisations must relate is matched by a significant shift in the nature of relationships. The 1980s and 1990s have seen a series of government-led initiatives internationally which have resulted in the 'marketisation' of education. The theoretical greater freedom of choice for parents and students this generates, allied to the link between pupil/student numbers and funding, has led to overt competition between institutions. The environment of each individual institution (its 'micro-market') may intensify or negate the degree of competition, but for many schools and colleges, the relationship with potential and current learners, their families, and with all those groups who may report on their performance, takes on a different significance to the previous era, where the supply of learners and funds was largely stable and secure. Scanning and responding to the external environment is no longer optional for schools and colleges but lies at the heart of ensuring a quality educational provision for pupils/students and surviving as a viable and credible learning organisation.

Though these developments have spanned two decades, still there remain many uncertainties about how educational institutions can manage the boundary between themselves and others, or indeed if such a boundary can any longer be discerned with any clarity. If the primary purpose of the institution is to manage learning, the fact that learning is now likely to take place in the home and the workplace as a lifetime experience has confronted educational managers with the need to rethink the definition of 'external' and take account of permeable borders.

The appropriate response has been seen by many as the adoption of 'marketing', a term common in business but relatively new to most educational institutions. The importing of a marketing philosophy and practice into the non-profit public sector has undoubtedly offered some useful ideas, but can also be dangerously misleading. Its translation to a sector which has social as well as financial aims requires caution. Many schools and colleges have interpreted the term as meaning selling or promotion. This may lead to a focus on attracting potential students and presenting a consistent positive public relations front to all, a stance which can be detrimental to the development of teaching and learning, and has been captured in a number of metaphors such as Hargreaves' 'Kentucky Fried Schooling' or Brighouse's 'bewildering bazaars'.

The pressures leading to such a response, the need to retain or increase student numbers, the frequent and public notice of successes and failures, are understandable, but the premise of this book is that they must be resisted, and that the management of external relations is a strategic responsibility of educational leaders which cannot be relegated to 'bolt-on' publicity and public relations activities. Rather, the primary task is to involve all staff in understanding the needs and wants of the immediate and wider community and to make decisions as to how a response will be shaped. Different imperatives will come into play. With some groups, such as parents, it may be important genuinely to build a sense of community by aligning values. With others, such as employers, the need for exchange and understanding may be uppermost. Other groups, such as the local authority or Ofsted, may require an account.

Such an approach envisages the proactive management of external relations as axiomatic to developing the quality of teaching and learning. The emphasis is on partnership and on enabling others to contribute the full richness of resource of the wider community to the education of learners of all ages. As such, educational leaders do not primarily need specialist expertise in the commercial tenets of marketing, nor extensive investment in glossy communication or 'marketing' staff. What is needed is a commitment to reflective analysis on what it means to be responsive, how the external environment can be understood and engaged, and a consequent refocusing of activities. This agenda is equally relevant across all phases of education.

This volume offers the stimulus for reflective analysis. The first section establishes the context for the management of external relations. Tony Bush examines the way in which external relations can be understood in an international context. David Scott explores the ever-increasing emphasis on accountability. The key concepts of external relations and marketing are placed in the context of strategic management by Nick Foskett. In the final chapter of this section, Valerie Hall explores the shifting tides of competition and partnership, and how far the two may be seen as different approaches. This introductory section establishes the key theoretical concepts which underlie the choices of how to act explored later in the volume.

The second section analyses managing relations with different groups of stakeholders. The different legislative base of schools and further education colleges and the difference in scale, with the latter often providing for many thousands of students, leads to differences in approach. This is reflected in the chapters which focus on one phase only. The first two chapters investigate the impact of legislation and government initiatives on schools and colleges. The number of changes and speed of introduction has demanded exceptional skills of response and these chapters scrutinise how far schools and colleges have managed the process. Keith Foreman uses a small sample of headteachers to establish how the demands of government have been experienced and managed. Jane Hemsley-Brown describes the plethora of initiatives changing the face of further education and their impact on colleges.

Governors are a particularly interesting case, in that they straddle the boundary between the school and the external environment. They are both part of the school and also represent external groups. As such their role is pivotal. The ways in which schools can work with governors are considered by Michael Creese and Peter Earley. Relations with parents are sometimes placed within the formal requirements to communicate and consult on parents evenings and at the annual governors meeting. David Middlewood makes the case for a more holistic and proactive stance, reflecting the international trend of greater expectations of involvement from parents and the potential of a genuine partnership. Reflecting the larger scale of activity in the further education sector, in terms of numbers of students and programmes, Peter Davies explores how colleges can meet the challenge of identifying the needs of so many disparate groups and individuals. If learners are to experience a coherent educational experience and if resources are to be used effectively within the education system as a whole, then working with other educational organisations is significant. Margaret Preedy demonstrates the ways in which collaboration can lead to school improvement and how competitive alliances can work to the advantage of individual organisations. The final group to be considered in this section is employers and business. The first part of the preface argued that there is a curriculum imperative for schools and colleges to use the full range of resource to support learning. The role of employers and business may be particularly critical as a link to wider society. Marianne Coleman explores the mutuality of well-managed relations with employers.

The final section approaches the management of external relations in a more holistic fashion by exploring the processes involved at a strategic level. A choice in relation to the environment depends on a full sense of knowing of what that environment consists. Stephen Waring analyses the ways in which educational organisations can establish systems to sense the external environment. Adopting a proactive stance to managing external relations will involve value judgements. Jacky Lumby explores the concept of responsiveness and argues that managing learning into the twenty-first century will involve an adjustment of values to ensure that relations with interested groups are based on equality and enabling. To conclude, Nick Foskett and Jane Hemsley-Brown turn the focus outwards to suggest ways in which the values and aims of the organisation can be communicated in a way which transcends simplistic promotion and engages the community in the excitement of supporting learning.

Throughout the volume the connection between the management of external relations and teaching and learning is at the heart. If learning is to infiltrate every aspect of our lives, the ways in which schools and colleges manage the permeability of their boundaries and establish a template for a learning organisation is potentially a powerful tool for metamorphosing individual learning organisations into a learning society.

The editors are grateful to all the contributors whose work appears in this volume. Thanks are also due for the advice, support and encouragement of the series editor, Tony Bush, and of Marianne Lagrange of Paul Chapman/Sage Publishing. We would also like to thank Christopher Bowring-Carr for preparing the index. Finally warm appreciation is given to Debbie Simister, Sue Robertson and Joyce Palmer for administrative support and producing the manuscript. We hope that readers of the volume may find the results of these labours as stimulating as we did.

Jacky Lumby and Nick Foskett
October 1998

NOTES ON CONTRIBUTORS

Tony Bush is Professor of Educational Management and Director of the Educational Management Development Unit at the University of Leicester. He was formerly a teacher in secondary schools and colleges and a professional officer with a local education authority. He was Senior Lecturer in Educational Policy and Management at the Open University before joining Leicester in January 1992. He has published extensively on several aspects of educational management. His main recent books are *Managing Autonomous Schools: The Grant Maintained Experience* (with M. Coleman and D. Glover, Paul Chapman, 1993), *The Principles of Educational Management* (with J. West-Burnham, Longman, 1994), *Theories of Educational Management* (Paul Chapman, second edition, 1995) and *Managing People in Education* (with D. Middlewood, Paul Chapman, 1997).

Marianne Coleman has extensive experience in education, mainly teaching in secondary schools, and also working in the advisory service of a large LEA. She is co-author of the book *Managing Autonomous Schools: The Grant Maintained Experience.* She has also published a range of materials as part of the EMDU's distance learning MBA, including *Marketing in Education* and *Women in Educational Management.* She has published articles on gender issues in management and contributed chapters to the widely read *Principles of Educational Management* (T. Bush and West-Burnham, Longman, 1994) and *Managing People in Education* (T. Bush and D. Middlewood, Paul Chapman, 1997). She has also written on the subject of mentoring. She is currently engaged in comparative research projects in China and South Africa.

Michael Creese taught physics before becoming the headteacher of a 13–18 school in his native county of Suffolk. He then moved into governor training and was awarded his doctorate for a thesis on governor–teacher relationships. His book *Effective Governors – Effective Schools; Developing the Partnership* was published in 1995. He now works as a freelance consultant/researcher and has recently concluded research into the role of governors in school improvement. He was a member of the team undertaking research for the DfEE into effective school governance.

Peter Davies is responsible for the management of FEDA-funded and contract research projects involving government departments, national and regional bodies, TECs, and individual colleges. He is also regularly involved in management training and consultancy, and is a member of the team of staff responsible for the delivery of FEDA's specialist Education Management MBA programme. Peter has played a leading role in the development of marketing management expertise in post-16 education for well over ten years, since marketing began to be recognised as a necessary activity for colleges. He is the joint author (with Keith Scribbins) of the first book on educational marketing to be published in the UK, *Marketing Further and Higher Education* (Longman, 1985), and has since written numerous articles and papers within the same field. He was instrumental in establishing the Marketing Network, the professional forum for marketing personnel in post-16 education, and has been a member of its Steering Group since its inception in 1987.

Peter Earley was a school teacher originally. He then worked for ten years at the National Foundation for Educational Research undertaking a number of projects in the areas of educational management, governance and professional development. He is currently a Senior Lecturer in the Management Development Centre at the Institute of Education, University of London, where he is also an Associate Director of the International School Effectiveness and Improvement Centre. He is currently researching school governing bodies and their role in school improvement. His most recent publications include *Improvement through Inspection? Complementary Approaches to School Development* (edited with B. Fidler and J. Ouston and published by David Fulton in 1996), and *School Improvement After Inspection? School and LEA Responses* (Paul Chapman, 1998).

Keith Foreman OBE was the principal of two community colleges in Cambridgeshire and Leicestershire before joining the Educational Management Development Unit of Leicester University in 1994 as Senior Tutor. He is a consultant to schools and LEAs, and was a member of the DES School Management Task Force from 1989 to 1992. His research interests lie in the broad field of school leadership, but much of his time currently is taken up with HEADLAMP and NPQH.

Nick Foskett is Senior Lecturer in Education at the University of Southampton, and Director of the Centre for Research in Education Marketing (CREM). His research is in the field of marketing in all sectors of education, and he has published extensively in relation to organisational systems developed by schools and colleges for marketing and also in relation to educational choice and decision-making by pupils and parents. Recent publications include *Managing External Relations in Schools*, an edited volume for Routledge (1992), and *Career Perceptions and Decision-making in Schools and Colleges*, a national survey of 'buyer behaviour' in education for Heist (1997).

Valerie Hall was formerly Reader in Education in the Graduate School of Education, University of Bristol. She has been a teacher and researcher in schools, further, higher and adult education for over thirty years. Throughout her career she has had a particular interest in the relationship between experience of work and personal biography, social context and adult learning processes. Her research on teaching, managing and leading in education has resulted in a number of publications, including her latest book *Dancing on the Ceiling*, which is study of women headteachers.

Jane Hemsley-Brown is Senior Research Fellow in the Centre for Research in Education Marketing (CREM) in the Research and Graduate School of Education, University of Southampton. Her background is in teaching, having taught in schools and colleges for over twenty years. She has worked on national research programmes, including career perceptions and student decision-making, and pupil awareness and understanding of higher education and its impact on education choices. Prior to joining CREM in 1997 she worked at the University of Greenwich as Research Fellow in Post Compulsory Education and Training.

Jacky Lumby is a Lecturer in Educational Management at the Educational Management Development Unit at Leicester University. She has previously taught in a range of educational settings, including schools, community and further education. Prior to joining Leicester University, she worked in a Training and Enterprise Council with responsibility for the development of managers in both business and education. Current projects include research in the management of vocational education in China and in South Africa. She has published articles on the management of the curriculum and the development of managers in the further education sector and also on strategic planning in colleges. She has published within EMDU's distance learning MBA and was a contributor to the first volume in this series, *Managing People in Education* (T. Bush and D. Middlewood, 1997) and joint editor of the second volume, *Strategic Management in Schools and Colleges*.

David Middlewood is a Senior Tutor in Educational Management and Director of School- and College-based Programmes at the Educational Management Development Unit of the University of Leicester. He taught in schools and community colleges for twenty-five years, including nine years as a headteacher, before joining Leicester University in 1990. His special interests are appraisal (in which he has extensive research experience), staff selection and development and management structures. His publications include work on appraisal, human resources and development planning, and most recently *Managing People in Education* (1997, with Tony Bush), the first volume in this series, and *Strategic Management in Schools and Colleges* (with Jacky Lumby), the second volume. Current research involves human resource management in South African schools, and teacher appraisal in New Zealand.

Margaret Preedy is a Lecturer in the Centre for Educational Policy and Management, School of Education, The Open University. Her recent publications include: *Educational Management: Strategy, Quality and Resources* (1997, with R. Glatter and R. Levacic, eds.) and *Organisational Effectiveness and Improvement in Education* (1997, with A. Harris and N. Bennett, eds.).

David Scott is a Lecturer in Educational Research Methods at the London University Institute of Education. He has carried out a number of research projects, in the fields of race, examinations, early childhood literacy and libraries. He has published some 40 articles in academic journals and chapters in books. He has written *Reading Research Texts* (Falmer Press), *Educational Research: Epistemology and Social Theory* (Falmer Press), *Researching Education: Data, Methods and Theory in Educational Enquiry* (Cassell) with Robin Usher, and edited *Effective Health Promotion: Evaluating Health Initiatives and Interventions* (Stanley Thornes Ltd) with Ros Weston, *Values and Educational Research* (Bedford Way Papers), *Understanding Educational Research* (Routledge) with Robin Usher, and *Accountability and Control in Educational Settings* (Cassell). He is the current editor of the *Curriculum Journal*.

Stephen Waring is Director of Corporate Services at Salisbury College of Further Education, where he is responsible for marketing and external relations. Previously Marketing Manager at Totton Sixth Form College in Southampton, he also spent twelve years teaching in Inner London comprehensive schools and in adult education. He was an Associate Lecturer of the Open University until 1997. His published work includes research into school governing bodies, as well as articles on marketing, teacher training, and equal opportunities.

GLOSSARY OF TERMS

AGIT	Action for Governors Information and Training
CAD/CAM	Computer aided design/computer aided manufacture
CBI	Confederation of British Industry
CBMA	College Business Managers Association
CEO	Community and Enterprise Office
CERI	Centre for Educational Research and Innovation
CTC	City technology college
DES	Department of Education and Science
DfEE	Department for Education and Employment
DLE	Demand-led element (of FEFC funding)
EAZ	Education action zone
EBP	Education Business Partnership
ERA	Education Reform Act (1988)
ESF	European Social Fund
FAS	Funding Agency for Schools
FE	Further education
FEDA	Further Education Development Agency
FEFC	Further Education Funding Council
FEU	Further Education Unit
GCSE	General Certificate of Secondary Education
GM	Grant maintained
GNVQ	General National Vocational Qualification
HEADLAMP	Headteacher Leadership and Management Programme
HEI	Higher education institution
ICT	Information and communication technology
IES	Institute of Employment Studies
INSET	In-service education and training (of teachers)
IT	Information technology
KS	Key Stage (of the curriculum)
LEA	Local education authority
LMA	Labour market assessment
LMI	Labour market information
LMS	Local management of schools
MSC	Manpower Services Commission
NACETT	National Advisory Council for Education and Training Targets

NAO	National Audit Office
NC	National Curriculum
NCC	National Curriculum Council
NEDO	National Economic Development Office
NFER	National Foundation for Educational Research
NPQH	National Professional Qualification for Headship
NQT	Newly qualified teacher
NTET	National Targets for Education and Training
NVQ	National Vocational Qualification
OECD	Organisation for Economic Co-operation and Development
PANDAS	Performance and Assessment Data
PASCI	Parental and School Choice Interaction Study
PFI	Private Finance Initiative
PI	Performance indicator
QCA	Qualifications and Curriculum Authority
QPID	Quality and Performance Improvement Division
SCIP	School Curriculum Industry Partnership
SDP	School development plan
SEN	Special education needs
SME	Small and medium-sized enterprises
SMT	Senior Management Team
SOC	Standard Occupational Qualification
SWOT	Strengths, weaknesses, opportunities and threats
TEC	Training and Enterprise Council
TES	*Times Educational Supplement*
THES	*Times Higher Education Supplement*
TNA	Training needs analysis
TQM	Total quality management
TTA	Teacher Training Agency
TUC	Trades Union Council
TVEI	Technical and vocational education initiative

Section I: Setting the Context

THE VANISHING BOUNDARIES: THE IMPORTANCE OF EFFECTIVE EXTERNAL RELATIONS

Tony Bush

INTRODUCTION: THE CHANGING CONTEXT

The growing importance of external relations

The external dimensions of school and college management have become more prominent during the 1990s. In previous decades it was rare for schools, in particular, to accord centrality to relationships with bodies and individuals beyond the boundary.

The traditional approach to outside groups was 'hands off', a stance apparently designed to maintain 'distance' between the institution and its clients. This was typified by the former practice of many primary schools which sought to separate the roles of parents and teachers by notices such as 'Parents: leave your children here', strategically placed at the school entrance.

By 1989, Sayer was able to detect a changing climate:

> The relationship of school and context was formerly a grey area, an extension of normal school organisation, little considered and less esteemed in the practice of schooling. It is now quite clearly and starkly the priority for future development in both the practice and the theory of management.
>
> (Sayer, 1989, p. 3)

Subsequently, the National Association of Head Teachers signalled the need for a new approach:

> Schools can no longer operate in isolation. The expectations of society, whether expressed by individual parents, identifiable groups, or government legislation, mean that schools need to be aware of views being expressed. They must take account of the public perceptions of how well they are performing and be prepared to respond to those articulated concerns which are genuinely representative.
>
> (quoted in Bagley, Woods and Glatter, 1996, p. 125)

The new climate was attributable largely to the impact of the Education Reform Act in England and Wales and a parallel shift to self-management in many other countries.

The impact of self-management

Schools and colleges have traditionally been controlled by national, regional or local governments which have determined or strongly influenced their character, funding and curriculum. This pattern was increasingly challenged in the 1980s as the post-war educational 'honeymoon' came to an end in many western countries because their former economic dominance was usurped by the success of Pacific Rim countries:

> In the USA, better educational productivity has become a national imperative because of the challenge we face in international competitiveness and the demands upon our national economy and workforce.
>
> (Boyd, 1997, p. 7)

The response to these economic pressures was to look for models from the private sector and seek to create self-managing units. This approach was reinforced by the ideological position of many governments, including the Thatcher-led Conservative administration in the UK. Their belief was that greater exposure to the discipline of the market place would serve to raise standards. The result was far-reaching educational change which one commentator on the New Zealand system (Holdaway, 1989) described as 'the earthquake approach to educational reform (shake everything up at once)' (quoted in Barrington, 1997, p. 148).

The aim was to make schools and colleges much more responsive to their clients by linking their funding to pupil and student numbers. This approach forces a closer relationship between organisations and their environments, a process described as 'resource dependency' by Hoy and Miskel (1989):

> Resource dependency theory views environment in terms of relative scarcity of resources ... if the school organisation cannot accomplish its goals without the resources controlled by the other organisation and is unable to secure

them elsewhere, the school organisation becomes dependent on the second organisation.

(Hoy and Miskel, 1989, pp. 36–37)

For self-managing schools and colleges, this dependence is on the decisions of hundreds of students, and parents as surrogate students, to 'purchase' education at their institution. School income is directly dependent on their collective decisions. The intention of policy-makers was 'to produce a shift in power from the producer to the consumer of services' (Harris, 1992, p. 110), a process which also dictated a sea-change in the importance of external relations for most schools. In England and Wales colleges have always been more dependent on student choice because they serve a post-compulsory market but their former links with local education authorities (LEAs) provided a measure of predictability which was greatly reduced with incorporation in 1993.

Fully-subscribed schools are able to thrive in the new climate but even they do not have unfettered power to determine their own future. As Bullock and Thomas (1997, p. 117) emphasise, 'the freedom schools have to make their own spending decisions, for example, is contingent upon it being used responsibly'. For undersubscribed schools, the need to be responsive to potential clients is palpable. Their very survival may depend on changing the public perception of the school so that it becomes more attractive to parents.

Colleges in England are further constrained by the strong role of the Further Education Funding Council (FEFC). While income levels are largely determined by student recruitment and retention, it is the FEFC which determines the criteria for funding, including the formulae. Randle and Brady (1997) claim that the FEFC is the dominant influence on the nature and scale of further education:

> In reality, therefore, further education is largely controlled by central government through this agency. Funding for educational provision is dependent on the college fulfilling certain performance targets ... it could be argued that it has driven the scale, shape and pace of change in the FE system in England since incorporation.

(Randle and Brady, 1997, p. 123)

The further education case serves to emphasise the precarious nature of self-management. Institutions can remain 'independent' only by meeting the needs of clients, whether students or parents seeking places or government bodies requiring adherence to national norms. Responsiveness is the vital element in effective management and this can be achieved only by an explicit external relations policy.

The range and variety of relationships

The advent of self-management has greatly increased the number and range of external links to be developed and maintained by schools and colleges. In England and Wales, these may be categorised as follows:

- formal relationships, including governing bodies
- funding relationships, including FEFC, local education authorities (LEAs), the Funding Agency for Schools (FAS) and bodies paying for specific services; for example, employers contracting with colleges for particular courses
- client relationships, including parents, students and feeder schools
- inspection, including Ofsted and FEFC;
- community relationships, including business and industry, and the local media.

These specific links are examined in subsequent chapters of this volume.

Defining the boundary

The notion of 'external' relations assumes a 'boundary' between the institution and its environment. Activities and people inside the boundary may be regarded as 'internal' to the organisation while those which are outside are deemed to be external. This distinction is clear at the conceptual level but it is blurred in practice; Glatter (1989, p. 2) describes it as 'arbitrary' and 'misleading'. Bolman and Deal (1989) also refer to the artificiality of the boundary in their definition of the external environment:

> Environment is typically seen as everything outside the boundaries of an organisation, even though the boundaries are often nebulous and poorly drawn. It is the environment that provides raw materials to an organisation and receives the organisation's outputs . . . Schools receive students from the local community and later return graduates to the community.
>
> (Bolman and Deal, 1989, p. 24)

The concept of boundary may be particularly ambiguous in explaining the position of governors. The legislation of the 1980s and 1990s has given governing bodies substantial formal authority to oversee the activities of schools and colleges. This would suggest a strong internal role. Radnor, Ball and Vincent (1997, p. 214), for example, argue that they 'could be described as "incorporated" into the school, not as external to it'. However, governing bodies are also a representative forum for the main external interests, including parents, employers, LEAs and the local community. In this sense, they appear to straddle the boundary, providing a conduit between the school or college and its environment. It is perhaps this dual role of formal authority and representation that best illustrates the uncertainty over the notion of the boundary. There is also a parallel issue about the permeability of the boundary and we shall examine this question in the next section.

CONCEPTUALISING EXTERNAL RELATIONS

Open systems theory

When schools operated an 'arms length' policy in relation to external bodies, they could be characterised as 'closed systems', seeking to minimise transactions with the environment. 'Closed systems are static or deterministic in their relations with the environment and in the interaction of their component parts. Their boundaries are set and tend to resist penetration' (Landers and Myers, 1977, p. 398).

The shift to self-management, and the associated requirement to interact closely with many groups and individuals, made it much more difficult for institutions to sustain a closed systems approach, as Boyd (1997) stresses in respect of the USA:

> The increasing environmental turbulence and external challenges to educational organizations ... showed that the closed system ... approach was inadequate for understanding or dealing with the most pressing problems of school administrators ... .Failing the test of practical relevance, the closed system model was abandoned and the search was on for more useful models.
>
> (Boyd, 1997, p. 10)

The alternative theory, identified by Boyd and others, was that of 'open systems' which assumes permeable boundaries and an interactive two-way relationship between schools and colleges and their environments:

> As a result of the search for more practically relevant models, organisations such as school systems are now viewed as open systems, which must adapt to changing external conditions to be effective and, in the long term, survive. The open-system concept highlights the vulnerability and interdependence of organisations and their environments.
>
> (Hoy and Miskel, 1989, p. 29)

The resource dependency referred to earlier (see page 4), means that external groups may be able to constrain the activities of the school. The problem is that these demands may conflict and school managers have to decide how to respond to these differing requirements in the light of their own values and strategic aims. Open systems theory assumes multiple and wide-ranging links across an increasingly permeable boundary but organisations are able to influence their environment and are not simply prisoners of external groups.

'Wild' environments

The climate of educational management in the late 1990s is very different from that of the previous decade. As we noted earlier, the Education Reform Act, and similar legislation in other countries, forced schools into the market place. The close link between success in recruiting students and pupils and income levels means that leaders of schools and colleges have to work hard to ensure their popularity with potential students and parents (Bush, 1995).

The shift from catchment areas to parental preference as the main determinant of school admissions illustrates Carlson's (1975) distinction between 'wild' and 'domesticated' organisations. When schools had clearly delineated catchment areas they could be regarded as 'domestic' organisations, protected from their environment:

> There is no struggle for survival for this type of organisation. Like the domesticated animal, these organisations are fed and cared for. Existence is guaranteed ... funds are not closely tied to quality of performance. These organisations are domesticated in the sense that they are protected by the society they serve.
>
> (Carlson, 1975, p. 191)

The new emphasis on parental choice and formula funding means that schools now match Carlson's description of 'wild' organisations which:

> do struggle for survival. Their existence is not guaranteed, and they do cease to exist. Support for them is closely tied to quality of performance, and a steady flow of clients is not assured. Wild organisations are not protected at vulnerable points as are domesticated organisations.
>
> (Carlson, 1975, p. 191)

Colleges have long been required to compete in the market place but this is a relatively new phenomenon for schools which might have been regarded as 'domesticated' until the legislative changes of the 1980s and 1990s. Now both schools and colleges exhibit many of the characteristics of 'wild' organisations, with their survival dependent on their ability to attract sufficient numbers of new clients (Bush, 1995).

Accountability

The advent of self-management has been accompanied by heightened accountability requirements for schools and colleges. Their autonomy is limited by the need to be answerable to a wide range of external bodies. Boyd (1997) shows that this is an international phenomenon:

> In many nations, schools are under a kind of scrutiny unknown in the past, as the demand for better results and more efficient use of resources keeps intensifying ... It's no accident, then, that school heads are retiring at a

record pace and that the job of school administrators has become more stressful and less attractive . . . in many nations, including the USA, Australia and Canada.

(Boyd, 1997, pp. 12–13)

MacPherson (1995, p. 475) traces the background to the concept of accountability and its application to education, arguing that 'the demand for accountability is intensifying and it takes many forms'. This emphasis is illustrated by the decision of the Teacher Training Agency (TTA) to include accountability as one of the compulsory elements of its National Professional Qualification for Headship (NPQH).

Scott (1989) distinguishes between accountability and responsiveness, claiming that the latter is arrived at freely while accountability is imposed:

> Responsiveness describes the willingness of an institution – or, indeed an individual – to respond on its or their own initiative, i.e. the capacity to be open to outside impulses and new ideas. Accountability, in contrast, describes the submission of the institution or individual to a form of external audit, its capacity to account for its or their own performance.
>
> (Scott, 1989, p. 17)

Scott's definition suggests a 'tough' interpretation of accountability and this view is also taken by Kogan (1984) whose analysis remains the best treatment of this important concept. His definition stresses the power of those demanding accountability:

> a condition in which individual role holders are liable to review and the application of sanctions if their actions fail to satisfy those with whom they are in an accountability relationship.
>
> (Kogan, 1984, p. 25)

The reference to 'sanctions' is important because they provide the 'teeth' for those seeking answers from schools and colleges. Sanctions in England and Wales include 'naming and shaming' underperforming schools and parents choosing other schools for their children or 'voicing' (Westoby, 1989) their complaints about actions by the school or its staff.

A full treatment of accountability may be found in Chapter 2.

Marketing

The shift to self-managing schools, and the concomitant requirement to compete with other institutions for students, means that effective marketing has become much more important for the success and vitality of schools. The increased emphasis on external relations, and the permeability of boundaries, means that education managers cannot ignore the need to market their institutions:

There is little doubt that increased competition has led to more consideration throughout the country's schools and colleges of the wishes and interests
of customers and their parents and employers.

(Gray, 1991, p. 9)

Bagley, Woods and Glatter (1996) point to the legislative imperatives
underpinning the shift to a quasi-market in education and explain the
rationale for increased competition between schools:

[There is] a great deal of emphasis on market forces as a means of improving education and giving parents more influence ... One of the intended
benefits of increased competition and choice is to motivate schools to
develop a closer relationship with parents as consumers in the educational
quasi-market ... schools will raise standards and become more 'customer
responsive' in order to compete for parental custom and to maintain or
increase pupil numbers, with good schools growing and bad ones closing.

(Bagley, Woods and Glatter, 1996, p. 126)

Similar trends are apparent in further education. While colleges have
always been more conscious of the market than schools, partly because
they serve the post-compulsory sector, there has been a heightened emphasis on the student as customer during the 1990s. Randle and Brady (1997,
p. 132) refer to the development of 'a customer/supplier relationship' and
express concern about 'the implications for lecturer control over the labour
process', a phrase which already seems old-fashioned in an era when
learning is stressed rather than teaching or 'control'.

Longhurst (1996) also discusses the concept of student as customer but
links it to the role of the FEFC:

Students as consumers do not exercise the monetary purchasing power
which is a normal feature of markets for commodities ... the reality of the
situation is that the FEFC is acting as surrogate purchaser for students ...
it is students who choose what course they will study and where; then the
FEFC picks up the tab at a price set by the FEFC.

(Longhurst, 1996, p. 53)

This comment illustrates the complex nature of the market in education
where the consumer does not pay for the service at 'the point of sale'
although they contribute to the cost through taxation. This means that
schools and colleges have to market themselves to the surrogate pur-
chasers as well as to students and parents.

The Institute of Marketing defines marketing as 'a management process
responsible for anticipating, identifying and then satisfying consumer
wants and needs with a view to making a profit' (quoted in Gray, 1991,
p. 2). Gray stresses the link between marketing and the concept of customers:

Services such as the education service are particularly vulnerable when they
fail to listen to their customers ... educational organisations need to reflect
upon their relationships with customers and those who sponsor customers,

starting from the recognition that those who use their services are customers with needs, rights and expectations.

(Gray, 1991, p. 2)

The development of a quasi-market has heightened awareness of the need for marketing without producing clear marketing plans in most schools although colleges are generally more effective in this regard. We shall return to the need for a marketing strategy in the final section of this chapter while the topic is given an extended treatment in Chapter 3.

STRATEGIES FOR EXTERNAL RELATIONS

Adopting a proactive approach

The growing importance of external relations suggests that schools and colleges should become proactive in relation to the environment and not simply respond to external demands. Hoy and Miskel (1989) argue that educational institutions should attempt to gain a measure of control:

> School organizations have the ability to define or enact their own environments . . . [they] do not have to be simple passive instruments of the external environment. Both internal and external coping strategies can be used to buffer environmental influences and actually to change the demands.
>
> (Hoy and Miskel, 1989, pp. 39 and 43–4)

This may require a fundamental change in the stance of the organisation, with external relations linked to the values and strategies of the school and college. Management needs to extend beyond the boundary to encompass the institution's stakeholders, those who have a legitimate interest in the way the school operates. Davies and Ellison (1997) claim that this requires a cultural change:

> The key shift in management is to develop a culture in the school which is outward-looking, client-focused and responsive to change. Staff, taking the lead from the senior management in the school, need to direct some of their in-service or professional development time to discussing broader strategic issues as well as current operational ones.
>
> (Davies and Ellison, 1997, p. 54)

Building partnerships with stakeholders

An important element of a strategic approach to external relations is to build partnerships with stakeholders. Governors and parents have an obvious stake in the school while local employers and other community representatives may have a legitimate interest. Hallinger and Heck (1998) show that the active involvement of stakeholders is a positive feature of successful schools:

> Several studies across a variety of national contexts indicated that more involvement from a variety of stakeholders in decision-making is character-istic of higher-producing schools . . . the principal [acts] as a boundary spon-sor, constantly seeking ways to involve community members.
>
> (Hallinger and Heck, 1998, pp.13–17)

Evidence of a growing appreciation of the need to build partnerships comes from the research of Radnor, Ball and Vincent (1997) who quote a secondary school head:

> I am listening to the market, and certainly the concept of self-governing schools where there is ownership by the community, by the community around the school, I don't mean the community 40 miles away, I genuinely believe that is the way forward . . . there are new partnerships which were not there to the same standard before.
>
> (Radnor, Ball and Vincent 1997, p. 220)

Partnerships with members of the governing body are particularly impor-tant. This is partly because they have the formal authority to oversee the activities of the school but even more significant is their role as the con-duit between the institution and its environment. Because the governing body represents the main stakeholders, a positive relationship is a vital element in building and sustaining the organisation's reputation.

Developing good relationships with parents, individually and collec-tive, is also an essential aspect of an external relations strategy. Bagley, Woods and Glatter (1996) echo Hallinger and Heck (1998) in pointing to the evidence linking parental involvement to school effectiveness and this goes beyond supporting their own child's learning to a wider association with the aims of the school.

These examples illustrate a philosophical stance that places schools and colleges at the heart of their communities, seeking and welcoming involve-ment for the benefit of pupils and students and to build the reputation of the institution.

Marketing and reputation management

All organisations have a reputation in their communities and this may be national or even international in some cases. This is most evident with large companies which have well-known brand names but may also apply to schools and colleges. Whatever the merits of national league tables, and the media interest in results, they do have the effect of making schools famous or notorious according to their performance on these criteria. Educational institutions may also earn a reputation because of their sporting or cultural achievements or as a result of the activities of their students or alumni.

The reputation of the school arises whether or not managers seek to develop it. A passive approach to this issue does not prevent an image of the organisation being held by people who know, or become aware of, its activities. Reputation management provides the prospect of the favourable aspects of the school being broadcast while a 'do nothing' stance may result in only negative images being projected in the community.

Marketing is the key element in a strategy to maintain and enhance the reputation of the school or college. Gray (1991) links marketing to a wider concern for customers and points to its centrality within the institution's overall strategy:

> A marketing orientation in an educational organisation is . . . one in which the interests and needs of the pupil or student as customer are central. Other clients – notably employers and parents – are also recognised, and due attention is given to their concerns and needs. These needs are regarded as the central reason for the organisation's existence, and are recognised as even more important than the needs of the enterprise's staff or owners.
>
> (Gray, 1991, p. 27)

Gray goes on to suggest that market knowledge is essential before the marketing strategy or plan can be developed, suggesting the need for effective market research. Colleges, for example, may consult employers or schools before deciding whether to introduce a new course or to modify an existing programme. A broader approach would be to conduct an audit of the attitudes of stakeholders to the institution as a step towards a more fundamental re-appraisal of the purpose of the organisation.

Internal marketing is a vital aspect of reputation management. Staff and students are potentially powerful advocates of the school or college in the community but will communicate positively about the institution only if they understand the mission of the organisation and, just as important, believe in it. Gray (1991, p. 33) describes this as 'selling the job to employees before an organisation can sell its services to customers'. He emphasises that internal marketing should include support staff as well as teachers:

> A marketing perspective should heighten teaching and non-teaching staff awareness of their roles in marketing the school services from the office, reception desk, telephone switchboard and the caretaker's office, as well as from the classroom.
>
> (Gray, 1991, p. 33)

There is evidence (James and Phillips, 1995) of increased awareness of the importance of reputation management but this aspect needs to be integrated into a coherent strategy for managing external relations.

EXTERNAL RELATIONS AND STRATEGIC MANAGEMENT

The increasing importance of external relations means that it has become a central element of strategic management for many schools and colleges and arguably should become so for all of them. What Hargreaves (1997) refers to as a fragmented education system means that the distinction between schools and colleges and their environments will become blurred. The boundaries will vanish as stakeholders increase their influence and learning is no longer confined to formal educational establishments; not least because of the growing importance of information and communications technology:

> It will become more difficult over the next 25 years to talk about 'the education system' in the sense of a distinctive, coherent and (state) managed system: in its place, what counts as education will merge with other social institutions whose boundaries are also melting – households, workplaces, religious centres.
>
> (Hargreaves, 1997, p. 11)

The three key aspects of an external relations strategy are 'scanning', the creation of specific management roles responsible for marketing, and environmental management strategies.

Scanning

Bagley, Woods and Glatter (1996) define scanning in terms of how, if at all, schools conduct activities aimed at knowing more about their environment. They identify the following examples:

- a one-off public opinion survey conducted by pupils using a questionnaire with members of the public in the town centre
- questionnaires to prospective parents at local primary schools.

Some of the schools did not engage in any scanning of parental or community perspectives. In respect of one school, Bagley, Woods and Glatter (1996, p. 33) comment that 'the relationship is still a top-down one, with the school convincing parents what it believes it is in their best interest to have'.

It is evident from this research that few schools accept Davies and Ellison's (1997) precept that they should engage in three levels of environmental scanning: global, national and local. They prefer to focus on promoting what they value rather than establishing the wishes of clients and prospective clients.

Foskett (in Chapter 3 of this volume) shows how the new headteacher of a village junior school used scanning as one of a raft of initiatives to improve the reputation of the school. The effect of this strategy was to increase pupil numbers by 40 per cent over three years.

Marketing roles

The second aspect of external relations strategy is to establish roles responsible for marketing. Hoy and Miskel (1989) stress that this is one way for organisations to manage the uncertainties arising from a turbulent environment:

> Creating internal roles that span organisational boundaries to link the school district with elements in the external environment is also an important strategy for coping with uncertainty and dependence. Two classes of functions are typically performed by boundary-spanning roles: to detect information about changes in the external environment and to represent the organisation to the environment.
>
> (Hoy and Miskel, 1989, pp. 39–40)

It is evident from the research of James and Phillips (1995, p. 85) that schools have a long way to go to develop the approach discussed by Hoy and Miskel. 'In none of the schools did anyone other than the headteacher have explicit responsibility for marketing.' Given the other pressures facing heads, this seems an inadequate way to address this important issue and suggests that schools, if not colleges, are still ambivalent about marketing, or even complacent about the need to enhance their reputation. This low-key stance may be unsustainable if external pressures on schools and colleges continue to mount.

Managing the environment

The third element in an external relations strategy is to develop and implement clear policies for relationships with external groups. Explicit plans for all aspects of environmental management are important if schools and colleges are to thrive in an era of mutual dependence. 'Environmental management strategies require broad-based planning and action. These strategies are tools that aid leaders in adapting to their environments and in modifying themselves to thrive in a given environment' (Goldring, 1997, p. 290).

Goldring (1997) identifies three broad strategies for managing the environment:

1. *Strategies aimed at reducing dependencies.* These strategies are directed at increasing the organisation's independence in relation to the environment. It may involve competing for additional sources of funding,

developing public relations strategies to enhance prestige, or reducing environmental influences through 'buffering'.

2. *Strategies aimed at environmental adaptation.* These strategies generally require the organisation to relinquish some autonomy in order to adjust to the environment. External groups may be 'co-opted' into the organisation or may form part of a coalition with the school to achieve common goals.

3. *Strategies aimed at redefining environments.* Environmental leaders may employ strategies to change the nature of the environment. This may involve targeting a different clientele or 'socialising' certain groups to accept the norms and values of the organisation.

These strategies are not mutually exclusive and leaders may employ one or more approaches at the same time. Using the intelligence acquired from 'scanning', leaders seek to use the most appropriate strategies based on situational analysis. In attempting to manage the environment for the benefit of students and staff, principals should ensure that they do not neglect internal management. Brighouse (1992, p. 217) claims that 'many leaders have lost their internal grip by becoming enchanted and preoccupied with the external'. In developing effective strategies for managing external relations, leaders should remember that the purpose of education is learning not marketing or reputation management.

CONCLUSION

The emergence of self-managing schools and colleges in many countries has given an enhanced value to the management of external relations. The reputation, the funding, and perhaps the very survival, of institutions depends on building and maintaining successful links with customers and surrogate customers such as parents and funding bodies. This increased dependence means that the notion of a 'boundary' between schools and their environments is increasingly difficult to sustain. Accordingly, educational institutions are being characterised as 'open systems' with permeable boundaries.

Effective leaders adopt a proactive approach to external relations through building partnerships with stakeholders, scanning the environment to anticipate and plan for change, and ensuring that marketing is an integral part of the organisation's strategic approach. The growing body of evidence showing that successful schools are those with an inclusive approach, involving all stakeholders, means that external relations must be a central aspect of management for educational institutions.

REFERENCES

Bagley, C., Woods, P. and Glatter, R. (1996) Scanning the market: school strategies for discovering parental perspectives, *Educational Management and Administration*, Vol. 24, no. 2, pp. 125–38.

Barrington, J. (1997) School governance in New Zealand: innovative change and persistent dilemmas, *International Studies in Educational Administration*, Vol. 25, no. 2, pp. 148–55.

Bolman, L. and Deal, T. (1989) Organisations, technology and environment, in R. Glatter (ed.), *Educational Institutions and their Environments: Managing the Boundaries*, Milton Keynes: Open University Press.

Boyd, W. (1997) Environmental pressures and competing paradigms in educational management, *ESRC Seminar Series Paper*, Leicester, June.

Brighouse, T. (1992) External relations and the future, in N. Foskett (ed.) *Managing External Relations in Schools*, London: Routledge.

Bullock, A. and Thomas, H. (1997) *Schools at the Centre? A Study of Decentralisation*, London: Routledge.

Bush, T. (1995) *Theories of Educational Management*, 2nd edition, London: Paul Chapman.

Carlson, R. (1975) Environmental constraints and organisational consequences: the public school and its clients, in J. Baldridge and T. Deal (eds.) *Managing Change in Educational Organisations*, Berkeley: McCutchan.

Davies, B. and Ellison, L. (1997) *Strategic Marketing for Schools*, London: Pitman.

Glatter, R. (1989) Introduction: coping with a new climate, in R. Glatter (ed.) *Educational Institutions and their Environments: Managing the Boundaries*, Milton Keynes: Open University Press.

Goldring, E. (1997) Educational leadership: schools, environments and boundary spanning, in M. Preedy, R. Glatter. and R. Levacic (eds.) *Educational Management: Strategy, Quality and Resources*, Buckingham: Open University Press.

Gray, L. (1991) *Marketing Education*, Buckingham: Open University Press.

Hallinger, P. and Heck, R. (1998) Can leadership enhance school effectiveness? *ESRC Seminar Series Paper*, Milton Keynes, June.

Hargreaves, D. (1997) A road to the learning society, *School Leadership and Management*, Vol. 17, no. 1, pp. 9–21.

Harris, N. (1992) Quality control and accountability to the consumer: an evaluation of the Education (Schools) Act 1992, *Education and the Law*, Vol. 4, No. 3, pp. 109–121.

Holdaway, T. (1989) An outsider's view of tomorrow's schools, *New Zealand Journal of Educational Administration*, Vol. 4, November, pp. 35–40.

Hoy, W. and Miskel, C. (1989) Schools and their external environments, in R. Glatter (ed.) *Educational Institutions and their Environments: Managing the Boundaries*, Milton Keynes: Open University Press.

James, C. and Phillips, P. (1995) The practice of educational marketing in schools, *Educational Management and Administration*, Vol. 23, no. 2, pp. 75–88.

Kogan, M. (1984) *Education Accountability: An Analytic Overview*, London: Hutchinson.

Landers, T. and Myers, J. (1977) *Essentials of School Management*, Philadelphia: W. B. Saunders.

Longhurst, R. (1996) Education as a commodity: the political economy of the new further education, *Journal of Further and Higher Education*, Vol. 20, No. 2, Summer, pp. 49–66.

MacPherson, R. (1995) Introduction, *International Journal of Educational*

Research, Vol. 23, no. 6, pp. 475–478.

Radnor, H., Ball, S. and Vincent, C. (1997) Whither democratic accountability in education, *Research Papers in Education*, Vol. 12, no. 2, pp. 205–222.

Randle, K. and Brady, N. (1997) Managerialism and professionalism in the 'cinderella' service, *Journal of Vocational Education and Training*, Vol. 49, No. 1, pp. 121–39.

Sayer, J. (1989) The public context of change, in J. Sayer and V. Williams (eds.) *Schools and External Relations: Managing the New Partnerships*, London: Cassell.

Scott, P. (1989) Accountability, responsiveness and responsibility, in R. Glatter (ed.) *Educational Institutions and their Environments: Managing the Boundaries*, Milton Keynes: Open University Press.

Westoby, A. (1989) Parental choice and voice under the 1988 Education Reform Act, in R. Glatter (ed.) *Educational Institutions and their Environments: Managing the Boundaries*, Milton Keynes: Open University Press.

2

ACCOUNTABILITY IN EDUCATION SYSTEMS: CENTRALISING AND DECENTRALISING PRESSURES

David Scott

INTRODUCTION

Education systems operate with different systems of accountability between their constituent parts. This chapter examines moves by the state to restructure public education in the United Kingdom, and emphasises the continuing tension between decentralising and centralising initiatives. Though each set of reforms has been made in response to, and in the context of, local conditions and arrangements, Whitty, Power and Halpin (1998) suggest that they represent a global trend:

> A common theme is the devolution of financial and managerial control to more local levels, either to municipalities and schools, as in Sweden, or more commonly away from regional and district levels to individual schools, as in the LMS policy in England and Wales, the 'direct resourcing' experiment in New Zealand and the USA Charter School Initiative. Another common characteristic is the promotion of parental rights to choose schools, sometimes articulating with changes to funding formulae, when the money follows the pupils, resulting in a move towards quasi-markets in education.
> (Whitty, Power and Halpin, 1998, p. 30)

They go on to argue that:

> However, it is evident that the liberalizing reforms are being implemented alongside others which consolidate power within central governments, at national and state levels. In particular, centrally defined goals concerning

what schools should teach, and how their performance should be assessed, are becoming commonplace.

(ibid.)

This trend is set to continue, as is evidenced by the new United Kingdom Labour Government's floating of the idea of Action Zones in deprived areas of the country. These will be jointly funded by government and the business community, and are designed to wrest yet more control from the regionalised tier of the education system, the Local Education Authorities (LEAs). Set against these decentralising moves are reforms which have sought to prescribe curricula for schools, for teacher training institutions and, to a limited degree, for further and higher education. However, it needs to be emphasised here that the extent of central control over the curriculum in the United Kingdom is not mirrored in other countries. For example, in Australia and New Zealand, national and state curricula allow flexibility of implementation in local contexts (Cowley and Williamson, 1998). Indeed, the re-evaluation of the National Curriculum in the United Kingdom being undertaken at present is designed to introduce more flexibility, with the consequence that more power over what is taught in schools is devolved to those who have to teach it.

These global trends influence the types of accountability systems with which schools and colleges have to operate. However, though different arrangements may be made, whether this comprises more direct control from the central authority or schools and colleges being subjected to the disciplines of the market place, it is important to understand these as colonising mechanisms. Though new systems of accountability undoubtedly have effects on the practice of teaching in schools and colleges, they do not and cannot preclude arrangements at the local level which do not conform to what is expected. This gap between intention and implementation (even when the policy process is reconstructed) allows educational institutions and teachers within them to behave in ways not prescribed by policy-makers.

The precise form accountability systems take is determined by policy-makers answering five questions in different ways (Halstead, 1994):

- Who is deemed to be accountable?
- To whom are they accountable?
- For what are they accountable?
- In what way are they accountable?
- In what circumstances are they accountable?

The post-war consensus in the United Kingdom on education policy engineered a settlement between competing stakeholders so that policy-makers rarely intervened in curriculum-making (Chitty, 1994). Schools in both the primary and secondary sectors were not considered to be accountable to government for the content of their curricula and thus were not required to justify decisions they made to policy-makers. When this post-war consensus broke down with the result that a National Curriculum was imposed in 1988, accountability relations between the different parts of the system changed and schools were required to teach a prescribed curriculum. This in turn meant that they were required to give an account of their curricular activities to those policy-makers.

However, simply giving an account to a government body of their procedures and the effect these have on their students does not mean that the government exerts any control over that institution's activities or over its future actions. For that to happen a number of other procedures have to be implemented. Either legislation is enacted which compels schools to follow the dictates of the government body or a mechanism is put in place which allows other stakeholders to exert pressure which in turn compels them to change their practice. In the first case this could be a quasi-governmental body like Ofsted which has been granted statutory powers to inspect each school and then to demand changes to that school's practice if the school is deemed not to have met the required standards. In the second case, governments can expose schools and colleges to market forces of choice, which means that the institution suffers financial and status penalties if it comes low down in a published league table. In each of these two examples governments can change the power relations between the different parts of the system by substituting one type of accountability system for another.

In the post-war settlement schools were relatively independent from government and parental pressures. The accountability ethic was of a professional kind. Schools organised their activities on the basis of a presumed expertise in curriculum and pedagogy. This was never absolute even before the introduction of the National Curriculum in the United Kingdom, since schools were accountable to LEAs and Her Majesty's Inspectorate, though these forms of inspection were infrequent. More importantly, headteachers and teachers were positioned within social discourses about how they should behave and perform. In other words, they were positioned in terms of how key educational concepts were understood in society, to do with, for example, relations between teachers and students, aims and objectives of education, epistemologies, status relations of teachers and so forth. The discourse theorist, Foucault, argues that:

> Truth is a thing of this world; it is produced only by virtue of multiple forms of constraint. And it induces regular effects of power. Each society has its regimes of truth, its general politics of truth, that is the types of discourse it accepts and makes function as true, the mechanisms and instances which enable one to distinguish true from false statements, the means by which each one is sanctioned, the techniques and procedures accorded value in the acquisition of truth, the status of those who are charged with saying what comes as truth.

> (Foucault, 1972, pp. 72–3)

Accountability was therefore implicit, rather than explicit. Control was exercised through hidden mechanisms of social discourse. However, as Foucault (ibid.) reminds us, 'discourse is the power to be captured'. Thus there was space within this discursive framework to challenge existing patterns of behaviour and to behave in ways which were generally not prescribed. This hidden mechanism works in a different way in accountability systems which explicitly define power relations in which schools and colleges suffer penalties if they seek to challenge the power of the central authority.

Governments can operate to change relations between the different parts of the system in three ways. First, they can regulate by passing laws which compel social actors to behave in certain ways. The National Curriculum, though subject to frequent changes in response to the actions of stakeholders in the system (Scott, 1994), prescribes content within publicly funded schools, and has changed the accountability mechanism and relations between society and schools.

Second, they can change the policy-making mechanism itself, so that some parts of the system have greater powers and others less. Two examples will suffice here. The government in 1993 limited the amount of coursework which could be set by examination boards as part of their syllabuses at GCSE. This had the effect of decreasing the amount of control exercised by teachers over the content of their teaching programmes and increasing the amount of control exercised by examination boards. Local financial management acted in a similar way. Here LEAs were compelled by law to give up some of their powers over schools, and headteachers and governing bodies were granted more financial autonomy. These changes to the relations between the different parts of the system led to different forms of accountability being set in place. Though LEA officials (except in the case of grant maintained schools) still exercised some powers over schools, now schools made decisions about schooling which they did not have to justify to them, that is provide good reasons for their implementation. It should be further noted that these changes to the system had contradictory outcomes, in that some of the reforms increased the powers of schools whereas others decreased them. It is not so much that those reforms became unworkable, but that because they were in tension with each other, the intended effects were not as expected. We will see later how policy-making mechanisms were also changed in relation to further education colleges.

The third way by which governments can influence the activities of schools is through control of their budgets. They can reallocate resources between different parts of the system (i.e. by handing over resources previously controlled by the LEAs to individual schools) and they can increase or decrease the total amount of resources within it (i.e. by changing the annual financial settlement for education). Again, this has effects in terms of accountability. If, for example, LEAs are restricted in terms of the amount of control they can exercise over school budgets, then schools themselves will feel that they are less accountable to LEA officials. They may still maintain the types of accountability relations which they had before the reforms, but this is merely an historical trace.

A further point needs to be made here before we look at different models of accountability and control. This concerns the epistemological dimension of these different models. Each model assumes a different form of knowledge. Central control models of accountability are underpinned by an output model in which schools as a whole are judged in relation to past performance (Boyson, 1975), or to standards achieved in other countries (Reynolds and Farrell, 1996), or to some projected ideal about what they should be achieving (Barber, 1996). Consumer-dominated systems of accountability, where the intention is to allow parents to make a choice between schools, demand an aggregated judgement between schools, usually in the form of published league tables. The evaluative state model (see page 27) demands accountability at the level of process and output, and is predicated on a notion of how schools should be organised. Since the demand made here is for information which is applicable across schools, methods of data collection have to be employed which are standardised. Self-evaluative models of accountability are less concerned with cross-school comparisons and more concerned with schools providing accounts of their practice which enable them to improve, not in any absolute sense, but in terms of how they understand their local circumstances and what they consider to be expert opinion. What this means is that different accountability systems have different epistemological bases by which judgements are made. Indeed, the desire to substitute one system for another is driven by different views of knowledge about educational institutions and systems. Systems which emphasise external accountability and control are more likely to subscribe to epistemologies which emphasise determinacy, rationality, impersonality and prediction (Usher, 1996). Systems of accountability and control which emphasise local knowledges and devolved systems of power are more likely to be holistic, interpretative, descriptive and ideographic. In short, the system of accountability adopted is underpinned by an epistemological framework, and a way of conceptualising both what goes on in schools and in what ways they can be changed. Knowledge therefore always serves particular interests and accountability systems are nothing if not interest-based (Habermas, 1972).

The further education sector in England and Wales offers us another example of the way accountability relations have changed. Though exhibiting some similarities to those operating within the school sector, there are also some significant differences. These reflect the different ways the sector was organised in the past and the different interests it serves.

THE FURTHER EDUCATION SECTOR

The administration of the sector comprised a partnership between the then Department of Education and Science and the LEAs, with the colleges accountable to both for the efficient use of their funding but to an extent free to decide on curricula for themselves. Deregulation and increased central control went hand in hand and were further cemented in place by subsequent legislation such as the 1992 Further and Higher Education Act.

This last created two Further Education Funding Councils, one for England and one for Wales, which took over funding responsibility for the sector. Their membership was decided by the Secretary of State, thus reinforcing the power of the central authority to influence decision-making at recontextualising stages of the policy process with subsequent effects at the level of implementation. The Act also required the Funding Councils to assess the quality of education provided by the sector. In order to achieve this, it established a quality assurance committee, which was authorised to work closely with the Training and Enterprise Councils (TECs). Though the Act itself did not impose a prescribed way of administering funding, the Funding Councils quickly moved to implement a system based on 'standard units' in the colleges. These standard units were calculated in terms of three aspects of student learning: entry, on-programme and exit, and the formula was partially driven by the need to express these aspects of learning in quantifiable forms.

In addition the Funding Councils set out to overhaul the then system of inspection, by setting up a new inspectorate. It operated in three ways: each college had its own designated inspector; subject specialist inspectors examined specific curriculum areas; and each institution was inspected every four years. This form of inspection differs from Ofsted school inspection in one fundamental respect: it incorporated both formative and summative elements, in that the first two types of inspection were private to the college itself, whereas only the last was public. Furthermore though aspects of the college's activities were graded, no overall grade was given to the college itself, thus restricting the ability of policy-makers and other influential bodies such as the press to create league tables of excellence. FE inspection is now based on self-assessment and only includes external inspection when self-assessment is not deemed appropriate.

The further education sector is enormously complex, in that the colleges offer a wide range of courses, both academic and vocational, which are validated by different examination bodies. Policy is therefore influenced at every level by different groups of people with different interests. For example, the further education sector has always been influenced by regional concerns, in the form of Regional Advisory Councils, funded by LEAs. These have now been established as independent companies, with a diminished role in influencing policy.

We have already noted the way successive governments have sought to both centralise and decentralise. This has meant removing financial powers from the LEAs and giving those powers to Funding Councils, appointed by government. The decentralising moves comprised the establishment of the colleges as semi-autonomous bodies, even though their activities are tightly regulated by quasi-governmental bodies, with subsequent effects on the types of accountability mechanism through which they operate. This works in two ways. The 1992 Act substantially changed the make-up of governing bodies. In the past, the majority of governors had been LEA appointees. After the reforms, existing members of the governing bodies were reappointed unless they had been specifically nominated by the LEAs before the reforms. This effectively broke the link between LEAs and the colleges, though some LEA representation remained, those governors having been appointed to represent community interests. It resulted in increased representation from business and industry, with representatives from the TECs statutorily appointed. Graystone *et al.* (1994) surveyed governing bodies after the reforms and found that the number of governors with direct experience of the FE sector had decreased and that there had been a similar decrease in the number of women members.

The second way that accountability relations were changed was by the incorporation of a competitive ethic into the system, driven by target-setting at central government level. Though client pressure was not formalised as part of the system as it was with the school sector, client pressure operated through competition between the colleges in terms of recruitment, stay-on rates and results. These were driven in part by the Funding Councils and the systems of quality assurance imposed on the colleges. One of the disadvantages of systems of accountability driven by external agencies which represent the central state is that curriculum-making becomes divorced from the process of implementing it. These reforms in both the school and further education sectors in the United Kingdom and the way accountability relations have been changed have been mirrored in recent years in other countries in the world, and, as we suggested above, need to be understood in global terms.

MODELS OF ACCOUNTABILITY

We now come to a discussion of possible models of accountability relationships between the different parts of the system. These are ideal models in that they are presented as self-sufficient and logically distinct. However, in practice such models operate in conjunction with other models, and thus schools and colleges have to operate with different and in some cases conflicting accountability relationships. Halstead (1994) suggests six different models:

- the central control model (contractual, employer dominant)
- the self-accounting model (contractual, professional dominant)
- the consumerist model (contractual, consumer dominant)
- the chain of responsibility model (responsive, employer dominant)
- the professional model (responsive, professional dominant)
- the partnership model (responsive, consumer dominant).

This framework for understanding issues of control and accountability in educational systems will be modified and simplified.

Central control model

Accountability is one-way. Schools and colleges in the United Kingdom are contracted to meet the requirements of government as laid down in Acts of Parliament. They are accountable for delivering a service whose purpose is defined by the state. Government may also stipulate how judgements are to be made about successful delivery (the evaluative dimension) and even how this should be achieved (the pedagogic dimension).

A number of criticisms of this model have been made. It assumes a policy framework which does not and cannot operate in practice. The central control model understands the policy process as uni-linear. The central authority, though frequently prepared to disguise its intentions, always operates to further the interests of capital (Hatcher and Troyna, 1994). Education policy serves this end and centre–periphery relations are understood as direct imposition by the one over the other. There are a number of problems with this. Those in positions of power rarely operate with such a coherent view of policy. Within democratic states, government directives and consultative documents are read in different ways by different social actors at different sites and this has an effect on how policy is implemented. This may be contrasted with a pluralistic model, where the policy process is understood as driven by diversity and influenced at every level by a variety of interests. In turn, this has been criticised because it is considered that all the relevant interests are not and cannot be equally represented and furthermore social actors do not have equal chances of influencing the construction of these policy texts. If we reject both these models, then we need to understand the policy process as continuous rather than cyclical. The policy text is never complete, but always allows itself to be written over at every stage of the process and at every level (not least at the stage of implementation). However, within this fluid model it is suggested that the state is centrally positioned to influence the outcomes of the policy process and thus is in a more powerful position than other stakeholders (Scott, 1996).

Furthermore, it has been argued that statist models of accountability are anti-democratic because they aim to limit the influence of other stake-holders, in particular teachers; and inefficient because effective teaching in part requires proactive curriculum-making. It operates through a form of strategic evaluation which is conducted on an a priori basis. Governments develop long-term aims, decide upon appropriate ways of resourcing them and put in place evaluative procedures to determine whether those goals have in fact been met (Whitty, Power and Halpin, 1998).

Evaluative state model

The state withdraws from the precise implementation of policy though it clearly has an important role in framing that policy. It creates a series of semi-independent bodies such as Ofsted which are accountable to government ministers, but which override existing forms of accountability such as LEA–school relations, and whose task is to set in motion ways by which schools will conform to government policy. Inspection is one such way. This hands-off approach means that responsibility for failure is to a large degree removed from government and transferred to quasi-governmental bodies which in turn command a variety of means to compel schools to behave in prescribed ways. Whitty, Power and Halpin (1998), for instance, suggest that:

> The strong evaluative state is a minimalist one in many respects, but a more powerful and even authoritarian one in others. In Britain, it is not just that policies of deregulation have allowed the government to abdicate some of its responsibilities for ensuring social justice, but in increasing a limited number of state powers (most notably through a National Curriculum and its associated system of testing) it has actually strengthened its capacity to foster particular interests while appearing to stand outside the frame.
>
> (Whitty, Power and Halpin, 1998, p. 46)

Again, the model has been criticised for being sectionalist (White, 1998) and inefficient, and because it results in a deprofessionalised teaching body which has the effect of lowering standards within schools and colleges.

Quasi-market model

Here government decides that it should not be directly involved with the making of education policy, though it is in the business of legislating about sources of influence and their respective powers, which in turn has an effect on how policy at the local level is determined. That is, government sets up a quasi-market which hands power to the consumer who exerts pressure on schools by either exercising or threatening to exercise the power of exit (Hirschman, 1970). Schools are financed on a per capita basis and thus they have to make decisions about whether to exclude disruptive children when this means losing funding. If they choose not to, this may result in a lower rank on a league table or interruption to the education of other children in the school which in turn depresses the overall results and the overall aggregate of school achievement. Indeed, Bowe *et al.* (1992) and Vincent *et al.* (1995) give examples of schools which have made these types of calculation, and excluded disruptive children.

The currency by which parents make a judgement about the school is based on examination or test results in a league table of achievement to allow comparisons between schools. A number of systems have been suggested:

- publication of raw examination and test results
- publication of value-added results which take into consideration achievement on entry to the school
- publication of value-added results which take into consideration achievement at entry to the school system (base-line assessment)
- publication of value-added results which take into consideration the different socio-economic circumstances of children.

Each of these is likely to produce a different order of merit and therefore choosing between them depends on the set of policy objectives formulated by the particular government in power. For example, if that set of policy objectives is underpinned by a belief that socio-economic circumstances are influential in how children perform in school, then the system which is used is likely to make reference to this. Whichever system is adopted, the accountability mechanism works by making schools and teachers within them responsive to parental wishes. This is an unequal relationship because collective parental wishes now dominate the relationship. The impulsion here is towards tradition, order and uniformity, and this is reflected in the evidence from school studies that there has in recent years been a revival of traditional values and traditional teaching and learning strategies (Woods, 1992; Whitty, Edwards and Gewirtz, 1993; Broadfoot, 1996 Halpin, Power and Fitz, 1997;). Innovation and experimentation is therefore discouraged.

A number of criticisms of this model have been made, not least that it has reinforced social and economic inequality (Bartlett, 1993). Walford (1992, p. 137), for instance, suggests that markets discriminate against 'working class children and children of Afro-Caribbean descent'. The market is, of course, a quasi-market, not least because some groups of parents have a greater capacity either to move to areas which have the school of their choice, or to be in a position to transport their children on a daily basis, or because they have a greater degree of cultural capital (Bourdieu and Passeron, 1980) which enables them to make more informed choices about possible schools for their children, and to display that cultural capital in a way which makes them more attractive to certain types of schools.

Professional expert model

The principle which underlies this model is that different decisions have to be made at different levels of the system. Those different links in the chain are usually thought of as government, local education authority, governors, headteachers, senior teachers and teachers. At government level, resource allocation is considered to be a priority, whereas at classroom level the professional expertise of the teacher predominates. In turn each level of the system is accountable to the next layer upwards, but not in terms of processes, only in terms of outputs.

We have already suggested that this model implies a flawed view of the policy process, in that stakeholders are not equally positioned in relation to the policy flow between the different parts of the system. Indeed, allocation of powers to each particular level cannot be accommodated within the model since decisions about who decides what have still to be made. For example, resource allocation may be considered to be the province of central government, local education authority or headteacher. Parental interests are excluded except through their role as governors (Deem, 1994). Various critiques of the professional expert model were made by influential right-wing thinkers in the 1980s (Scruton, 1980; Sexton, 1987; Lawlor, 1988). They questioned the idea of expert professional knowledge and the ability of teachers to deliver when their prime concern was to protect their own vested interests. They further argued that it was possible to achieve a consensus on what should be taught and indeed on how it should be taught. The practitioner is therefore understood as accountable to other stakeholders in the system for efficient and effective delivery and not for the development of curricula and pedagogy. Those advocates of the professional expert model understand the theory–practice relationship in a different way. Pedagogic theory developed by policy-makers and the research community cannot be understood as binding on teachers, but only as valid when reconstructed by the practitioner working in situ (Scott and Usher, 1998).

Partnership model

The principle of accountability underlying this model is that since values underpin all aspects of educational decision-making, and since there are no absolute ways of determining the correctness of particular sets of val-

ues, decisions within educational systems have to be made through negotiation between all the different stakeholders. This means that no one
stakeholder has a monopoly of power over any other, or can claim a special status, but that the various partners negotiate with each other and
come up with agreed solutions. What this also means is that the means
of reaching agreement has to be, in some ideal sense, stripped of those
power relations which privilege one stakeholder over another. This in turn
means that teachers are now accountable to other partners in the system,
and change their practice if prompted to do so by parents or policy-makers. Governments, in turn, forsake their privileged position in the policy
process, avoid sectionalism (White, 1998) and properly enter into the
deliberative process.

IMPLICATIONS FOR MANAGERS IN SCHOOLS AND COLLEGES

Since it has been argued in this chapter that accountability systems are
value-laden and that the state has the means to substitute one system for
another, resistance to this has to operate in the first instance at the political level. However, it has also been argued that systems of accountability or indeed policy-making can never be imposed absolutely. There is, in
other words, space within any imposed model for local initiatives. Thus
it is possible for managers of schools and colleges to:

- influence the various sites of policy deliberation
- negotiate with inspection bodies about both the criteria with which they
  operate and how they come to make the judgements they do
- operate proactively to establish productive relations with their various
  partner bodies and thus influence the types of accountability relations
  within which they are positioned
- privilege some of these accountability relations and de-emphasise the
  importance of others – schools in the United Kingdom, for example,
  are already learning to present a public face to inspection bodies, whilst
  at the same time paying more careful attention to the needs and wishes
  of their main client body, parents
- adopt internal evaluation systems which are intended to improve the
  education they offer to their students and which operate outside the
  formal accountability mechanisms which successive governments in the
  United Kingdom and elsewhere have imposed on them.

Indeed, these externally operated systems have had two consequences.
First, the gap between the public face of the educational institution and
its private reality has widened as it has sought to protect itself in a cul-

ture of 'naming and shaming'; and second, there has been a reduction in the amount of reliable and valid information about the system made available to the public. Accountability relations, which are an important part of educational systems, always operate more effectively if open and accurate descriptions of them are made available.

REFERENCES

Barber, M. (1996) *The Learning Game: Arguments for an Education Revolution*, London: Victor Gollancz.

Bartlett, W. (1993) Quasi-markets and educational reforms, in J. Le Grand and W. Bartlett (eds.) *Quasi-markets and Social Policy*, London: Macmillan.

Bourdieu, P. and Passeron, J. C. (1980) *Reproduction*, London: Sage.

Bowe, R. and Ball, S. with Gold, A. (1992) *Reforming Education and Changing Schools: Case Studies in Policy Sociology*, London: Routledge.

Boyson, R. (1975) *The Crisis in Education*, London: Woburn Press.

Broadfoot, P. (1996) *Education, Assessment and Society*, Buckingham: Open University Press.

Chitty, C. (1994) Consensus to conflict: the structure of educational decision-making transformed, in D. Scott (ed.) *Accountability and Control in Educational Settings*, London: Cassell.

Cowley, T. and Williamson, J. (1998) A recipe for success? Localised implementation of a (flexible) national curriculum, *The Curriculum Journal*, Vol. 9, no. 1, pp. 79–94.

Deem, R. (1994) School governing bodies: public concerns and private interests, in D. Scott (ed.) *Accountability and Control in Educational Settings*, London: Cassell.

Foucault, M. (1972) *The Archaeology of Knowledge*, London: Routledge.

Graystone, J. with Bayliff, W., Evans, S. and Reece, I. (1994) *FE Governors and their Contribution to a Quality Learning Service*, Blagdon: FEU/FESC, Research Report RPT 16.

Habermas, J. (1972) *Knowledge and Human Interests*, London: Heinemann.

Halpin, D., Power, S. and Fitz, J. (1997) Opting into the past? Grant maintained schools and the reinvention of tradition, in R. Glatter, P. Woods and C. Bagley (eds.) *Choice and Diversity in Schooling: Perspectives and Prospects*, London: Routledge.

Halstead, M. (1994) Accountability and values, in D. Scott (ed.) *Accountability and Control in Educational Settings*, London: Cassell.

Hatcher, R. and Troyna, B. (1994) A ball by ball account, *Journal of Education Policy*, Vol. 9, no. 2, pp. 155–70.

Hirschman, A. (1970) *Exit, Voice and Loyalty: Response to Decline in Firms, Organisations and States*, Cambridge MA: Harvard University Press.

Lawlor, S. (1988) *Correct Core: Simple Curricula for English, Maths and Science*, London: Centre for Policy Studies.

Reynolds, D. and Farrell, S. (1996) *Worlds Apart? A Review of International Surveys of Educational Achievement involving England*, Ofsted Reviews of Research, London: HMSO.

Scott, D. (1994) Making schools accountable: assessment policy and the Education Reform Act, in D. Scott (ed.) *Accountability and Control in Educational Settings*, London: Cassell.

Scott, D. (1996) Education policy: the secondary phase, *Journal of Education*

Policy, Vol. 11, no. 1, pp. 133–40.

Scott, D. and Usher, R. (1998) *Examining Educational Research: Data, Methods and Theory*, London: Cassell.

Scruton, R. (1980) *The Meaning of Conservatism*, London: Macmillan.

Sexton, S. (1987) *Our Schools – A Radical Policy*, London: Institute of Economic Affairs Education Unit.

Usher, R. (1996) A critique of the neglected assumptions of educational research, in D. Scott and R. Usher (eds.) *Understanding Educational Research*, London: Routledge.

Vincent, C., Evans, J., Lunt, I. and Young, P. (1995) Policy and practice: the changing nature of special education provision in schools, *British Journal of Special Education*, Vol. 22, no. 1, pp. 4–11.

Walford, G. (1992) Educational choice and equity in Great Britain, in P. Cookson (ed.) *The Choice Controversy: Current Debates and Research*, Newbury Park, CA: Corwin Press.

White, J. (1998) New aims for a new National Curriculum, in J. White and R. Aldrich (eds.) *Bedford Way Paper*, Institute of Education, University of London.

Whitty, G., Edwards, T. and Gewirtz, S. (1993) *Specialisation and Choice in Urban Education: The City Technology College Experiment*, London: Routledge.

Whitty, G., Power, S. and Halpin, D. (1998) *Devolution and Choice in Education: The School, The State and The Market*, Buckingham: Open University Press.

Woods, P. (1992) Empowerment through choice? Towards an understanding of parental choice and school responsiveness, *Educational Management and Administration*, Vol. 20, no. 4, pp. 329-341.

3

STRATEGY, EXTERNAL RELATIONS AND MARKETING

Nick Foskett

MARKETISATION AND THE GROWTH OF EXTERNAL RELATIONS MANAGEMENT

Schools and colleges have always interacted with their external environments in both pro-active and reactive ways. Until the 1990s, however, educational institutions were emphatically 'domesticated' environments (Carlson, 1975) protected from the impact of market forces – funding was guaranteed, catchment areas were delimited and protected, and their quality of education/training was not linked to funding in any explicit way. Building an external relations component into institutional planning or strategy was simply a matter for professional judgement, and its presence or absence depended on the management's view of what the proper relationship was with external stakeholders. Political and social change, however, embedded in a commitment to the ideology of the market and of consumer choice in pursuit of the three 'Es' of economy, efficiency and effectiveness (Farnham, 1993), has been steadily absorbed into the educational culture and given statutory authority through legislation. Schools and colleges have moved into a 'wild' environment (Carlson, 1975), characterised by market accountability, financial responsibility, and a key focus on explicit demonstrations of quality that enable consumer comparison of institutions.

Marketisation has characterised the public sector in many western countries in parallel to the processes in the UK, shifting schools and colleges to focus on marketing and external relations management – but to varying degrees. In some states – for example, the USA and Denmark – the tradition of school engagement with the community has always supported the notion of partnership with a wide range of external stakeholders (OECD, 1997). In Spain, Sweden and France some elements of competition between state schools and colleges have been enhanced, and the need to take stronger account of public perceptions of school quality has become established in schools (Agudo, 1995; Van Zanten, 1995). In contrast, in Australia and New Zealand, as in the UK, the implanting of models of parental choice into the school system has pushed schools strongly towards adopting competitive stances in external relations management (e.g. Waslander and Thrupp, 1997).

The challenge of managing the external relations of schools and colleges has clearly been increased by marketisation. This chapter examines the nature of external relations management and marketing, its interpretation and development by schools and colleges, and its place in institutional strategic planning.

EXTERNAL RELATIONS AND MARKETING – DECONSTRUCTING ALIEN CONCEPTS

The concept of marketing is for most educationists an imported, even alien, concept. Foskett (1996) has shown how there is a wide range of interpretations of marketing amongst managers in secondary schools and confusion about its relationship to public relations, promotion, advertising and external relations management – an idea confirmed in the FE sector by Pieda (1996), Smith, Scott and Lynch (1995) and Foskett and Hesketh (1997).

Many definitions of marketing have emerged from within the discipline of 'management' (e.g. Christopher, McDonald and Wills, 1980), but it is possible to identify two specific perspectives – marketing as an overall philosophy for an organisation, and marketing as a functional area of management. As a functional area marketing involves the application of strategies to effect the sale of a product or service. As an overall philosophy, however, marketing is central to the operation of an organisation and 'is not a specialised activity at all (but) encompasses the entire business – it is the whole business' (Drucker, 1954, p. 56).

Three types of organisational orientation may be identified from this analysis. Product-oriented organisations are concerned primarily with the product, be it a 'good' or a 'service', that they have the expertise in producing. Sales-oriented organisations recognise that selling is central to their survival, and an emphasis is placed on promotion of their 'products' through advertising and sales techniques. Foskett suggests that

Such a sales-oriented culture is often the marketing stereotype. . . . The first response of an educational institution moved from the market-protected positions of monopoly power (e.g. impermeable school catchments or LEA allocation of particular courses to particular FE colleges), or of great excess demand over supply (e.g. applications to higher education in the 1970s) is to seek to sell what it already offers very vigorously.

(Foskett, 1998, p. 49)

A market-oriented organisation, in contrast, is one in which the customer is central to its operation, and its emphasis is on satisfying customer requirements by providing goods and services that customers want. Such an orientation has implications for the organisation and its management, for each element of the organisation's operation, from strategic planning to 'front-of-house' activities, will be dictated by the customer-focus.

Marketing in education, however, is complicated by two important issues. Firstly, service industries, even in the private sector, have not traditionally taken a strong marketing perspective. Cowell (1984) explains this in a number of ways:

- Service products are inherently intangible which makes their promotion difficult, particularly where the 'product' is long term in its rewards (e.g. education).
- Services in the professional sector may see marketing as unethical, compromising the objectivity of their relationship with their 'client'.
- Some service sectors experienced demand far in excess of their ability to provide it (e.g. higher education), so promotion was unnecessary.
- Most educational organisations have enjoyed monopoly power (e.g. over a specified type of provision or a tightly demarcated catchment area), and so have perceived no need for marketing.
- Little professional guidance or training on adopting a marketing perspective has been available.

Secondly, traditional concepts of professionalism and public service in education do not sit easily with the notion of marketing. The view of the professional as 'expert' and the monitor of quality may be interpreted to mean that responsiveness to the market is unnecessary. Indeed, in education the customer may be seen not as the pupil or parent, but in terms of professionally defined notions of either an academic discipline or the needs of society as a whole. As Gray has suggested:

The purposes for which public sector institutions such as schools were established go far beyond mere customer satisfaction. (They) have public service duties and responsibilities . . . (to) tackle real needs which may not be appreciated by those customers.

(Gray, 1991, p. 25)

Educational institutions, therefore, have many different external links which go beyond transactional or exchange relationships. While such relationships do exist – for example, in the recruitment of students/pupils – they are only a small component of the totality of external relations which must be sustained. These are illustrated in Figure 3.1.

These functions are not, of course, distinct and the overlap and feedback between them is very important. For example, a school's role as community partner, if effective, will contribute to its recruitment of pupils, as will its performance in the quality assurance processes operated by Ofsted. The importance of this is emphasised by Foskett and Hesketh (1997) who identify the significance of 'word of mouth' in parents' and students' choice of school or college, which, although a secondary product of the school's activities, may account for two-thirds of the influence on parental choice of school (Foskett, 1995; Carroll and Walford, 1997).

While managing these external relationships is of great importance to the institution, each is embedded in its internal processes. Worcester's Law (Worcester, 1985) asserts that 'no organisation can sustain a good rep-

---

(a) Transactional-based external relations

- As an education/training provider in the education/training market – for example, in 'selling' FE courses, or selling a 'primary education' to parents for their children.
- As professional client – for example, in purchasing advisory services from the LEA.
- As commercial customer – for example, in the purchase of supplies.
- As a competitor – for example, in bidding for commercial contracts, or for a share of earmarked funding from LEA/FEFC or EU sources.

(b) Relationship-based external relations

- As partners with 'customers' – for example, the relationship with parents in supporting pupils' development.
- As professional partner – for example, relationships with service providers such as educational psychologists
- As community partner – for example, relationships with community organisations such as the church or the police.
- As political player – for example, in responding to consultations on educational initiatives.
- As professional adviser – for example, in providing advice to parents on special needs support.

(c) Public accountability external relations

- As political servant – for example, in receiving delegated funds through LMS or FEFC funding, or in implementing government literacy initiatives.
- As accountable public body – for example, in being subject to LEA, Ofsted or FEFC inspection, or generating public examination results that appear in league tables.

Figure 3.1. External relationships of schools and colleges

utation that it does not deserve'. A perception that marketing is simply about choosing the message the institution wants to convey and then communicating that by public relations and promotional activity ignores the importance of underpinning the image with effective quality assurance. This, in turn, suggests three important issues for managers:

1. External relations management cannot be the domain of only a small group. It is neither something that only senior managers do nor can it simply be delegated to junior colleagues. While in a large institution specific functions (e.g. media relations) may be undertaken by specialists, and the whole process will need co-ordination from senior management, each member of the organisation has an important role.
2. Effective external relations will probably require significant 'internal marketing' (Robinson and Long, 1985) to support it. This is the process of sharing vision amongst the whole organisation and generating strategies for actioning the vision from internal consultation.
3. Staff are key players within this process, since their activities define the quality of the organisation, and they represent a key stakeholder group with whom 'management' must manage relationships with great care. This link between staff support, quality and external relations is recognised in much of the quality management research in education (Murgatroyd and Morgan, 1993; West-Burnham, 1997), and is exemplified by the Investors in People movement.

So what is the relationship between external relations management and marketing? External relations management relates to:

> Those aspects of an organisation's activities that in any way cause it to relate to an audience beyond its own boundaries. This includes both processes with an overtly external connection and those processes which, while largely internal to the organisation, have a direct impact on some external (stakeholder).
>
> (Foskett, 1992, p. 6)

Such processes need management whether or not an organisation is market-focused. Putting up a sign which says 'Parents must not proceed beyond this point' at the school gate is managing external relations, but is probably not very effective marketing! Where an institution is market-focused, however, all external relations management has a marketing component, since it is designed to support the notion that all of the organisation's activities are focused on customers and clients, that marketing is an holistic philosophy for the school or college. Such a perspective means that the harsh equation of 'marketing = selling' can be replaced by a perspective which is much more in tune with educational philosophies.

Figure 3.2 is a model of marketing that includes both traditional educational values and the discipline of the market. Marketing is represented as

Figure 3.2. The marketing triad model

a 'field', with an individual's or organisation's precise conceptual location representing a balance between recruitment, quality and community responsiveness. Such a location will depend on the 'micro-market' conditions the organisation finds itself in, and will change over time. A college under threat from declining student numbers may focus its marketing perspective on the bottom left of the model, while a neighbouring institution in a more secure market position might be located more centrally or towards one of the other corners. In all cases, however, there is a component of each of the three elements in the marketing perspective that a school or college must adopt – quality and community relationships can never be ignored in favour of 'pure' recruitment activity. This emphasis on links with stakeholders in non-transactional relationships emerges strongly from an analysis of marketisation in a number of European countries (OECD, 1997), and Cardno (1998) emphasises the centrality of the community links in the context of government guidance on strategic planning in New Zealand schools.

This model links to an important concept that has emerged in the marketing of small businesses (Payne *et al.*, 1995; Gronroos, 1997) – relationship marketing. This recognises that small organisations (and all schools and most colleges are small organisations) sell not just a product or service but a relationship which is based on partnership, mutual trust and confidence (Stokes, 1996). A number of ideas emerge from this:

- Such an approach reflects what has traditionally been regarded as good 'educational' practice in most schools and colleges, and sits more comfortably with educationally driven philosophies.
- It emphasises the importance of managing all external relations in support of effective long-term relationships with external client groups.

- It confirms Drucker's (1973, p.4) perspective that effective marketing almost removes the need for 'selling', for 'the aim of marketing is to know and understand the customer so well that the product or service fits him and sells itself'.
- Most schools and colleges have extensive experience in developing these relationships, so that 'even while claiming an innocence of marketing, or more vehemently, an antipathy towards it, (schools and colleges) are actually rather good at it' (O'Sullivan and O'Sullivan, 1995).

STRATEGY, MANAGEMENT AND EXTERNAL RELATIONS

Accountability and autonomy have made a commitment to strategy a core requirement for educational institutions, both statutorily and pragmatically. Strategic management is, in essence, taking proactive responsibility for the future and long-term development and direction of the whole institution. Middlewood (1998), drawing on the work of Mintzberg (1995), Fidler (1996) and Weindling (1997), distinguishes clearly between strategic thinking and operational management. Strategic thinking is long-term, reflective, conceptual and creative, emphasising the identification of opportunities in response to a continuous scanning of the environment, and is concerned with achieving the institution's vision. Operational management is short-term and immediate, leading to action in a small time frame, and concentrates on concrete, often routine, functions focusing on the internal context of the institution. Strategic thinking and operational management are clearly not separate, indeed they must not be so for each must inform the other, but they represent opposite ends of a management activity spectrum.

Strategic management is intimately involved with the institution's external environment. Hanson and Henry (1992) emphasise the importance of 'strategic marketing' to educational institutions, where most of the organisation's planning is intimately linked to its awareness of the environment in which it operates. This they distinguish from 'project marketing' ('the most-practised form of marketing' (ibid, p. 258), which is short-term and is the management of specific market needs.

Johnson and Scholes (1993) indicate that the whole concept of strategic management comprises three components, within each of which we can identify external relations components:

- strategic analysis
- strategic choice
- strategic implementation.

Strategic analysis

Strategic analysis is about ensuring that strategy is linked to the market. The organisation's environment provides the parameters within which it may operate, and comprises the market environment and the socio-political environment. Every organisation is constrained by external economic circumstances, and the political environment in which policy decisions are made. While the opportunities for actively influencing these are limited, no organisation needs to be entirely the victim of external circumstances. A key aspect of strategic analysis is collecting sufficient 'intelligence' and data to be able to make reasoned judgements about future trends, scenarios and patterns. Sensing this component of the external environment is often highly subjective and requires astute political judgement, but the view from the crow's nest this provides means that careful adjustments of the tiller can avoid the ship foundering on the rocks (Foskett, 1997).

Sensing the market environment is also subjective, but much less so. Market analysis seeks to describe the organisation's present and future markets in terms of:

- market characteristics – size, constraints, character, patterns of change and future development
- competition – the nature and behaviour of competitors
- buyer behaviour – the decision-making processes of customers

Such market intelligence can be obtained formally through a marketing research programme (Davies and Scribbins, 1985) or informally through gathering information from inside or outside the organisation (Martin, 1995). (See Chapter 12 for a detailed consideration of marketing research.)

While strategy must be informed by market considerations, many other factors are also of importance, for schools and colleges have a broad social remit in addition to the market imperatives. The FEFC (1997) has identified a number of factors which impact on college strategy, including:

- the overall direction of the institution
- needs and market analysis
- staff skills
- finance and estate management issues
- the local labour market.

Planning and marketing are tightly linked, therefore, but are not the same thing. It is the role of management to make judgements about the importance of the market in their planning decisions and strategic choices. Gray (1991) sees strategic planning as deriving from strategic analysis, however, with all strands of institutional plans building from marketing analysis techniques. The product of this process has three components:

1. An institutional plan
2. Thematic plans for each component of the institutional plan (e.g. curriculum, estates, finance)
3. A marketing plan, which identifies both future marketing activity (e.g. promotion, public relations) and future marketing research and evaluation activities.

Strategic choice

Strategic choice is, in essence, choosing the broad approaches that the organisation will take to achieve its aims. Kotler and Fox (1995) identify three elements of marketing strategy formulation, which are intended to ensure that the institution 'plays' in the market in the most effective way. These are explored in detail in Chapter 14, but are outlined here:

1. *Target market strategy.* This involves identifying which segments of the market the institution wishes to operate in – a college may choose to focus, for example, on 16–19-year-old academic-track students rather than vocational courses. Schools, while constrained because of statutory curriculum requirements, may still focus on particular market segments (e.g. as a technology school).
2. *Competitive positioning strategy.* This involves identifying the distinguishable features of the institution that make it distinctive from competitors in the same market segments – for example, a small school may emphasise its friendly, community ethos, while a large school may emphasise its range of facilities.
3. *Marketing mix strategy.* This involves identifying the specific combination of elements that the organisation will present to promote itself, and is often characterised by the idea of the five Ps (Product, Place, Price, Promotion and People).

Strategic implementation

The final stage in Johnson and Scholes' (1993) model is strategic implementation, which involves turning the strategy into practice. This includes establishing appropriate systems, acquiring and applying the relevant resources, operating the systems, and evaluating/measuring their effect. Within this process, two important management issues can be identified. Firstly, the establishment of effective internal quality assurance systems should ensure that the service or product meets customer expectations.

Secondly, it is important to develop mechanisms for collecting external data on how programmes and activities are perceived – what the FEFC calls 'confirmatory evidence' (FEFC, 1997).

CASE STUDIES IN THE MANAGEMENT OF MARKETING AND EXTERNAL RELATIONS

How far do these principles operate in the 'real world' of educational institutions, though? Few detailed research-based case studies exist either in the school sector or in FE. From the research of Foskett (1995), Gewirtz, Ball and Bowe (1995), James and Phillips (1995), Glatter, Woods and Bagley (1996) and Woods, Bagley and Glatter (1998), the following features of external relations management in schools emerge:

- A steady cultural shift towards accepting the need to operate actively in a market environment.
- A very varied interpretation of marketing, but with a strong 'product-centred' perspective in schools.
- A reactive, ad hoc approach to marketing, with the dominance of short-term promotional activities.
- An emphasis on short-term 'crisis management' approaches, dealing with recruitment issues.
- A failure to recognise the dynamic nature of markets and the presence of market threats even to institutions in currently strong positions. Schools successful with their image and recruitment are frequently complacent and do not seek to scan the market.
- The absence of any coherent form of marketing research.
- The adoption of undifferentiated marketing strategies by schools, most seeking to be 'all things' to all potential pupils. Glatter, Woods and Bagley (1996, p. 22) suggest that popular schools 'have no incentive to differentiate further' and less popular schools seek 'not to sharpen but to blunt any difference and thereby share the mutual benefits from being similar'.

In primary schools, practice is similar to that of secondary schools, but is even more 'conservative' in approach (Stokes, 1996; Minter, 1997). As Foskett (1998, p. 54) indicates:

> A strong commitment to educational values drives them, together with the establishment of strong relationships with the community. The role of word-of-mouth is so important that a 'selling' orientation is of little assistance, so many primary schools have, by default, and without reference to the 'canons' of marketing, adopted a strategy that is 'relationship marketing'.

Although marketing has become a major preoccupation for FE institutions and a substantial marketing function has been developed in larger colleges with significant specialist marketing teams, many smaller colleges still place marketing as a peripheral activity in the job portfolios of middle and senior managers. Research into FE marketing by Smith *et al.* (1995), Hemsley-Brown (1996), Pieda (1996) and Foskett and Hesketh (1997) suggests that:

- There is considerable diversity in the organisation and systems adopted to deal with marketing.
- As with schools, the emphasis is on short-term 'project' marketing rather than strategic marketing integrated into long-term institutional planning.
- Considerable expertise has been developed in the use of promotional strategies traditionally associated with large commercial organisations.

The three case studies below are presented to provide a more detailed perspective on these developments, although it is important to recognise the unique character of the market places within which each of the institutions operates. They are not presented here as being 'typical', but serve to illustrate some of the pressures and responses schools and colleges have experienced in the market place.

Case study 1 – Grove Primary School

Grove Primary School is a 7–11 junior school in a small village in a rural part of central southern England. It takes most of its pupils from the village infant school, and in 1996 had 75 pupils on roll. This represented a steady decline from 95 three years earlier, indicating a growing disenchantment in the village with the school. In 1996 the headteacher left and the new head was appointed by the governors with a brief to reverse the decline in numbers. The strategy employed by the head was not based *explicitly* on any marketing principles (the head denies any knowledge of marketing!), but on a clear five-element approach:

1. recognition that word-of-mouth is the most important promotional tool for any school, especially in a strong community like the village
2. personal relationships between all the staff and all external stakeholders (parents, neighbours, suppliers, LEA) must be positive, optimistic, welcoming and indicative of the pursuit of quality
3. quality is identified by good achievement in school performance league tables
4. the head must take the lead in spending as much time as possible with parents of potential pupils, and respond to all invitations for the school to participate in local activities

5. the head scans the external environment for opportunities to enhance the school's relationships with stakeholders, and to identify potential threats as they arise.

The school has no formal marketing plan, and marketing is not mentioned in the School Development Plan. While the governors monitor the results of marketing, they take no active part in the process, and the head is clear that 'I am the school's marketing'. Such a pattern of activity is clearly based on relationship marketing rather than transactional marketing, but indicates a school which is, in reality, highly responsive to its market environment. In this school, the success is:

- a roll for 1998/9 of 105
- a number of pupils now admitted from infant schools at some distance from the school
- a number of affluent parents in the village opting to use the school rather than preparatory schools
- the appointment of an additional member of staff.

A number of key principles emerge from this example. The importance of seeing marketing in the primary school as relationship marketing is underlined, which in turn emphasises the need to be concerned with all external relations processes and not just recruitment. Linked to this is the centrality of quality assurance and the pursuit of measurable success in underpinning external perceptions, which in itself requires the engagement of all staff with responding to the external environment. Thirdly, the importance of monitoring the environment is clear, as is the identification of a clear set of strategies and priorities.

Case study 2 – Greenstreet Community School

Greenstreet Community School is an 11–16 mixed comprehensive school serving, principally, a large local authority housing estate in a city in southern England. While its performance in public examinations has improved in recent years, and it performs well in relation to its intake of pupils, it is still amongst the poorest performers in the LEA. It has never recruited up to its maximum intake number, and has substantial competition from other local schools, including a similar school at the other end of the estate. Important threats are the school's reputation for bullying and boys' underperformance, and new buildings at its major competitor school. Significant strengths include a strong community education programme, a highly regarded staff, a strong sports tradition and an attractive campus. A new head was appointed in 1997.

The school has never had an explicit marketing plan and external relations management had always been a (poorly developed) responsibility of the headteacher, who had never spent much time promoting strong links with external organisations. The new head, on appointment, established a primary aim of filling all the places in the next year's intake and establishing Greenstreet as the first choice school in the locality through:

- short-term promotional developments to address current under-recruitment through, for example, establishing good links with the education reporter of the local newspaper, and feeding regular stories in relation to pupil achievement
- focusing in the medium term on improving examination results through establishing teaching and learning issues as the key focus for all staff, addressing in particular boys' under-achievement and the linked issue of behaviour; innovative developments included a cross-curricular literacy programme and the introduction of vocational programmes for 14–16-year-olds
- identifying the characteristics that might make Greenstreet distinctive within the local schools market; this included, for example, emphasising and developing the community character of the school with internal appointments of staff to develop strong literacy and music outreach programmes
- establishing mechanisms for sensing the external environment – for example, commissioning a survey of feeder school pupils and parents to gain their perceptions of the school and its competitors
- developing appropriate political links through the generation of good relationships with the LEA, community groups and the local post-16 institutions.

Despite these developments no explicit marketing plan was created. Each approach was either a feature of a short-term component of the development plan or else a strategy developed in the head's own practice. The strategy, though, demonstrates clearly the recognition of both short-term and long-term marketing needs, the link between long-term aims and issues of broad external relations management, the focus on partnership as much as 'exchange' relationships, and the importance of quality assurance and teaching and learning as guarantors of future success in the market.

Case study 3 – Lowlands College

Lowlands College is an urban further education college in north-west England. At the time of incorporation in 1992 it emphasised strongly traditional vocational and craft-based programmes, with a small 'academic-track' sector and some self-funding business training programmes. Its strengths were its industrial links and its reputation for quality vocational training. Its weaknesses were its traditional 'dirty hands' image, and its location in a declining inner city area. Prior to incorporation, the local authority had channelled 'academic' work to two sixth form colleges in the city. Marketing was the responsibility of a Vice Principal and the Head of Business Studies, but no explicit marketing plan or strategy existed. Following incorporation the college was faced with a declining Average Level of Funding (see Chapter 6) and a highly competitive market with expansion targets of 25 per cent over four years.

Lowlands reorganised its marketing organisation and operations. A Marketing Officer and Assistant were appointed, line managed by the Vice Principal (Planning), with a responsibility for promoting the college's programmes. A separate Community and Enterprise Office (CEO) was established, led by a middle management appointee, reporting to the Vice Principal (Curriculum), with a brief to review the needs of the college's client groups, to identify new markets and to generate new sources of income. The CEO was also charged with establishing a marketing database and undertaking appropriate marketing research. The integration of these activities fell to the Senior Management Team with the responsibility for the college's strategic plan. The Strategic Plan contains a section on 'Marketing' which focuses on promotional activities. Other sections in the plan include a theme within 'Curriculum' on 'New developments and potential', and a further section on 'Managing relationships with external partners'.

Key decisions on strategy included the choice not to expand substantially 'academic-track' provision, but to focus on vocational and business-funded training programmes. The college chose, despite the decline in engineering employment, to establish a high quality IT-based engineering provision for training, and to develop a training and conference suite for the regional business community. A franchise Year 1 engineering programme was established with a local university. In the period 1992–95 the college expanded its market share of engineering and business programmes in the region, but overall expansion meant that FEFC targets were not met. The funding gap this left was only bridged by the use of demand-led (DLE) funding (see Chapter 6) from the FEFC. By 1998 the college's financial position has deteriorated, and a merger with one of the local sixth form colleges is being negotiated.

Lowlands demonstrates the challenges of managing external relations in a highly competitive post-compulsory environment. The college adopted a strong sales-oriented approach which, in turn, led to the planning of external relations and marketing being diluted within the college's strategy. The decision to focus on existing areas of expertise was not based on external scanning, although this choice recognised the need to be distinctive in the market. The college was handicapped by its own inexperience with marketing as it moved from a 'domesticated' to a 'wild' environment, and the inclusion of marketing into the strategic planning process for the college was a bolt-on to existing planning. A college of similar history nearby used its market analysis to re-focus the college's programmes towards business education, with an aggressive pursuit of the academic-track market of local school sixth forms. Its future is much more secure than that of Lowlands.

CONCLUSION

Managing external relations and managing marketing are tightly linked processes for all institutions. At a strategic planning level, the strategy needs to be driven by the institution's interaction with its external environment, including its markets. In turn the strategy drives the way the institution operates directly in the market, and shapes the character of the wide spectrum of relationships that influence external perceptions of the 'quality' of the institution. The education system is characterised by considerable diversity in marketing and external relations practice. The 'sales-oriented' perspective still dominates, with marketing detached from mainstream institutional planning. However, since most schools and colleges are small businesses, an approach based more strongly on the concept of 'relationship marketing' may link together more firmly an institution's educational mission and its market situation. In conclusion, Smith, Scott and Lynch's perspective on marketing in FE still describes the situation across the educational world:

> Marketing is on the march, (but) ... institutions are at different stages of development in marketing terms, marketing philosophies are often poorly articulated, marketing functions have yet to be adequately defined, and the organisation of marketing remains inchoate (and occasionally illogical).
>
> (Smith, Scott and Lynch, 1995, p. 110)

REFERENCES

Agudo, J. (1995) The education market in Zaragoza. *Paper presented to the European Conference on Educational Research*, Bath, UK.

Cardno, C. (1998) Working together – managing strategy collaboratively, in D. Middlewood and J. Lumby (eds.) *Strategic Management in Schools and Colleges*, London: Paul Chapman.

Carlson, R. (1975) Environmental constraints and organisational consequences: the public school and its clients, in J. Baldridge and T. Deal (eds.) *Managing Change in Educational Organisations*, Berkeley, Ca: McCutchan.

Carroll, S. and Walford, G. (1997) Parents' response to the school quasi-market, *Research Papers in Education*,Vol. 12, no. 1. pp. 3–26.

Christopher, M., McDonald, M. and Wills, G. (1980) *Introducing Marketing*, London: Pan.

Cowell, D. (1984) *The Marketing of Services*, Oxford: Butterworth.

Davies, P. and Scribbins, K. (1985) *Marketing Further and Higher Education*, Harlow: Longman for FEU.

Drucker, P. (1954) *The Practice of Management*, New York: Harper and Row.

Drucker, P. (1973) *Management Tasks, Responsibilities and Practice*, London: Harper and Row.

Farnham, D. (1993) *Managing the New Public Services*, Basingstoke: Macmillan.

FEFC (1997) *Identifying and Addressing Needs: A Practical Guide*, Coventry: FEFC.

Fidler, B. (1996) *Strategic Planning for School Improvement*, London: Pitman.

Foskett, N. H. (1992) An introduction to the management of external relations in schools, in N. H. Foskett (ed.) *Managing External Relations in Schools*, London: Routledge.

Foskett, N. H. (1995) *Marketing, management and schools – a study of a developing market culture in secondary schools*. Unpublished PhD thesis, University of Southampton.

Foskett, N. H. (1996) Conceptualising marketing in secondary schools – deconstructing an alien concept, in *Proceedings of the 'Markets in Education, Policy, Process and Practice' Symposium*, University of Southampton.

Foskett, N. H. (1997) Staring into the Black Hole, *Management in Education*, Vol. 11, no. 4, pp. 3–6.

Foskett, N. H. (1998) Linking marketing to strategy, in D. Middlewood and J. Lumby (eds.) *Strategic Management in Schools and Colleges*, London: Paul Chapman.

Foskett, N. H. and Hesketh, A. J. (1997) Constructing choice in contiguous and parallel markets: institutional and school-leavers' responses to the new post-16 market place, *Oxford Review of Education*, Vol. 23, no. 3, pp. 299–320.

Gewirtz, S., Ball, S. and Bowe, R. (1995) *Markets, Choice and Equity in Education*, Buckingham: Open University Press.

Glatter, R., Woods, P. and Bagley, C. (eds.) (1996) *Choice and Diversity in Schooling: Perspectives and Prospects*, London: Routledge.

Gray, L. (1991) *Marketing Education*, Buckingham: Open University Press.

Grönroos, C. (1997) From marketing mix to relationship marketing – towards a paradigm shift in marketing, *Management Decision*, Vol. 35, no 4, pp. 322–9.

Hanson, E. M. and Henry, W. (1992) Strategic marketing for educational systems, *School Organisation*, Vol. 12, no. 2, pp. 255–67.

Hemsley-Brown, J. (1996) *Marketing post-sixteen colleges; A qualitative and quantitative study of pupils' choice of post-sixteen institution*. Unpublished PhD thesis, University of Southampton.

James, C. and Phillips, P. (1995) The practice of educational marketing in schools, *Education Management and Administration*, Vol. 23, no. 2, pp. 75–88.

Johnson, G. and Scholes, K. (1993) *Exploring Corporate Strategy*, 3rd edition, Hemel Hempstead: Prentice-Hall.

Kotler, P. and Fox, K. (1995) *Strategic Marketing for Educational Institutions*, 2nd edition, New York: Prentice-Hall.

Martin, Y. (1995) What do parents want? *Management in Education*, Vol. 9, no. 1, pp. 12–14.

Middlewood, D. (1998) Strategic management in education: an overview, in D. Middlewood and J. Lumby, (eds.) *Strategic Management in Schools and Colleges*, London: Paul Chapman.

Minter, K. (1997) *Marketing in the primary school*. Unpublished MA (Ed) thesis, University of Southampton.

Mintzberg, H. (1995) Strategic thinking as seeing, in B. Garratt (ed.) *Developing Strategic Thought*, London: Harper Collins.

Murgatroyd, S. and Morgan, C. (1993) *Total Quality Management and the School*, Buckingham: Open University Press.

OECD (1997) *Parents as Partners in Schooling*, Paris: OECD.

O'Sullivan, C. and O'Sullivan, T. (1995) There's beauty in candlelight: relationship marketing in the non-profit sector, in *Proceedings of the Annual Conference of the Marketing Education Group*, Bradford: MEG.

Payne, A., Christopher, M., Clark, M. and Peck, H. (1995) *Relationship Marketing for Competitive Advantage: Winning and Keeping Customers*, Oxford: Butterworth-Heinemann.

Pieda (1996) *Labour Market Information for Further Education Colleges: A Handbook for Practitioners*, Manchester: Pieda.

Robinson, A. and Long, G. (1985) Substance v. trappings in non-advanced FE, *Journal of Further and Higher Education*, Vol. 12, no. 1, pp. 23–40.

Smith, D., Scott, P. and Lynch, J. (1995) *The Role of Marketing in the University and College Sector*, Leeds: Heist Publications.

Stokes, D. (1996) Relationship marketing in primary schools, in *Proceedings of the 'Markets in Education, Policy, Process and Practice' Symposium*, University of Southampton.

Van Zanten, A. (1995) Market forces in French Education. *Paper presented to the European Conference on Educational Research*, Bath, UK.

Waslander, S. and Thrupp, M. (1997) Choice, competition and segregation: an empirical analysis of a New Zealand secondary school market, in A. Halsey, H. Lauder, P. Brown, and A. Wells (eds.) *Education, Culture, Economy and Society*, Oxford University Press.

Weindling, D. (1997) Strategic planning in schools: some practical techniques, in M. Preedy, R. Glatter, and R. Levacic (eds.) *Educational Management: Strategy, Quality and Resources*, Buckingham, Open University Press.

West-Burnham, J. (1997) *Managing Quality in Schools*, 2nd edition, London: Paul Chapman.

Woods, P., Bagley, C. and Glatter, R. (1998) *School Choice and Competition: Markets in the Public Interest?* London: Routledge.

Worcester, R. (1985) Familiarity breeds favourability, *The Times*, 7 November.

4

PARTNERSHIPS, ALLIANCES AND COMPETITION: DEFINING THE FIELD

Valerie Hall

Managing external relations requires schools and colleges to form partnerships, alliances, and, in some cases, be in competition with other individuals, groups, institutions and federations with whom they may have little in common in terms of values, behaviours and even goals. There is evidence everywhere of new partnerships in educational provision accompanied inevitably by the tensions created by predispositions and contexts as a result of the new and often unfamiliar combinations of people working together. These tensions are exacerbated in education systems where there is a need to demonstrate competitive success and where collaboration or competition are requirements not options. In order to set the scene for the collaborative and competitive processes that characterise school and college approaches to external relations, I have identified (in Figure 4.1) four arenas for collaboration and competition. Within each of these arenas internal and external struggles take place that have implications for how partnerships and alliances develop or fail to develop.

ARENAS FOR COLLABORATION AND COMPETITION

All four arenas have implications for the management of the varieties of external relations that are the focus of this book. Whichever is the more fashionable of the two terms (and fashions change with political allegiances), both collaboration and competition are taken for granted as processes which are easy to achieve. A commitment to the values that under-

	Preferences	
Arena	**Collaboration**	**Competition**
Intrapersonal	Relational	Autonomy
Interpersonal	Win-win	Win-lose
Intra-institutional	Teamwork	Individual effort
Inter-institutional and extra-institutional	Partnerships	Go-it-alone

Figure 4.1. Arenas for collaboration and competition

pin each strategy accompanies the belief that each represents a form of natural and desirable behaviour on the part of the individuals and groups who make up our educational institutions. In fact, both these strategies constitute highly complex processes which, however desirable each may seem, depend for their effectiveness on the actors and settings involved.

Within the *intrapersonal* arena, individuals vary in their preferences for collaborating (emphasising the relational) or competing (emphasising autonomy). Their self-identity is shaped by this preference and exhortations to behave in ways which challenge this preference can lead to resentment and withdrawal. Those who favour collaboration value, and even depend on, the close, mutually supportive relationships this way of working entails. They are prepared to forego praise for individual achievement in favour of their intrinsic enjoyment of mutual support. Those who favour competition are prepared to accept the possible isolation from others it creates, since the reward of autonomy is greater.

Interpersonal relations among staff in schools and colleges, in spite of education's context of professional collegiality, can manifest competition as readily as collaboration. In recent years schools and colleges have moved towards increasing use of task and management teams to achieve their objectives, but research (e.g. Wallace and Hall, 1994) shows that teamworking can be fraught with difficulties over the balance between equity and hierarchy. Not everyone wants to work in a team, yet the joint work that teamwork represents depends on the commitment of all involved. Rewarding outstanding individual teacher performance, an increasingly popular mechanism in many education systems, creates schisms between teaching colleagues who prefer to see young people's learning as the outcome of their combined efforts. These interpersonal differences are writ large *intra-institutionally* in the form of departmental empires competing for limited resources or collaborating across subject boundaries to achieve school or college goals.

As examples elsewhere in this volume show, exhortations to schools and colleges to collaborate with each other (as well as compete through league tables) have led to many imposed partnerships, as well as voluntary alliances. As we shall see later, the success or otherwise of these depends not least on their appropriateness for the purposes for which they have been formed. These inter-institutional arrangements usually share, at the very least, an educational identity that sets them apart from people and organisations outside education, whether they be clients of the service or contributing in other ways. *Extra-institutional* collaboration can imply working with partners who hold different values, purposes and conceptions of what needs to be done to achieve them. Schools and colleges are continuously faced with the decision as to whether to take up a competitive or collaborative posture in relation to managing external relations. To ensure that their decision is the right one (or, where it is imposed, a workable one), all involved in the partnerships and alliances, as well as those following a competitive strategy, need to take account of the intra-personal, interpersonal, intra-institutional, inter-institutional and extra-institutional factors influencing outcomes. It is all too easy for schools and colleges to claim the rhetoric of collaboration with particular groups of people (e.g. parents) or organisations (e.g. within the commercial sector) and, in reality, continue to dominate and set an agenda which fails to be responsive to their partners' concerns.

In the rest of this chapter I aim to show how two factors are fundamental to the range of possibilities for collaboration or competition in contexts which contain driving forces for both: the individual (personal or institutional) will to collaborate or compete; and the political context. The two are, of course, related. Collaboration between institutions, whose staffs are demoralised by government acts that demean their professional status, will have little chance of success. In the context of the advent of a Labour Government in Britain, after years of Conservative rule, Lumby (1998) quotes one college principal's perception of the effect of a changing government on attitudes to collaboration and competition:

> I think the context for colleges is changing. Certainly the change of government with a different set of values has changed the agenda for further education. This will mean that one of the key issues for strategic planning will be to recognise that partnership and collaboration will need to be addressed in some way in both process and content. Within our strategic plan there is an emphasis on partnership but there is a hard edge there relating to the competitive element. The balance will change. The balance has swung since incorporation very much towards secrecy, non-partnership. Over the last two years we have seen that ease off slightly and over the next two years it will be swinging the other way.
>
> (Lumby, 1998, p. 60)

This principal's optimism obscures the fact that collaboration must be modelled and invited, not commanded. 'We have ways of making you collaborate' remains the same death knell to collaboration that it has always been. Would-be partners all too commonly remain sceptical of enthusiastically advocated partnerships that obscure hidden agendas and conflicting interests. A local education authority's proposal to bring in a company that runs state schools for profit in North America to run one of its failing schools has been viewed by some as opening the back door to the privatisation of education. Critics remain unconvinced by the company's claim that they are not about privatisation but about private–public sector partnerships (Rafferty, 1998). The same scepticism characterises responses to government plans for education action zones that rely on, in the government's words, 'imaginative ways of working using sustainable local partnerships built on the roles of schools, local communities and LEAs' (DfEE, 1998, p. 4). The range of partners proposed for these zones is indeed wide, to include local clusters of schools working with the LEA, local parents, businesses, Training and Enterprise Councils and others. Yet within this complex set of co-operative relationships, the spectres of individualism and competition are still present. The collaborative efforts are centred around the curriculum, through the sharing of resources including teachers and accommodation. Differentiation rears its head in the form of flexible contracts to attract 'outstanding educational leaders', additional rewards for outstanding performance by individuals and teams, and the creation of specialist schools with additional resourcing. The injection of these divisive strategies into a set of arrangements described in the language of collaboration threatens to undermine the validity of the enterprise. The projects are further potentially compromised by their financial dependency on funds and other resources from the business world which, for many educators, represent commercial values that are inimical.

COLLABORATION AND COMPETITION: FRIENDS OR FOES?

So far in this discussion, collaboration and competition have been presented as seemingly antithetical processes, representing different beliefs about appropriate strategic action or means to achieve shared or individual goals. The debate around the precise meanings of collaboration particularly can appear semantic, yet it is essential if those responsible for managing the ensuing processes are to make the right strategic decisions. If the rhetoric advocates a shift to greater collaboration through partnerships and alliances, then leaders and managers have to understand the practical issues and underlying cultural change that need to be addressed. Kennedy (1997), in her proposals for widening participation in further education in Britain, recommends the establishment of a national system of permanent local partnerships which involve the community in planning the further education sector. In her view, competition has inhibited the collaboration necessary to widen participation (p. 35). Such partnerships enable alignments and collaborations to be created as a result of continuous discussion around a clear and urgent common purpose (p. 4). The Kennedy Report's powerful advocacy of partnerships must be complemented by an understanding of the dynamics of forming and sustaining partnerships across diverse groups, and the tensions that arise from the often disparate values and goals of those involved.

Elsewhere Wallace and I have written of 'collaboration as a subversive activity', proposing it as a feasible strategy for improving education and reflecting professional service values, in the face of central government pressure upon schools and colleges to compete against each other as a means of raising educational standards (Hall and Wallace, 1993). A review of the words associated with collaboration and competition show each to have a dark side to the positive characteristics that their proponents claim. However, the 'dog eat dog' identity of competition prevails in the eyes of many educators, who are suspicious of its emphasis on survival of the fittest, confrontation and conflict, coalitions to represent different interests, gamesmanship. Goals achieved through competition are inevitably at someone else's expense. Competition is, after all, a 'win-lose' game, in which players may start on equal or unequal terms, are motivated by the status that comes with winning, and may or may not play by the rules to achieve that status. When each student represents a pot of money (as is the case in self-managing schools and colleges), then any means may become acceptable to win their custom, including inventing student enrolments, exaggerating institutional successes, and sweeping out of sight whatever detracts from a public image shaped for success. Glatter (1995, p. 25) quotes the examples of schools who have been massaging their truancy figures to avoid being held up to ridicule. There has been more than one case in the last two years of colleges hauled over the coals for similarly massaging their enrolment figures to increase their income. On the other hand, proponents of competition would argue that, in reinforcing individual and institutional autonomy, it promotes creativity, as well as being more responsive to the demands of different constituencies. In this way, it is argued that competition leads to increased quality.

Advocates of collaboration would point to what individualistic colleagues lose by being locked in competition with each other rather than engaging in mutually enriching relationships, but collaboration has a negative side too. Dog helping dog, after all, has a soft ring to it, implying possible submission, compliance, acquiescence. In the context of war, for example, collaboration is seen as treachery, a betrayal. Leaders, particularly women, who adopt collaborative strategies are often seen as weak leaders, unable to stand on their own two feet. Reviewing research on women as leaders, Shakeshaft says:

> The collaborative approach to decision-making that shares power may cause women to be initially evaluated as weak or ineffective. Women who manage from a collaborative framework do so within a system that stresses the values of competitive individualism and personal achievement at the expense of community goals.
>
> (Shakeshaft, 1989, p. 207)

That same system is the one in which collaboration by all, women and men, is encouraged.

At a time when many government initiatives in education are pushing for more collaboration between institutions and community groups with different expectations about leadership styles, both men and women educational leaders are faced with establishing their authority without reneging on their commitment to collaborative styles of working. The expectations that parents, governors and employers in a community have of 'strong' leadership may include characteristics (such as a unilateral rather than relational use of power and a preference for leading from the front) that contradict the principles of collaborative leadership. As well as its negative associations, collaboration is associated with more positive concepts of relatedness, connectedness, affinity, mutuality. It implies interconnectedness as a basis for sharing, co-operating, exercising joint control. From the agreement to collaborate come alliances, contracts, partnerships. Consortia, for example, of schools or schools and colleges, represent patterns of connectedness in which individual strengths are also recognised and drawn upon. By coming together (unless it is to conspire and plot), partnerships provide possibilities for involvement and engagement, moral support and protection. Ideally working together means working harmoniously, shoulder to shoulder, as one. Striving for individual success, whether of the individual, the group or the institution, takes second place to creating the synergy required for success for the whole enterprise.

COMPETITION AND COLLABORATION: FRIEND AND FOE

So far I have presented collaboration and competition as mainly dichotomous, except in situations where collaboration internally is used to compete more successfully externally. Another way of viewing these strategic ways of working is as a continuum (Figure 4.2).

The typology represented in Figure 4.2, based on a notion of a continuum from conflict to collaboration, reflects two dimensions. The first covers the degree to which strategies encompass the aim of achieving

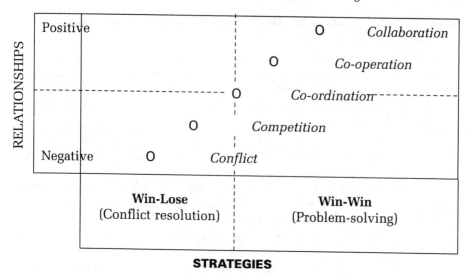

Figure 4.2. A continuum of ways of working

success for all those engaged in the interaction (a win-win scenario), or for one individual or group to the detriment of the other (a win-lose scenario). Bringing together individuals and groups who have previously believed in winners and losers (industrialists with educators, for example) needs careful handling. The second dimension addresses how far relationships are positive and mutually supportive, or negative, where one individual or group achieves goals at the expense of the others' feelings. The amount of shared effort, pooling of resources, and commitment distinguishes collaboration from co-operation or co-ordination, both of which involve working together but with less commitment to joint goals. Competition implies one group or individual striving to achieve goals at the expense of another, but within acknowledged parameters – the rules of the game. The term 'conflict' represents overt struggle where anything may go.

Glatter (1995) argues that the commonly accepted dichotomy between 'competition' and 'collaboration' is misleading and that they should not be seen as mutually exclusive processes (p. 27). He uses evidence from the PASCI Project (looking at the interaction between parental choice of secondary school and school decision-making in a competitive climate, fully reported in Woods, Bagley and Glatter, 1998) to support his view that schools do collaborate for instrumental purposes of competitive advantage, as well as in many other ways. He concludes that, since collaboration clearly does have a place in the quasi-market model, the necessary infrastructures must be put in place and maintained to support its continuation. Collaboration then becomes an appropriate strategy for preserving education as a public service offered by professionals, motivated by a desire to serve the common good. Research in both North America and Britain confirms that collaboration within schools is one of the key factors associated with effective pupil learning. Sammons, Thomas and Mortimore (1997) show that more effective schools in Britain are proactive in harnessing parental support (extra-institutional); and intra-institutionally, heads of more effective departments attach considerable importance to teambuilding and teamwork. Collaboration thus becomes not only possible when education is in the market place but all the more to be fought for, whatever the constraints.

Many of the new partnerships being proposed for education resemble arranged or even shotgun marriages. The partners may come from different sectors with different values and perceptions of the purposes of education and the practices of those who work in it. If some educators have objected to central government's imposition of competition on their ways of working, others, as professionals, balk against being required to collaborate. They perceive it as a threat to their professional autonomy and devise strategies, as Hargreaves (1991) has so cogently argued, to circumvent its imposition. He points to the dangers of contrived collegiality that ignores or damages the spontaneity, voluntariness, development-orientation, pervasiveness and unpredictability that characterise collaborative working relationships between teachers and their colleagues. He questions the possible results of replacing these characteristics with collaboration that is administratively regulated, compulsory, implementation-oriented, fixed in time and space and predictable. Arguments about the extent to which teachers should be technicians or artists provide another example of the different perceptions that those within and outside education bring to its purposes and processes. The educators who contributed to Macbeth, McCreath and Aitchison's (1995) volume focusing on collaboration or competition in a range of educational contexts, come firmly down on the side of collaboration as being the most appropriate strategy for the culture of education, supported by the testimonies of the book's contributors.

So far I have argued that collaboration and competition are engaged in by individuals and groups (the actors) who bring with them values, cultural expectations and an understanding of what the different approaches involve, based on their experience. Central to their participation are the accountability relations and the way they perceive their accountability to the partnerships and alliances of which they are a part. Competition engendered by education in the market place has made many schools and colleges inward looking and, at the same time, strengthened their accountability to their own constituencies. Partnerships muddy the waters of accountability by requiring accountability to a whole group (of people and institutions) rather than to a single unit. For some, the advantages of separatism outweigh the benefits of unity.

Sometimes the decision to collaborate rather than compete is more obvious than others, assuming that the choice of appropriate strategy still exists. Levacic and Woods (1994), based on their examination of a number of examples of collaboration, conclude that a partnership between a secondary school and its feeder primaries seems to be the type most likely to develop successfully, a conclusion supported by the PASCI studies referred to earlier. It is unambiguously in the interests of staff from institutions providing for a later phase of schooling to build strong links with potential feeder schools who are their suppliers. Similarly, as Evans and Lunt (1995) show in their study of an LEA's responses to the reorganisation of special education needs provision, pooling resources for that purpose would enable schools to form a team that could support pupils who might otherwise be suspended or sent into segregated provision. However, changing the individualistic cultures in legally autonomous schools and colleges is not an easy task for those responsible for coordinating newly formed clusters.

COLLABORATIVE AND COMPETITIVE LEADERSHIP

The role of leadership becomes crucial in determining the success of new partnerships and alliances and is itself transformed by the collaborative (or competitive) nature of the setting of which it is a part. Sayer (1989) argues for a collegiate form of school management that involves other professional services, parents and other interest groups in real decision-making. As he strikingly expresses it, managing outwards is not just about managing the ship but the currents around it and even the mud in which it is stuck (p. 145). When new groups start working together, questions are inevitable about where leadership does and should reside. Who has responsibility for making the partnerships work? Each of the groups involved (e.g. a further education college, a secondary school, a governing body) will have its own identified leader, whose status may be undermined in a different setting with competing leaders. Yet for collaborative efforts to be successful, leaders have to be skilled in managing the specific behaviours and processes that collaboration requires.

Headteachers and principals are no more likely to be expert in engaging in or managing collaboration than their colleagues and wisely look to share responsibilities for managing this way of working with outsiders. In whatever context the decision to collaborate is taken, the process of developing collaboration between individuals and groups unaccustomed to working together is a major innovation. If implementation is to be more than superficial and transient, those presently concerned and any newcomers have to learn new practices and change their beliefs and values in a way that cannot be imposed. The first gamble for a leader choosing or being forced to collaborate is whether more will be gained than lost by the group they represent. A further challenge comes from the extent of the congruence between collaborative styles of working and their own preferred leadership style.

Based on our development work with leaders of collaborating groups (Hall and Oldroyd, 1992), we observed the use of a range of styles, differentiated in terms of the relative amount of influence over decisions exercised by the leaders or followers. Figure 4.3 shows how, while all three types of collaborative group shown require both leaders and managers, the leadership function is more likely to be shared as the group moves towards a Type Z mode of operating and the formal leader becomes principally a facilitator.

Although Type Z might be the ideal goal of collaborating groups, many teachers may prefer a Type X situation, particularly when pressured by the immediate demands of the classroom, with little time to manage. On the other hand, leader-directed collaboration may be more appropriate when one or more of the following conditions exist, i.e. when groups:

- are at the early stages of their development, or have a finite lifespan
- have clearly defined tasks, tight deadlines
- have participants who are not yet fully committed to collaboration or are unsure of what it involves.

	Type X	**Type Y**	**Type Z**
	LEADER-DIRECTOR COLLABORATION	NEGOTIATED COLLABORATION	DELEGATED COLLABORATION
Formal leader Influence on Decisions	High	High	Low
Follower Influence on Decisions	Low	High	High
Process Role	•persuade •'the boss'	•negotiate consensus •'primus inter pares'	•delegate •'the facilitator'

Figure 4.3. Types of collaboration and leadership style

In the initial stages of collaboration, for example, the group's members may, as a result of shared uncertainty and conflicting interests, look to the group leaders or manager to provide the 'vision'. This situation was common in groups in all sectors that we studied, which had been set up for specific purposes, involving collaboration as a means to achieve their goals. Where these goals had been defined by outside agencies, the leader's task was to find ways of helping colleagues transform the goals into ones of which they could take ownership. As one co-ordinator said, 'Collaboration is a way of making visions a reality'.

Leading collaborative efforts also requires leaders to decide how much they are willing to share. In countries where more powers are being given to school boards or governing bodies, many principals have been forced to question how they work with governors and how much they will share power with them. The choices made by designated leaders relate to their own beliefs, values, actions, leadership style and the support they give others as autonomous individuals. Different contexts present different leadership challenges for implementing strategy and require different responses. Decisions have to be made about whether strategic action taken now in the interests of the school may work later against a longer-term strategy for the improvement of the education service as a whole. Adopting a collaborative strategy means involving individuals and groups internal and external to the school in its affairs. Stoll and Fink's (1996) research on effective schools highlights the links between school improvement and collaborative leadership styles. In this situation, where collaboration is in the interests of both the individual institution and the common good, leaders must make strategic choices about whether they will manage their staff members as individual units or assume that they are inherently connected. Chairs of collaborative groups have the task of converting an aggregation of autonomous individuals into a functioning unit. They have to overcome insistent individualism and promote connections in order to cultivate a sense of collective responsibility for the groups whose educational needs they serve. As well as titled leaders, successful collaborative efforts require untitled leaders, whose work oils the machinery of collaboration. This function becomes particularly important when the collaborating groups involve partners with differential status, though the intra- as well as interpersonal struggles of high-status leaders forced to work together can create tensions of their own.

PARTNERSHIPS, ALLIANCES AND STRATEGIC CHANGE

Cardno's model for the collaborative management of strategic change includes 'managed collaboration' which requires the leader to make several decisions about managing the collaborative process itself before engaging others in the partnership (Cardno, 1998, p. 106). She cites the example of schools and colleges in New Zealand who must, in drawing up required organisational charters, consult stakeholders. The process is overseen by the principals who in turn must know who these stakeholders are. She describes how getting a collaborative approach to strategic management wrong can lead to alienation and a lowering of the sense of a community endeavour. Its strengths, however, outweigh the dangers:

> At the governance–management interface the benefits of a collaborative approach include the development of skills in strategic thinking and planning, the creation of commitment to strategic decisions and a general unity about priorities and direction. The collaborative approach also has advantages at the organisation–departmental interface by increasing staff's knowledge of and commitment to a chosen direction of change.
>
> (Cardno, 1998, p. 110)

She proposes three tests to determine participation of stakeholders. First is the test of jurisdiction, that is, always involve those who have jurisdiction and clarify its parameters in terms of official roles and responsibilities. Second is the test of relevance, that is, always involve those for whom the decision is one they will be required to implement and be accountable for the results. Her third rule of thumb for collaboration is the test of expertise. Those for whom the decision is highly relevant should only be involved selectively according to whether they also have official jurisdiction, in which case they may need their expertise developing. I would add a fourth requirement to hers; a meta-requirement that all involved should be aware of and preferably trained in the skills of collaboration, something which is rarely addressed on training programmes for laypeople and professionals working in the interests of education.

In his proposals for a framework for new relationships between school and community, Williams (1989, p. 151) includes the need for schools to have objectives that are dependent on those involved recognising that it will be essential to achieve integration or fusion of school/community aspirations, objectives and interests for the success of schools in all aspects of their work. Communication systems that are direct, unfiltered, accurate and two-way are crucial to the process though not easily achieved while competition still has a part to play. Even if competition was eliminated, as the basis of a market place philosophy and a set of practices for education, the micropolitics of organisations would ensure the continued undermining of collaborative attempts. Hoyle (1986) describes micropolitics as 'almost a separate organisational world of illegitimate, self-interested manipulation' (p. 126) Coalitions, from this micropolitical perspective, become divisive devices for pursuing interests rather than goals.

Creating the openness required for successful collaboration involves identifying the appropriate boundaries between closeness and distance. Churchill was overheard to remark, 'My wife and I tried to breakfast together but had to stop or our marriage would have been wrecked.' As suggested earlier, partnerships and alliances in education have many of the characteristics of voluntary and shotgun marriages, including the need for the newly-weds to start constructing their joint rather than distinctive versions of reality.

Drawing together the skills required to lead collaboration, Figure 4.4 shows the twelve characteristics of effective managers of collaboration that were the outcome of the development work I referred to earlier.

Effective managers of collaboration:
• promote joint work for joint purposes
• support positive relationships
• achieve a high level of sharing in order to solve problems
• use collaboration to respond to curriculum change
• use collaboration to enhance both individual and institutional effectiveness
• realise that individuals and groups vary in their readiness to collaborate
• use different forms of collaborative leadership
• use leadership styles that give a similar emphasis to structuring group activities and motivating group members
• recognise that collaboration needs time for and commitment from participants
• diagnose the setting (culture and climate) before promoting collaboration
• operate in settings that are open, collegial and consultative
• influence the setting in which it occurs.

Figure 4.4. Twelve characteristics of effective managers of collaboration

CONCLUSIONS

In this chapter I have aimed to show how the prescriptions for collaboration, particularly in contexts where competition continues to be valued, need to be accompanied by a thorough understanding of the essence of different forms of collaboration and the skills required to ensure that they are successful. Leading and managing collaborative efforts means managing people for collaborative ends, managing cultures which support collaboration and managing processes. The three are interlinked. Managing people for collaboration means creating conditions which support the will to collaborate and the growth of a commitment to joint work as creative not threatening. It means shaping cohesive groups from a diverse range of people ingredients, not all of whom were selected specifically for their ability or desire to work together. Williams, for example, talks of creating cohesive groups and not just making 'human cocktails' (1989, p. 156). It means providing opportunities for exchange and knowing how to manage the dynamics of group meetings, where conflict may be more apparent than consensus. It means creating a culture which values learning from each other. The communities of learning which the Kennedy Report advocates are more likely to have fuzzy than rigid boundaries, thereby creating opportunities for collective learning which becomes more than the sum of the individual learner parts. It has become commonplace in education as elsewhere to talk of the learning organisation. Partnerships and alliances as collaborative efforts are potentially the perfect learning organisations. As Pedler, Burgoyne and Boydell (1991) have shown, the energy flows of learning companies enable individual purpose to come about through shared identity which in turn fires collective purpose. Similarly collective purpose gives meaning to an individual's life and place in the company (p. 31).

For critics of the commercialisation of education, becoming responsive to the needs of individuals need not mean becoming individualistic. Even if, as I have shown, it is possible to collaborate to be different, it is also possible to collaborate for a common purpose and a common good. Intra-institutional collaboration, which we know contributes to effective schools, has to be accompanied by extra-institutional partnerships and alliances that will contribute to effective communities for lifelong learning. Global electronic educational opportunities threaten the sanctity of the individual school or college and require new forms of collegiality. At the same time the virtual relations that are created through these new technological forms have to be accompanied by real relations between schools and colleges and the communities of people they serve.

REFERENCES

Cardno, C. (1998) Working together: managing strategy collaboratively, in D. Middlewood and J. Lumby (eds.) (1998) *Strategic Management in Schools and Colleges*, London, Paul Chapman.

DfEE (1998) *Education Action Zones*, London: HMSO.

Evans, J. and Lunt, I. (1995) Meeting special educational needs through partnerships, in Macbeth, McCreath and Aitchison, *op. cit.*

Glatter, R. (1995) Partnership in the market model: is it dying? in Macbeth, McCreath and Aitchison, *op. cit.*

Hall, V. and Oldroyd, D. (1992) *Development Activities for Managers of Collaboration*, Bristol: NDCEMP.

Hall, V. and Wallace, M. (1993) Collaboration as a subversive activity: a professional response to externally imposed competition between schools? *School Organisation*, Vol. 13, no. 2, pp. 101–117.

Hargreaves, A. (1991) Contrived collegiality: the micropolitics of teacher collaboration, in J. Blase (ed.) *The Politics of Life in Schools: Power, Conflict and Co-operation*, London: Sage.

Hoyle, E. (1986) *The Politics of School Management*, London: Hodder & Stoughton.

Kennedy, H. (1997) *Learning Works: Widening Participation in Further Education*, London: HMSO.

Levacic, R. and Woods, P. A. (1994) New forms of financial co-operation, in S. Ranson and J. Tomlinson (eds.) *Autonomy and Independence in the New Governance of Schools*, Harlow: Longman.

Lumby, J. (1998) Restraining the further education market: closing Pandora's box, *Education and Training*, Issue no. 2, March–April, pp. 57–62.

Macbeth, A., McCreath, D. and Aitchison, J. (eds.) (1995) *Collaborate or Compete: Educational Partnerships in a Market Economy*, London: Falmer Press.

Pedler, M., Burgoyne, J. and Boydell, T. (1991) *The Learning Company*, London: McGraw Hill.

Rafferty, S. (1998) US firm in bid for Surrey school, *Times Educational Supplement*, 17 July, p. 3.

Sammons, P., Thomas, S. and Mortimore, P. (1997) *Forging Links: Effective Schools and Effective Departments*, London, Paul Chapman.

Sayer, J. (1989) Issues for management training, in J. Sayers and V. Williams (eds.) *Schools and External Relations: Managing the New Partnerships*, London: Cassell.

Shakeshaft, C. (1989) *Women in Educational Administration*, 2nd edition, Newbury Park, Ca: Sage.

Stoll, L. and Fink, D. (1996) *Changing Our Schools: Linking School Effectiveness to School Improvement*, Buckingham: Open University Press.

Wallace, M. and Hall, V. (1994) *Inside the SMT: Teamwork in Secondary School Management*, London: Paul Chapman.

Williams, V. (1989) Schools and community: a framework for new relationships, in J. Sayer and V. Williams. (eds.) *Schools and External Relations: Managing the New Partnerships*, London: Cassell.

Woods, P. A., Bagley, C. and Glatter, R. (1998) *School Choice and Competition: Markets in the Public Interest?* London: Routledge.

Section II: Relating to Stakeholders

5

SCHOOLS AND THE STATE

Keith Foreman

In a review of international education systems, Levin (1997) stated that 'large-scale educational reform is widespread across the industrial world'. Schools have been, and remain, subject to changes demanded by governments determined to raise standards of student learning and achievement. Basing his analysis on an OECD summary of more than two dozen countries (OECD, 1996), Levin argued that this period of reform is sharply different from earlier periods of major change:

> If these were characterised by a strong desire for growth, a sense of optimism and a focus on the positive contribution of schooling to social and economic welfare, the current wave of reform is linked to feelings of fear, retrenchment and cynicism. . . . Educational change is occurring in the context of large-scale criticism of schools. Government policy documents typically take the view that school systems have failed to deliver . . . and that the failure is especially lamentable in view of the high level of spending on schools.
>
> (Levin, 1997, p. 254)

The underlying cause of the wave of reform has been economic, to ensure future global competitiveness. An earlier OECD survey (1993) described the position in this way:

> Only a well-trained and highly adaptable labour force can provide the capacity to adjust to structural change and seize new employment opportunities created by technological progress. Achieving this will, in many cases, entail a re-examination, perhaps radical, of the economic treatment of human resources and education.
>
> (OECD, 1993, p. 9)

Levin argues that the failure of schools is attributed to their 'capture' by teachers and managers resistant to change. This explains why this era of reform is not generally accompanied by large-scale funding. The concern is for improved outcomes at lower unit cost.

Another feature is the increased influence of ideological groups intent on removing power from 'the state' – from politicians and bureaucrats – and handing it to 'the market'.

> The market solution ... currently holds politicians around the world in its thrall ... (it) provides (them) with all the benefits of being seen to act decisively and very few of the problems when things go wrong.
>
> (Gewirtz, Ball and Bowe, 1995, p. 1)

While national leaders may have been attracted by notions of competition and business practice, they have not been easily persuaded to hand over powers. In countries where educational authority was formerly exercised at central and regional levels (e.g. USA, Canada, UK) the former have been strengthened at the expense of the latter. Education has thus become much more prominent politically. This has led to heightened public and media interest in school performance and has forced schools to devote much more attention to external relations.

TRENDS IN INTERNATIONAL EDUCATIONAL REFORM

Although details vary from country to country there are three trends which are common to many reform packages.

1. *Self-management of schools:* the devolvement of authority, particularly over finance, to school principals/headteachers, and the creation of councils or governing bodies to share that authority. This, according to Caldwell and Spinks (1992), is the 'international megatrend'.
2. *Centralisation:* increasing central government control of education policy and practice, particularly over curriculum, assessment and the training and employment of teachers.
3. *Competition and consumer preference:* legislation giving parents and students more choice through the creation of market-like mechanisms – often referred to as quasi- or regulated markets.

But governments face major problems in achieving their objectives. First, there is the obvious contradiction between local management and choice on the one hand and increased centralisation on the other. The former encourages diversity, the latter conformity. If all schools are expected to teach the same curriculum why bother with devolution and parental choice?

Then there is the resistance of professional and institutional organisations to changes forced upon them. Hargreaves (1994) summed it up in this way:

> Schools *and especially classrooms* are remarkably resilient to change, much to the consternation of politicians, policy-makers and innovators (. . .) Professional and institutional structures . . . withstand many an assault and have powerful capacities to maintain and reproduce themselves despite surface changes.
>
> (Hargreaves, 1994, p. 10, original emphasis)

A third difficulty is related to the change process which is 'uncontrollably complex' and requires 'a two-way relationship of pressure, support and continuous negotiation. . . . We have known for decades that top-down change doesn't work . . . leaders keep trying because they don't see any alternative and they are impatient for results' (Fullan, 1993, p. 37). Politicians may apply varying degrees of pressure and support, but 'continuous negotiation' on a national scale is simply not possible. 'Consultation' is the best option but it may be greeted with cynicism by those who may reasonably doubt its authenticity.

A fourth problem is that education and politics, by their very nature, are contentious. For any theory, argument or proposition there are others in opposition. Furthermore, education policies arrived at through the cut and thrust of central political processes still require implementation by professionals who may be deeply opposed to them, but whose support and commitment are essential to success.

Finally, there is the sheer length of time needed to achieve significant change, for instance, to pedagogical practice. Dalin concluded that 'There is no quick fix . . . it is a complex and long journey' (Dalin *et al.*, 1993, p. 119). But the very nature of politics requires rapid results – to prove that 'schools can be turned round' in response to central direction. Thus initiative is heaped upon initiative, target on target, risking confusion and disenchantment among practitioners.

This chapter focuses on the relationship between the state, the supreme political authority, and state schools in England. There is general agreement that changes in educational management in the UK have been among the most radical. Johnson (1997) assessed the position in this way:

> It is difficult to overestimate the scale and profundity of changes that have occurred within the English education system and the whole of the British public sector over the last 17 years or so. Many . . . institutions . . . have been dismantled or significantly redesigned. Relations at all levels reshaped and reweighed. . . . A country accustomed and conditioned to expect incremental, evolving adjustment in the public domain has experienced a New Right project of radical and systematic changes.
>
> (Johnson, 1997, p. 52)

The debate about the effectiveness of these reforms is not concluded. There is certainly 'no consistent view' about how successful they have been in 'transforming teachers' practice' (Hargreaves and Evans, 1997).

Between 1988 and April 1997 Conservative governments were in power; from May 1997, with a landslide majority, a 'New Labour' administration. The Conservatives placed their emphasis on structural changes to the school system, a national curriculum, inspection and parental choice. Labour emphasises 'excellence for all' while maintaining many of the practices begun by their predecessors. Excellence for everyone means increasing central influence and control over teaching and learning.

This chapter will examine each of the three international trends in educational reform noted above (see p. 68). The focus is not so much on *impact* in the sense used by the government researchers and inspectors seeking evidence of improvement resulting from particular reforms. Nor is the focus on *responsiveness*, i.e. sensitivity and adaptability to external pressure or stimulus (see Lumby, Chapter 13). Rather it is on the *reaction* of schools to a plethora of government reforms.

Evidence has been gathered by interviewing seven headteachers selected because they had been in post for a decade, four of them in the same school. Their schools are situated in four local authorities: two are primary (4–9); two middle (9–13); three secondary (11–16, 13–18, 11–18). Numbers on roll vary from 200 to 1,800 (see Figure 5.1). Semi-structured interviews were conducted in February and March 1998. Questions invited heads' personal perceptions of the impact, practicability and consequences of major reforms, and also what they had done to introduce and incorporate them into their schools. Given the sheer volume of reform, selection of topics was inevitable, and only brief reference is made to existing research findings.

These seven schools may be regarded as an opportunity sample. What

School	Phase	Age group	LEA	No. on roll	Teaching staff (FTE)
A	primary	4–9	W	208	9
B	primary	7–11	X	232	9
C	middle	9–13	Y	515	22
D	middle	9–13	Y	285	14
E	secondary	11–16	Z	400	32
F	secondary	13–18	W	868	59
G	secondary	11–18	X	1,830	95

Figure 5.1. Details of sample schools

their heads provided was their personal response to a barrage of external mandate, pressure and criticism. Organisations subject to generalised complaints about performance present extraordinary challenges to the people who lead in them, and they react in different ways. These are the reactions of seven leaders.

SELF-MANAGEMENT

Local management of schools (LMS) increased the powers of governors, heads and staff, at the expense of local education authorities (LEAs), to determine the specific purposes of their schools and to deploy resources in pursuit of these aims. Income was linked to pupil/student numbers, encouraging competition. Grant maintained status provided even more freedom from LEAs.

Self-management is based on the theory that decisions for individual schools will be more effective and efficient if made by people within them who are able to tailor spending to the perceived needs of pupils/students. Making governors responsible for a school and headteachers accountable to them reflected an uneasiness about putting too much power into the hands of professionals. In practice, LMS meant that headteachers became more powerful and created the potential for conflict between professional and lay interests (see, for instance, Baginsky, Baker and Cleave, 1991; Thody, 1994; Esp and Saran, 1995; Deem, Brehoney and Heath, 1995). However, most governing bodies 'far from being overactive, are still lethargic, while others are working in amiable co-operation with their schools' (Johnson, 1997, p. 15).

An OECD synthesis of studies in nine countries gave a cautious welcome to self-management.

> Greater autonomy in schools ... (leads) to greater effectiveness through greater flexibility in and therefore better use of resources; to professional development selected at school level; to more knowledgeable teachers and parents, so to better financial decisions; to whole-school planning and implementation with priorities set on the basis of data about student (outcomes) and needs.
>
> (quoted in Thomas and Martin, 1996, p. 28)

Other researchers have not been so welcoming. Ball (1994) argues that:

> Self-management is a mechanism for delivering reform rather than a vehicle for institutional initiative and innovation. Furthermore, it gives apparent autonomy to the manager while taking apparent autonomy from the teacher. It drives a wedge between the curriculum – the classroom-orientated teacher – and the market – the budget-orientated manager.
>
> (Ball, 1994, p. 71)

A majority of the interviewee headteachers saw the financial freedom that LMS provided as the reform they had most welcomed because, in the words of the head of school A, 'it allowed us to prioritise expenditures and be creative, to act quickly without waiting on the LEA'. Savings allowed this school to 'make major purchases or prepare for a rainy day'. But three of the seven had faced serious problems. One secondary head with a declining roll in a previous school had grappled with the problem of 'concealing overspending from governors' – until 'sleepless nights caused a rethink'. Another had been a 'loser' by the LEA formula and had to manage subsequent staff redundancies. One, unable to balance a budget deficit *and* meet the requirements of the National Curriculum, had handed responsibility for the budget back to the LEA.

All the headteachers interviewed had found ways of working out relationships with governors by themselves taking a major role 'either with governors' approval or by default or by outmanoeuvering (them)' (Johnson, 1997) or by pursuing definition in their respective roles. They worked hard to avoid conflict, giving much more time to governors than had been the case prior to 1988. Sub-committee work had been extended and other staff, particularly deputies, invited to share in their work. One primary head (school B) had a taxing experience with an ineffective governing body – 'they were simply not interested in the responsibilities they bore in law'- and was grateful to move on to another school and another (more effective) set of governors.

CENTRALISATION

The list of actions taken by central governments to improve standards in their schools since 1988 is extensive. The focus here is upon the following:

- curriculum and assessment
- inspection
- measures to extend control over teachers
- actions to limit the powers of LEAs.

Curriculum and assessment

The first National Curriculum (NC), introduced in the 1988 Reform Act amid much controversy and opposition (Barber, 1996), was supported by a complex structure of national testing at 7, 11, 14 and 16 based increasingly on test data measured against national standards. The impact in primary schools has been extensively researched (see, for instance,

Campbell and Neill, 1994; Osborn and Black, 1994; Croll *et al.*, 1994). They found teachers to be working conscientiously (perhaps too much so) for longer hours with more of their time taken up with professional development, preparation, administration and, above all, assessment. In secondary schools the major concerns were assessment (Ball and Bowe, 1992), the degree of prescription (Ribbins, 1993) and subject specialisms (Campbell and Neill, 1991). The controversy and opposition that it engendered led Barber (1996, p. 72) to assert that 'it is dangerous, damaging and sometimes humiliating to run roughshod over the teaching profession' and that 'policy is brought into disrepute if it is changed on a (ministerial) whim'.

The headteachers consulted for this research were asked about their reactions to the NC and how their staff had responded. All the heads accepted that it was needed though deploring the way it had been introduced – without teacher consultation – and managed, and its 'great cost'. They reported some resentment especially amongst older teachers against over-prescription and the unsettling changes that a succession of ministers had made to both the curriculum and its assessment. The head of school C believed that the NC reduced teachers to 'operatives'. Another suggested that it made teachers 'do what they must rather than their best', while another asserted that it 'restricted creativity because of the detail laid down'. A primary head (school B) made the point that subject skills have become too critical a factor in staff appointments. 'If someone has the combination you want, he/she gets the job in preference to someone who reveals all sorts of other, very desirable qualities'. The Labour government focus on literacy and numeracy were welcomed by the primary and middle school heads, though again there were doubts about its prescriptiveness and detail. Nevertheless, the impression created by these experienced heads was that they would cope with any change required of them. The keys to success were interpretation and prioritisation – assisting the teaching staff to prepare for new demands by building them into the school's planning processes.

Inspection

The 1992 Act introduced Ofsted. No state school was exempt from systematic public scrutiny. The aims were higher standards and increased accountability – 'improvement through inspection'.

While inspection and other forms of external evaluation are common in OECD countries, practice in England gives *less attention to internal self-review* than is the case elsewhere and *more attention to published tables of performance* (CERI, 1995).

The literature on the effects of inspection is copious. Ouston *et al.* (1996) found 'abundant evidence ... of the stress and anxiety which inspections engender' (p. 103) but they tentatively suggested that, with greater experience, schools 'may be developing a more mature and confident approach to inspection, coming to terms with the inspection process' (p. 101). Ouston *et al.* (1996), investigating the relationship between school development plans and inspection in 170 secondary schools, reported that most headteachers thought that inspection had been valuable to their school's development. On the other hand, Gray and Wilcox (1995, p. 96) having surveyed 24 schools following inspection, reported that 'Only about a quarter or so of the recommendations could be said to be at best substantially implemented and nearly 40 per cent remained essentially unimplemented'.

The views of headteachers in this survey broadly reflected these research findings. On the positive side, the head of school A recognised its thoroughness and the benefits of knowing what was to be expected and the criteria to be used. 'We prepared very carefully – including a mock inspection. The report was good; it raised morale.' A middle school head (school D) said that the inspection, the grading system and public reporting proved an excellent lever for moving staff to 'consider their present positions'. But negative comments were more in evidence. One middle school head (school C), who had been inspected twice, described his inspections as 'a complete and utter nonsense in terms of school improvement'. He resented its high cost and asserted that the process of preparation had deflected the school from its planned development.

A number of heads criticised inspection because it was not coupled with advice. 'The process should be developmental – a springboard to greater things – but it was not' (school B). The head of the 13-18 upper school suggested that managing inspection has become merely a matter of routine. It 'was keeping the path clear'. The other secondary headteacher, able to compare inspections in his two schools, had serious doubts about their reliability. In the first case 'we got a caning', in the other 'it was glowing' but there were only marginal differences in examination performance and other criteria. The first school was struggling to recruit following an earlier crisis over its leadership, but was improving rapidly. The second school was the most popular in the borough and oversubscribed.

The 'failing' school has been a feature of the inspection process. The 1993 Act inaugurated a 'special measures' regime and by January 1997 over 250 schools had been thus designated, leading to regular re-inspection. The government believed that such measures would shock schools into action. 'Naming and shaming' was adopted by New Labour creating intense opposition among heads and teachers.

Failure is a growing area of international concern and the subject of an OECD study (OECD, 1997). Kovacs (1997) found a distinct difference between those countries, a majority, which emphasised *failure at school* (i.e. the failure of students) and the minority, including the UK, which talked of school *failure* (i.e. the failure of those responsible – heads, teachers, governors).

The reaction of survey headteachers to the policy on failing schools reflected the controversy which it engenders. It was recognised that the strategy seemed to work in some cases. It led to extra support and gave staff and governors a great sense of urgency, once the initial shock had passed. School E was in special measures. The head said that it had made his colleagues 'more resilient' but also 'more hard-edged and practical. It made us very conscious of our dependency on the outside world – and much more skilled in dealing with the media.' In contrast, there was condemnation of a blunt weapon which failed to take into account the differing social and economic contexts in which schools were placed. 'Naming and shaming' received severe criticism, reflected in the comment by the head of school E that 'we would not dream of treating staff or children in that way – it is psychologically wrong'. But this can be compared with the reaction of two heads of 'named' schools – writing anonymously – who argued that 'the policy works . . . it had the desired effect' (*TES*, 1998).

Control of teachers

Teachers' strikes in the early 1980s led to a number of measures to control and regulate the profession, including:

- excluding unions from pay bargaining
- laying down detailed conditions of service
- compulsory training and funding targeted at government priorities
- compulsory appraisal
- directed time – determined by headteachers.

Many of these measures led to difficulties and tensions between unions and government and also between headteachers and their staff. Teachers felt disempowered (see, for instance, Whitty, Power and Halpin, 1998; Busher and Saran, 1995).

Appraisal has been the subject of much debate and controversy (see Middlewood, 1997). Reactions of interviewee headteachers varied from 'I welcomed it. If I'm carrying a white clipboard, the staff know I am observing them' (school A) to more typically, 'a time-consuming, cumbersome and unnecessary process . . . it's on the back burner' (school F). All the schools had implemented some form of annual review which might or might not include classroom observation. As one head put it, 'We had to interpret the legislation to make it work'. Training days and directed time had been 'absorbed'. All illustrated ways in which they had tried to make it easier for their teachers: setting government requirements in some order of priority; working together to find practical solutions; motivating measures to raise self-esteem; maintaining a positive image for the school in the local community; or setting up working parties – for example, on staff development. But they also recognised the dangers of 'over protection' in an era of increasing transparency and accountability.

Schools and LEAs

Under the 1944 Act, LEAs were to provide 'a varied and comprehensive education service'. They built and maintained schools, recruited and paid teachers, and provided a wide range of services to schools, parents and local communities. But relations between central and multi-purpose local authorities were 'perennially fraught' (Ball, Vincent and Radnor, 1997) and in the 1980s Conservative governments began an attack on the local authority role in educational management.

The thrust of Conservative legislation was to 'circumscribe LEA involvement in the management and governance of the education service' (Audit Commission, 1998, p. 9) leading to a position where LEAs were described as having 'very little power and no clear role' (Brighouse, 1996). The key reform was LMS, forcing LEAs to hand over a large percentage of their budgets to schools. Measures to limit local government processes and finances came in close order including allowing, indeed encouraging, schools to opt out of LEA control. Heads and governors of the first GM schools cited 'independence from the LEA' as the most important reason for their decision (Bush, Coleman and Glover, 1993). The position of the 1997 Labour government is that there is a need for an intermediate body in the management and governance of education, and LEAs should have this role (DfEE, 1997).

None of the headteachers in this survey had sought to break away from their LEAs and they did not approve of GM status. The head of school F saw the initiative as 'a gross misuse of public expenditure'. Another (school C) accused GM schools of encouraging selection, and weakening the ability of LEAs to provide an effective service to all parents. They all welcomed the intention of the Labour government to return GM schools to the LEA fold. Their response to the prospect of LEAs with more responsibilities for school performance varied with their experience of relationships during the previous decade. All of them had invested funding in LEA services, sometimes made available through privatised agencies, welcoming the choice available to them. One primary head (school B) spoke warmly of the LEA's support in the introduction of the 1994 Code of Practice for Special Educational Needs. This was a measure introduced by DfEE following unusually extensive consultation between central and local government. Another primary head (school A) welcomed his LEA's compilation and distribution of comparative performance data, regretting that 'it had only recently got round to it ... it had not grasped early enough the nettle of underperformance'. If there were still some concerns about 'paternalism' and 'patronage', there was also clear recognition that their LEAs were striving to support them in response to central government demands. However, much depended on the quality of the relationships these heads struck with advisers/inspectors. One (primary) head, now into his fourth appointment since 1986, could look back over several 'link advisers'. 'Some have simply been much more effective than others – and this helps to determine my response to and use of the LEA.'

Thus, a position of some stability in the forty years after the 1944 Act (the Golden Age of the LEAs) has been disturbed by, first, an outright attack upon their position and, since 1997, a reassertion of their role, subject to stringent accountabilities. For school leaders this has presented both threats and opportunities. For the great majority, however, there has been no wish to rid themselves of an often helpful and supportive ally. 'Many schools still look to the LEA for support and guidance' (Ball, Vincent and Radnor, 1997 p. 153). The headteachers in this sample have reflected this position.

MARKETS, COMPETITION AND CONSUMER CHOICE

Levin (1997), basing his assessment on OECD research, asserts that those advocates of the market in education have had most success in England (p. 252). Parents are, in principle, able to choose the schools their children will attend while schools are required to provide information to assist parents in making their choice. League tables of assessment results are published by central government, as are Ofsted inspection reports.

Critics argue that choice and market mechanisms lead to more selection and more provision for the most able at the expense of the least able (see, for instance, Ball, 1994). Fewer parents than anticipated appear to take advantage of the choice offered to them. The wishes of the student, the location of the schools, the choices of friends, the atmosphere in the school, appear to be as significant as the school's academic performance (West and Varlaam, 1991). Schools have responded by improving their advertising and public relations and monitoring the action of competing schools if not by producing substantial changes in teaching and learning (Gewirtz, Ball and Bowe, 1995; Bagley, Woods and Glatter, 1996) – the ultimate test of greater effectiveness.

All of the heads in this survey recognised that competition is a spur. They had produced more elaborate brochures and used the local media to enhance their image. Secondary schools have courted local primary schools. However, in pursuit of collaboration, 'pyramids' or local cross-

phase organisations, sometimes encouraged by LEAs, had been strengthened, though, as the head of school D suggested, 'not all heads wished to
join in'. Local agreements about admissions were often in use. One head
(school A) stated that 'town primary heads will always ask non-catchment
parents if they have checked with their "local" schools'. Collaborative
working was 'deliberately pursued' in several cases – in others, where
competition for students was high, 'it was harder to achieve'.

The publication of league tables with 'raw' data was universally con-
demned. 'Transparency' itself was not opposed – but the use of data which
were unreliable and misleading was. Benchmarking was given both a cautious ('reliability depends on the criteria you adopt') and an enthusiastic
('it provides a valid basis for comparison with other schools in similar
contexts') welcome.

AN OVERVIEW

When headteachers in this survey were asked to sum up their reactions
to a decade of national reform, their answers reflected their perception of
themselves as leaders and their schools as organisations. The head of
school D was totally disillusioned and looking for early retirement. 'I
cannot do any more . . . even a Labour government keeps piling on more
and more initiatives!' Another (school C) saw himself as being in 'constructive opposition' to every innovation, though he also spoke of his
'much greater sense of accountability'. This was underlined by a common
view among headteachers that their roles had become more complex and
demanding. They had to give much more attention to staffing issues, the
budget, working with governors and strategic planning. They also felt
obliged to give more of their personal time to external relations, especially
to marketing and public relations. More than one reflected the position
suggested by Gewirtz, Ball and Bowe (1995) that the government was
making policy and then blaming schools for under-achievement. But there
was also universal recognition that 'the wave of reforms now made the
position of the headteacher central to a school's success', confirming
earlier research findings.

All the headteachers had introduced a number of changes in management structures and practices. Greater financial responsibility had led
larger schools to appoint bursars. All schools had invested more or less
heavily in computer technology for administrative purposes. Secondary
schools had been forced by curriculum priorities and budgetary pressures
to reassess, in some cases reduce, the number of academic and pastoral
middle management posts. The head of the 11–16 secondary school
described the pressure on Heads of Department during an inspection as

'the toughest job in any school!' Primary schools had appointed curriculum or achievement co-ordinators. All staff were multi-roled. There was regular reference to 'more committees and more consultation' and to a sharper focus on 'vision, core purpose, mission' and above all, on the issue most central to a school's purpose, the quality of learning.

There was, inevitably, some scepticism and cynicism: for example, on the state's requirement for 'worship' and Ofsted references to requirements for daily assemblies not being met, but these were outweighed by a strong sense of commitment to teachers, support staff, students, pupils and parents, and to the improvement of an education service which had gone through a period of confusion and contradiction.

CONCLUSION

The main conclusion to be drawn from this study is that schools interpret and adapt national policies to suit their particular circumstances and the particular needs of their students. It demonstrates the contradictions between local management and centralisation, the resilience of professional organisations to external changes and the complexities inherent in raising educational standards. Regardless of what national governments may believe, 'one of the great fallacies of educational change is that policy directives from any level, have a direct impact on student achievement . . . the greater impact on student progress is achieved by those innovations or adaptations of practice that intervene in or modify the learning process' (Hopkins, 1998, p. 218). These innovations and adaptations of practice are, in the end, only made possible by the heads and teachers in the schools – those who were blamed for the failure of schools and whose apparent resistance to change, as Levin (1997) argued, was a central cause of this particular wave of reform.

However, it is abundantly clear that, over a decade, schools have learnt that change is permanent, have become much more aware of their corporate accountability and their responsibility for raising standards. It may also be argued that a Labour government recognises that a balance between pressure, support and continuous negotiation/consultation with a central focus on learning is more likely to raise standards than the 'brute sanity' of earlier administrations. If the relations between 'schools and the state' are to remain cordial and productive then programmes for change ought to focus on matters pertinent to learning rather than straying into the wasteful extravagances of political ideology.

REFERENCES

Audit Commission (1998) *Changing Partners: A Discussion Paper on the Role of the Local Education Authority*, London: Audit Commission.

Baginsky, M., Baker L. and Cleave, S. (1991) *Towards Effective Partnerships in School Governance*, Slough: NFER.

Bagley, C., Woods, P. and Glatter, R. (1996) Scanning the market: school strategies for discovering parental perspectives, *Education Management and Administration*, Vol. 24, no. 2, pp. 125–38.

Ball, J. and Bowe, R. (1992) Subject departments and the implementation of National Curriculum policy: an overview of the issues, *Journal of Curriculum Studies*, Vol. 24, no. 2, pp. 97–115.

Ball, S. J. (1994) *Educational Reform: A Critical and Post-Structural Approach*, Buckingham: Open University Press.

Ball, S., Vincent, C. and Radnor, H. (1997) Into confusion: LEAs, accountability and democracy, *Journal of Education Policy*, Vol. 12, no. 3, pp. 147–163.

Barber, M. (1996) *The National Curriculum: A Study in Policy*, Keele: Keele University Press.

Brighouse, T. (1996) *A Question of Standards: The Need for a Local Democratic Voice*, London: Politeia.

Bush, T., Coleman, M. and Glover, D. (1993) *Managing Autonomous Schools: the Grant-Maintained Experience*, London: Paul Chapman.

Busher, H. and Saran, R. (eds.) (1995) *Managing Teachers as Professionals in Schools*, London: Kogan Page.

Caldwell, B. and Spinks, J. (1992) *Leading the Self-Managing School*, London: Falmer Press.

Campbell, R. and Neill, S. (1991) *The Workloads of Secondary School Teachers*, London: AMMA.

Campbell, R. and Neill, S. (1994) *Teacher Commitment and Policy Failure*, Harlow: Longman.

CERI (Centre for Educational Research and Innovation) (1995) *Schools Under Scrutiny*, Paris: OECD.

Croll, P., Abbott, D., Broadfoot, P., Osborne, M. and Pollard, A. (1994) Teachers and education policy: roles and models, *British Journal of Educational Studies*, Vol. 42, no. 4, pp. 333–47.

Dalin, P. with Rolff, H. in co-operation with Kleekamp, B. (1993) *Changing the School Culture*, London: Cassell.

Deem, R., Brehony, K. and Heath, S. (1995) *Active Citizenship and the Governing of Schools*, Buckingham: Open University Press.

DfEE Standards and Effectiveness Unit (1997) *From Targets to Action*, London: DfEE.

Esp, D. and Saran, R. (1995) *Effective Governors for Effective Schools*, London: Pitman.

Fullan, M. (1993) *Change Forces: Probing the Depth of Educational Reform*, London: Falmer Press.

Gewirtz, S., Ball, S. J. and Bowe, R. (1995) *Markets, Choice and Equity in Education*, Buckingham: Open University Press.

Gray, J. and Wilcox, B. (1995) Inspection and school improvement: rhetoric and experience from the bridge, in *Good School: Bad School: evaluating performance and encouraging improvement*, Milton Keynes: Open University Press.

Hargreaves, A. and Evans R. (eds.) (1997) *Beyond Educational Reform: Bringing Teachers Back In*, Buckingham: Open University Press.

Hargreaves, D. (1994) A road to the learning society, *School Leadership and*

Management, Vol. 17, no. 1, pp. 9–21.

Hopkins, D. (1998), Powerful learning, powerful teaching and powerful schools, in B. Fidler, S. Russell, and T. Simpkins, *Choices for Self-Managing Schools*, London: Paul Chapman.

Johnson, D. (1997) *Governors in Schools and Further Education Policies*, University of Leicester, Educational Management Development Unit.

Johnson, H. (1997) England's funding agency for schools: making and implementing policy without accountability? *International Studies in Educational Administration*, Vol. 25, no. 1, pp. 52–59.

Kovacs, K. (1997) Combating failure at school: an international perspective, in L. Stoll and K. Myers (eds.) *No Quick Fixes: Perspectives on Schools in Difficulty*, London: Falmer Press.

Levin, B. (1997) The lessons of international educational reform, *Journal of Education Policy*, Vol. 12, no. 4, pp. 253–266.

Middlewood, D. (1997) Managing appraisal, in T. Bush, and D. Middlewood (eds.) *Managing People in Education*, London: Paul Chapman.

OECD (1993) *Education at a Glance*, Paris: CERI/OECD.

OECD (1996) *Meeting of the Education Committee at Ministerial Level: Lifelong Learning for All*, Report of the Secretariat, Paris: OECD.

OECD (1997) *Combating Failure at School: Dimensions of the Problem, Country Experiences and Policy Implications*, Paris: OECD.

Osborn, A. and Black, E. (1994) *The Changing Nature of Teachers' Work: Developing the National Curriculum at Key Stage 2*, London: NAS/UWT.

Ousten, J., Earley, P., Fidler, B. (eds.) (1996) *Ofsted Inspections: The Early Experience*, London: David Fulton.

Ribbins, P. (1993) Telling tales of secondary heads: on educational reform and the National Curriculum, in C. Chitty, (ed.) *The National Curriculum: is it Working?* Harlow: Longman.

TES (1998) Naming and shaming works, 17 April, p. 15.

Thody, A. (ed.) (1994) *School Governors: Leaders or Followers?* Harlow: Longman.

Thomas, H. and Martin, J. (1996) *Managing Resources for School Improvement*, London: Routledge.

West, A. and Varlaam, A. (1991) Choosing a secondary school: parents of junior school children, *Educational Research*, Vol. 33, no. 1, pp. 22–30.

Whitty, G., Power, S. and Halpin, D. (1998) *Devolution and Choice in Education: The School, the State and the Market*, Buckingham: Open University Press.

6

THE STATE AND COLLEGES

Jane Hemsley-Brown

INTRODUCTION

The predominant contemporary discourse in further education (FE) in the UK has dramatically changed since the incorporation of colleges in April 1993 when the 'new' sector for post-16 education was created. It is widely accepted by those involved in further education that since the early 1980s the government is 'imposing an economic paradigm on education' (Elliot, 1996, p. 9) and there has been a shift from a 'collectivist' (Beardshaw *et al.*, 1998) operational environment, dominated by a culture of collegiality and a humanistic philosophy with colleges working in partnership with LEAs (local education authorities) to a culture of managerialism within a rational-economic philosophy, operating in a competitive market environment managed by the Further Education Funding Council (FEFC). Despite this philosophical shift, however, there is less evidence to suggest that the operational environment is now more market-driven – although the rhetoric of the market-place is much in evidence (Scott, 1996). This chapter examines the changing relationship between the FE sector and government and provides an analysis of the ways in which significant policy changes have impacted on the management of external relations in colleges, in relation to:

- the policy framework
- the operational environment
- the culture.

POLICY FRAMEWORK

In broad terms the philosophy of further education could be described as having moved from 'humanistic' to 'rational economic', with a shift in the policy and missions of further education institutions from a predominant concern with professional issues to a concern with economic ones. Those working in the FE sector prior to the 1992 Act believe that the dominant philosophy was more collaborative with a 'liberal humanist curriculum which appeared to consider the needs of the students' (Leonard, 1998, p. 78). Reeves supports this view observing that:

> individuals working in colleges will have been accustomed to a more liberal, less directed, traditional regime reflecting a range of values. They will notice a diminution in personal autonomy and freedom of choices as they are forced to participate in the national economic mobilisation.
>
> (Reeves, 1995, p. 35)

The aims of further education have been redefined by government through a new emphasis on effectiveness, efficiency and expansion (FEFC, 1996) and a move away from professional integrity, autonomy, pedagogy and student-centredness (Elliot, 1996). Legislation implemented throughout the 1990s has changed the philosophy of the FE sector and affected the relationship between the state and FE colleges in a number of significant ways. These will be considered here in relation to:

- the impact of the 1992 Further and Higher Education Act
- the rhetoric of the market
- competition
- National Targets for Education and Training (NTETs)
- lifelong learning.

The impact of the 1992 Act

The Further Education Funding Council (FEFC) was set up to:

> ensure sufficient and adequate further education facilities throughout England to meet the need of students; to contribute to the development of a highly skilled workforce (. . .); [and] to promote access to further education for people who do not participate in education and training, but could benefit from it.
>
> (FEFC, 1996, p. 8)

'The incorporation of colleges following the Act meant that major financial decisions are now taken at college level' (Bradley, 1996, p. 379), whereas previously they were the domain of the LEA. Colleges had to adapt their management systems rapidly to take account of their new financial responsibilities. On the credit side, however, there was the idea that the move might 'free colleges from the shackles of inept or reactionary local authorities, raise the status of FE and help to establish an expanded and more coherent system' (Hyland, 1992, p. 106)

The new funding methodology has been the driver for implementing the government's agenda of 'economic efficiency', rapid growth through 'increased participation' and the 'raising of vocational skill levels' (FEFC, 1996). Although the government believed that linking funding to achievement would 'act as a powerful lever to improved performance' (DfEE, 1996, p. 10), the funding methodology is having more effect on encouraging growth than any other factor (NAO, 1997c, p. 20) and has fundamentally changed the philosophy of FE from an emphasis on human relations and curriculum, to an emphasis on financial imperatives (Foskett and Hesketh, 1996). The FEFC appears to want to manage the sector as if it were 'a homogeneous entity driven by an accountancy model with secondary regard to the educational process' (Evans, 1994, p. 7). The funding methodology has created 'a new value system and forced colleges into developing a market ideology' (Jephcote *et al.*, 1996, p. 35). The rhetoric of the market is examined in the next section.

The rhetoric of the market

Since the early 1990s there has been an escalation in the emphasis on market systems throughout the world as the 'best' solution to the problem of allocating scarce resources (Scott, 1996). In practice 'there has never existed a perfectly free market economy' (Seddon, 1987, p. 44) or a pure planned economy (Isachsen, Hamilton and Gylfason, 1995). In a predominantly market system 'an organisation matches its own human, financial and physical resources with the wants of its *customers*' (Wills *et al.*, 1983, p. 9). The key issues presented to support a market-driven education system are that enhanced choice for the consumer places organisations in a competitive environment which leads to greater 'cost effectiveness' (Sexton, 1990, p. 18); 'improved efficiency' (Bredo, 1987, p. 69); 'greater diversity' (Ball, 1990, p. 6); 'an improvement in standards' (Leonard, 1988, p. 52); 'higher quality' (Elmore, 1987, p. 80) and 'greater responsiveness' (Elmore, 1987, p. 87). The language of policy-making in further (and higher) education is suffused with the 'rhetoric of the market' (Scott, 1996), competition and choice – but 'the underlying objectives of policy have little to do with the promotion of market relations *per se* and much to do with increasing participation and reducing costs' (Scott, 1996, p. 26). Competition is central to the operation of a market, and is discussed in the next section.

Competition

Competition between providers has been the central focus of the new FE sector – because 'competition between institutions is seen as the best way to achieve cost-effective expansion' (Scott, 1996, p. 28). Competition in a *free* market, however, is viewed as the most effective way to ensure that individual interests are met – that *customer* needs are satisfied (Elmore, 1987). In the new further education sector, competition has not been introduced as a way of improving responsiveness to customer needs, but is viewed as a way of ensuring cost savings whilst meeting government-defined objectives. Colleges are forced to compete (FEFC, 1997a; Lumby, 1998) but they are also urged to work in partnership (DFE, 1992; DfEE 1998a) to improve skill levels. The notion of competition in the post-1992 FE sector relates to the need for colleges to compete with other providers to attract increasing numbers of students to avoid finance being 'clawed back' and the possibility of eventual closure (Ainley and Bailey, 1997). Such a competition-based perspective is not universally valued in the sector, however, and the Kennedy Report (FEFC, 1997a) 'deplores some of the effects of the free market and competition, describing some colleges and schools as wanting to go it alone' (Lumby, 1998, p. 59).

A competitive market environment is claimed to improve quality (Leonard, 1988) because providers are under pressure to meet customer demands and offer greater choice. Since 1992, however, the customer emphasis of a market ideology no longer prevails for students' interests are being represented by the 'paymaster' (Gravatt and Sorrell, 1996) – the FEFC – who pays colleges on their behalf and the government itself has maintained and reinforced its old position as the near-monopoly customer. This shift in power has re-defined education beyond compulsory schooling, by emphasising extrinsic rather than intrinsic reasons for participation. Skills for an effective working life have become more important than 'education' (McGinty and Fish, 1993) and the FEFC is funding 'qualifications' (Gravatt and Sorrel, 1996) rather than investing in training. The major objective is to up-skill the workforce to help Britain compete in a global market – but with virtually no additional financial investment (Reeves, 1995). The competitive environment has fundamentally shifted the philosophy and missions of colleges to an economic agenda drawn up by government, and colleges are expected to meet government targets in order to maintain funding.

National Education and Training Targets

Colleges are crucial to the creation of a highly trained and flexible workforce and in providing the skilled people businesses need (Reeves, 1995) in an ever more competitive global market (*TES*, 1997). As part of this strategy, the National Targets for Education and Training (NTETs) were launched by the CBI (Confederation of British Industry) in 1991. They drew attention to the serious skills gap that existed between the UK and a number of its foreign competitors. The Targets aim to 'improve the UK's international competitiveness by raising standards and attainment levels in education and training to world class levels' (NACETT, 1995, p. 12).

The relationship between the state and colleges has been significantly changed by the introduction of NTETs with colleges forced to relinquish power over the curriculum to the DfEE, through the FEFC – in a 'partnership' (DFE, 1992). Hyland and Turner argue that:

> In such a climate, it is nationally defined government targets, enforced through funding regulations, which dictate the FE curriculum not local needs and community interests.
>
> (Hyland and Turner, 1995, p. 42)

One of the characteristics of a planned economy is that 'targets are set by a central authority' (Isachsen, Hamilton and Gylfason, 1995). The government strategy for meeting the NTETs is characteristic of bureaucratic systems, where 'central government makes decisions about production' (Seddon, 1987, p. 42) and this increases accountability and dependency on the state rather than enhancing independence. Targets for educational development elsewhere in the world are more ambitious than in the UK and the levels of investment are higher. Government and private investment in education in the Pacific rim, for example, far exceeds the systems of western Europe (Cantor, Roberts and Pratley, 1995). In the UK, however, the strategy for raising standards and attainment levels in education and training has been implemented in conjunction with a strategy to drive down unit costs. For example, colleges with a predominantly 16–19-year-old intake are finding it increasingly difficult to attract extra students because of local competition, especially from 11-18 schools where funding is often higher and offers more flexibility. Development of subjects which require specialist facilities and equipment can also present financial problems.

Increasing the supply of highly educated people and maintaining high and sustainable levels of employment have led to recommendations for 'a new learning society' (DfEE, 1998b, p. 18) and a *National Strategy for Lifelong Learning* (Coffield, 1997).

Lifelong learning

The new Labour government elected in 1997 signalled its commitment to cradle-to-grave education within three months of being elected when Bob Fryer was charged with drawing up a blueprint for *Learning for the Twenty-First Century* (1997). There is growing support for the view that the UK needs to develop a learning culture if people are to meet the challenges of the next century. The philosophy behind the lifelong learning strategy is based on a finding that the UK performs poorly in international comparisons in both training and educational attainment – notably in 'basic and core skills' (Tuckett, 1997, p. 3).

The creation of a learning society is economic in origin and is based on the need to cope with the unpredictability of change. The Green Paper *The Learning Age* indicates that:

> equipping people with the right knowledge and skills will be crucial to maintaining high and sustainable levels of employment and price stability. It will improve productivity.
>
> (DfEE, 1998b, p. 33)

There is an acknowledgement, however, that the Learning Age is more than just improving productivity and employment opportunities and that 'the development of a culture of learning will help to build a united society' (DfEE, 1998b, p. 10). The Kennedy Report recognises the unique contribution of further education towards a 'self-perpetuating learning society' (FEFC, 1997a, p. 25) and argues that further education is the key to widening participation in lifelong learning. Current approaches to lifelong learning differ from those previously promoted and stress not only the importance of further education colleges and the LEAs, but:

> the vital importance of the role played by various kinds of partnership in learning, rather than concentrating chiefly on the role of government as a monopoly provider of formal education and training.
>
> (Chapman and Aspin, 1997, p. 117)

This vision of lifelong learning for all is expected to embrace both compulsory and post-school education and requires the collaborative efforts of government, the CBI, the TUC, employers, TECs, funding bodies, training providers and colleges, and LEAs (DfEE, 1998a). The new strategy also recognises the key role of local authorities as strategic planners, co-ordinators, partners and providers (Fryer, 1997). While the LEAs will probably have a co-ordinating role, it will need to operate in a way which focuses on securing adequate provision for a wide range of groups in society, including under-represented groups. It has also been recognised that if FE is at the core of the government's lifelong learning strategy 'there is a need to focus more resources there' (*THES*, 1998, p. 12). The partnership approach to creating and promoting a learning society in which local authorities will play a major role potentially changes the relationship and environment in which FE sector colleges currently operate, and suggests a need for greater collaboration. Changes in this operational environment are examined in the next section.

OPERATIONAL ENVIRONMENT

'In post-compulsory education (as opposed to schools) there have been surprisingly few policies deliberately designed to encourage the growth of markets' (Scott, 1996, p. 27). There has been a significant change in who the major customers of further education are – a shift from student-con-sumers to employers and the government – but there is little evidence to support the conjecture that a market in further education was created by the 1992 Act:

> Factors usually associated with the market in education, including perfor-mance indicators, accountability and vocationalism have been key features of the FE sector since the mid-1980s, and arguably for much longer than that.
>
> (Elliott, 1996, p. 7)

The operation of a market system in FE, for many managers, has been overshadowed by the complexities of a new FEFC bureaucracy and both before and after 1992 the operational environment in colleges has exhib-ited elements of both a market and a planned system. The 'marketisation' of the FE sector, however, has affected the operational environment of col-leges significantly through policy developments affecting the following areas:

- funding
- growth
- widening participation
- alternative sources of funding.

Funding methodology

A decade ago the funding of the education system in England could be described as a national system locally administered, a partnership between the then Department of Education and Science (DES) and the local edu-cation authorities (LEAs). The Further and Higher Education Act (1992) made colleges 'independent bodies and established funding councils for England and Wales to administer the central government grant for the further education sector' (NAO, 1997c, p. 9). Education and training pro-grammes were converted into 'funding units by means of a tariff which gave standard values of units to different aspects of provision' (McClure, 1997). 'The tariff is probably the most important set of numbers in further education because it creates the link between the FEFC's policies and their implementation via funding allocations' (Gravatt and Sorrell, 1996, p. 17). Two key observations emerge from this development. Firstly, the diversity between providers (Evans, 1995; Glatter, Woods and Bagley, 1996; Foskett,

1998) which characterised the FE sector is decreasing, generating a more homogeneous system nationally. Secondly, the further education sector has gained little from 'independence' and has exchanged one bureaucratic system (LEAs), for another (the FEFC) (Jephcote *et al.*, 1996).

The new funding arrangements had a negative impact on the operational environment in which FE sector colleges operated. (A more detailed summary of how the funding methodology is applied in practice is provided by the National Audit Office (NAO, 1997c).) For example, prior to incorporation a college might have only two main demands for performance data – to prepare the annual Further Education Statistical Return (FESR2) and to make recoupment claims to other local authorities. Since 1993, however, the FEFC's funding guidance lists the much increased audit evidence required to support funding claims. An FE college, for example, with 10,000 students, one-third of whom were under 19, one-third of whom were eligible for fee remission and 5 per cent of whom were eligible for additional support, would have to keep over 30,000 pieces of paper as evidence (Gravatt, 1996, p. 25).

The FEFC claims to aim to ensure that the funds allocated are used 'effectively' and 'efficiently' and, therefore, some colleges have been under considerable pressure to reduce costs or to increase growth rates to bring costs in line with other colleges as the FEFC has been working towards 'convergence' (DfEE, 1996, p. 6) so that by 2002, all colleges will receive the same amount of money per unit (Hemsley-Brown, 1997). The security under the LEA, which was gained through historical funding and an emphasis on local needs, had provided stability and afforded some collaboration between local education providers who believed that they were able to respond to the needs of students and local employers. Relationships between the LEAs and colleges varied widely prior to the incorporation of colleges and this affected not only the financial situation which colleges inherited when joining the newly incorporated sector, but also perceptions of the reforms (Ainley and Bailey, 1997).

Significant changes in the funding of colleges have fundamentally changed the operational environment in which the FE sector operates although the system remains 'a mixed economic environment' (Seddon, 1987, p. 44) with some characteristics of a market and some elements of a planned economic system. The economic goal has become paramount and colleges are forced to implement significant efficiency measures to avoid closure (Reeves, 1995) or 'mergers with other colleges' (Ainley and Bailey, 1997, p. 114). Pressure to improve the efficiency of public utilities has also resulted in additional problems for some institutions. Colleges, for example, relying on employees taking day-release programmes from the public sector have faced growth problems because the public sector is also facing cuts. Training areas such as construction have also been hit because of cyclical depression in the industry (Frampton, 1995). The funding mechanism has emphasised the need to expand above any other factor, and growth is discussed in the next section.

Growth

The move to free colleges from LEA control and raise the status of FE was expected to support considerable growth in participation among 16–19-year-olds. The Kennedy Report (FEFC, 1997a) acknowledges that growth has taken place at an impressive pace and gives credit to colleges and other providers who rose to the challenge. The Council's funding of colleges had two strands – the demand-led element (DLE) and the main allocation. The DLE was intended to encourage colleges to expand, particularly in areas where there is demand and their marginal costs are low. Financial constraints, however, led to the DfEE removing demand-led funding from 1997, and a key pathway to growth for colleges was thereby removed.

Colleges cannot afford to remain static because failure to grow would set a college budget on a downward spiral (Ainley and Bailey, 1997). The funding system does not give colleges more independence but encourages dependence on the state through the funding council. The funding is structured in such a way that colleges are forced to compete in the same or similar markets for students who are most likely to meet the FEFC criteria – securing entry, staying on the learning programme and gaining qualifications (Stanton, 1996). For example, a sixth form college in a middle class area which already concentrated on full-time 'A' level programmes, retained a high proportion of students, and provided high levels of additional support would, at least initially, have been favoured because it was 'already doing what the FEFC wanted them to be doing' (Gravatt and Sorrell, 1996, p. 64). However, an FE college in inner London, with a high intake of students on benefit taking workshop-based programmes, such as computing or engineering not funded directly by an employer and with higher drop-out rates, might be treated less favourably.

Reeves (1995, p. 29) argues that colleges will be 'forced to shed activities that are not funded, marginally funded, or cannot be funded by other means'. Colleges intending to expand are thus not free to operate in a market environment but are dependent on complex funding constraints and regulations issued through the FEFC. Emphasis on growth within the constraints of the funding mechanism has led to concerns about social inequality and the need to widen participation (FEFC, 1997a).

Widening participation

The Kennedy Report (FEFC, 1997a) highlighted concerns about widening participation and expressed serious reservations about the competitive market environment operating in the FE sector. It is suggested that what is needed 'are more systematic strategies to address persistent patterns of under-participation and under-achievement among some groups' (FEFC, 1997b, p. vii). Recent support for this analysis has been provided by the DfEE (DfEE, 1998a) which now aims to 'make this country both more competitive and a fairer and more cohesive society' (NACETT, 1998, p. 1). The Kennedy Report argues that 'learning is central to economic prosperity and social cohesion' and claims that:

> a dramatic shift in policy is required to widen participation in post-16 learning and to create a self-perpetuating learning society.
>
> (FEFC, 1997a, p. 15)

The DfEE is only now acknowledging that faith in the competitive market system may have contributed towards social inequality in participation. Market systems are charged with producing unacceptable levels of inequality and 'governments are forced to intervene in markets to alleviate the worst excesses' (Beardshaw *et al.*, 1998, p. 65). Under the FEFC there are lucrative markets, which are funded, and there are poor markets – those which are not funded (Gravatt and Sorrell, 1996). Further education colleges have experienced a highly conflicting relationship with the market, therefore, as they have been encouraged to carry out the directives imposed by the FEFC, which exhibits characteristics of a planned economic system, by behaving competitively as though operating independently in a market system. Despite this strait-jacket, however, some colleges have been innovative and proactive in seeking new markets and have sought alternative funding for additional growth.

External links and alternative funding

'Not all income derives from the FEFC, although it constitutes well over half for most colleges' (Harper, 1997, p. 65). In 1997 the National Audit Office recommended that 'colleges should consider the opportunities for growth in areas of activity not funded by the Funding Council' (NAO, 1997a, p. 4). Colleges receive funds from, for example, Training and Enterprise Councils (TECs), local employers, the National Lottery, schools, the Higher Education Funding Council (HEFC) and residence and catering operations (Harper, 1997, p. 65). College managers are expected to be innovative in seeking alternative sources of funding (Crequer, 1997) through other bodies including:

- *The Private Finance Initiative (PFI).* The government expects that the private sector will play an increasing part in the funding of the public sector, although the Association of Colleges has warned that few colleges will be able to attract investment from the private sector, even through the PFI Project (Russell and Munro, 1998). Schemes such as

PFI involve considerable negotiation and contracts are complex although a small number of colleges have secured funding for proposed building schemes.

- *The European Social Fund (ESF)*. The European Union, through the European Commission, also provides funds for work and technology related projects. For FE colleges and voluntary organisations, the main source of money from Europe has been the European Social Fund (ESF). However, its utility is limited for 'the Fund is quite specifically about employment issues – and only supports schemes which help people get or keep work, such as vocational training and guidance' (ESF, 1998, p. 1).

- *Franchising*. Some colleges have achieved rapid growth through collaboration with employers, private training providers, schools, community and voluntary organisations and other institutions to deliver further education provision on a franchised basis (NAO, 1997c, p. 20). Since 1992 franchising has been one of the most rapidly developing ways of generating additional funding but the demise of demand-led funding is likely to make the economics of franchising less attractive from 1998–99 onwards (NAO, 1997b, p. 4). Franchising is an alternative method of achieving growth and relies on collaborative efforts between a number of partners, usually, but not necessarily, in the local area. For example, a home counties FE college arranging franchising agreements with a large number of companies in London and Essex could have surpassed its student number targets by 40 per cent in 1995–6. This would have reduced its average level of funding down to one of the lowest in the area (Gravatt, 1997).

The need to bid for funding from a range of non-FEFC organisations potentially changes the relationship between the state and the FE sector significantly. Governing bodies were advised that the change in status of colleges to corporate institutions would bring about 'a new form of independence, a new maturity, which brings with it new rights, duties and responsibilities' (Cuthbert, 1988, p. 5). Colleges have the potential to extend their autonomy and increasingly acquire the appearance of business organisations rather than state-dependent monopolies by increasing non-FEFC income. However, applying such a business model to education would be against the ideological position of many lecturers who are fearful of the shift in the 'core business and focus of colleges' (Elliot, 1996, p. 13) and a significant shift in culture. The issue of cultural change is considered in the next section.

CULTURAL CHANGE

One of the outcomes of significant and widespread reforms of the structure and curriculum of FE has been to create contradictory and oppositional forces within the sector. Senior managers working within the ideology of a market have embraced a 'control ethos' and a 'managerialist culture' (Elliot, 1996, p. 16) which clashes with the democratic ideology and commitment to student-centred learning which underpins the practice of many lecturers. Changes in the structure and funding of the FE sector have impacted on the culture of FE colleges in two key ways:

1. an emerging culture of managerialism
2. dependence, independence and collaboration.

Managerialism

The wide ranging reforms since incorporation, many of which are designed to increase efficiency and meet performance indicators, were imposed (rather than negotiated) by senior managers in response to government pressure (Elliot and Crossley, 1994). Following incorporation, in some institutions, there has been a cultural shift away from 'negotiated collegiality' (Elliot, 1996, p. 20) towards rationalistic new managerialism. Smaller, more cohesive management teams have also emerged as a way of avoiding the 'old interdepartmental rivalries' which might hamper the whole college's chances of survival in the new and uncertain environment (Ainley and Bailey, 1997).

Leonard (1998) argues that since incorporation a managerialist culture has developed, which is more masculine, authoritarian and traditional compared with the collegial, democratic style of the 1980s. The management style which has emerged is highly structured with little dialogue with members of staff further down the structural hierarchy. A significant change in management style also has implications for the relationship between the LEA and the FEFC and individual colleges, and a move towards greater collaboration.

Dependence, independence and collaboration

The market paradigm offers at one and the same time constraint and opportunity. The incorporation of colleges was hailed as an end to the dependency culture created by the LEAs and the beginning of a new independence (NAO, 1997c) under the FEFC. Incorporation, particularly the new funding arrangements, had the reverse effect and forced colleges to compete for a larger share of those markets which are funded by the funding council. This has increased dependence rather than promoting independence from the state although the rhetoric has continued to focus on independence in a competitive market. The new managerialist culture and the policies of the FEFC and its requirements have also reduced the space and scope for 'the exercise of teachers' professional autonomy' (Ainley and Bailey, 1997, p. 72). Many teachers feel they have lost control over their own working lives through increasing regulation imposed from outside, and through a significant change in management style.

The government's response to the report *Learning Works* (FEFC, 1997a) supports the view that the way forward is through 'collaboration' and 'strong partnerships' (DfEE, 1998a). It is now recognised that 'excessive emphasis on market competition in the past has inhibited collaboration and strong partnerships are now needed to develop local strategies for learning' (DfEE, 1998a, p. 9). Educational institutions have a wide range of external links (Foskett, 1998) which go beyond relationships with funding bodies and government and the ethos of FE relies on providing a 'service to the community and responding to the needs they have got' (Ainley and Bailey, 1997, p. 66) which can only be achieved through collaborative effort.

CONCLUSIONS

This chapter has examined three opposing elements which have characterised FE institutions since incorporation, their philosophy, operational environment and culture. Since FE sector colleges were removed from local authority control they have been coerced by the funding methodology into implementing the government's agenda of economic efficiency, rapid growth through increased participation and the raising of vocational skill levels. These legislative changes have fundamentally changed the ethos and culture of the sector, and the operational environment has shifted away from a customer-orientated market system towards a rational-economic market system. However, in recent years there has been growing interest regarding business practices in Asia (Arias, 1998) and a new approach to marketing has emerged stressing 'partnership' (DfEE, 1998a) and 'collaboration' (Lumby, 1998; Elliot, 1996) which stresses:

> the importance of managing relationships and building a highly loyal customer base and marketing networks, in the longer term.
>
> (Grönroos, 1997, p. 323)

The best way forward would appear to be to 'find strategies which replace the dominant discourse with one which is predicated upon collaboration rather than competition' (Elliott, 1996, p. 22).

REFERENCES

Ainley, P. and Bailey, B. (1997) *The Business of Learning*, London: Cassell.

Arias, J. T. G (1998) A relationship marketing approach to *guanxi, European Journal of Marketing*, Vol. 32, no. 12, pp. 145–56.

Ball, S. (1990) *Markets, Morality and Equality in Education*, London: Tufnell Press, Hillcole Group No. 5.

Beardshaw, J., Brewster, D., Cormack, P. and Ross, A. (1998) *Economics: A Student Guide*, Edinburgh: Addison Wesley Longman.

Bradley, D. (1996) Who dares wins: intended and unintended consequences of the Further Education Funding Council methodology, *Educational Management and Administration*, Vol. 24, no. 4, pp. 379–88.

Bredo, E. (1987) Choice, constraint and community, *Journal of Education Policy*, Vol. 2, no. 5, pp. 67–78.

Cantor, L., Roberts, I. and Pratley, B. (1995) *A Guide to Further Education in England and Wales*, London: Cassell.

Chapman, J. D. and Aspin, D. N. (1997) *The School, The Community and Lifelong Learning*, London: Cassell.

Coffield, F. (1997) *A National Strategy for Lifelong Learning*, Newcastle Upon Tyne: Department of Education, University of Newcastle.

Crequer, N. (1997) Hackney hard hit by funding policy, *Times Educational Supplement News and Opinion*, 3 January, *TES* Online Archives: http://www.tes.co.uk.

Cuthbert, R. (1988) *Going Corporate*, Bristol: Further Education Staff College.

DES (Department for Education and Science) (1992) *Further and Higher Education Act*, London: HMSO.

DFE (Department for Education) (1992) *Education for Adults in FE Colleges*, A Report by HMI, London: DFE.

DfEE (1996) *Funding 16–19 Education and Training Towards Convergence*, DfEE London: TSO.

DfEE (1997) *Widening Participation in Life Long Learning*, DfEE: TSO.

DfEE (1998a) *Further Education for the New Millennium, Response to the Kennedy Report*, Sudbury: DfEE Publications Centre.

DfEE (1998b) *The Learning Age*, DfEE: TSO.

Elliot, G. (1996) Educational management and the crisis of reform in further education, *Journal of Vocational Education and Training*, Vol. 48, no. 1, pp. 5–23.

Elliot, G. and Crossley, M. (1994) Qualitative research, educational management and the incorporation of the further education sector, *Educational Management and Administration*, Vol. 22, no. pp. 188–197.

Elmore, R. F. (1987) Choice in public education, *Politics of Education Association Year Book*, pp. 79–98.

ESF (European Social Fund) (1998) *European Social Fund*, ESF Internet Web Site: http://www.funderfinder.org.uk/pack/esf.html.

Evans, R. (1994) Further Vision, *Education*, Vol. 183, no. 2, p. 7.

Evans, I. (1995) *Marketing for Schools*, London: Cassell.

FEFC (1996) *Introduction to the Council*, Coventry: FEFC.

FEFC (1997a) *Learning Works: How to Widen Participation*, Report by Helena Kennedy QC, Coventry: FEFC.

FEFC (1997b) *How to Widen Participation: A Guide to Good Practice*, Coventry: FEFC.

Foskett, N. H. (1998) Linking marketing to strategy, in D. Middlewood and J. Lumby (eds.) *Strategic Management in Schools and Colleges*, London: Paul Chapman.

Foskett, N. H. and Hesketh, A. J. (1996) *Student Decision-Making and the Post-16 Market Place*, Southampton: Centre for Research in Education Marketing/Leeds: CREM/Heist Publications.

Frampton, D. (1995) *Towards a Nation of Shopkeepers: The Devocationalisation of the FE Curriculum*, Lewisham College Praxis Papers, 2, December, Lewisham: Management Monographs.

Fryer, R. H. (1997) *Learning for the Twenty-First Century*, First Report of the National Advisory Group for Continuing Education and Life Long Learning, London: DfEE.

Glatter, R., Woods, P. A. and Bagley, C. (1996) *Choice and Diversity in Schooling: Perspectives and Prospects*, London: Routledge.

Gravatt, J. (1996) *ISR Institutional Surveillance and 'So Called Data'*, Lewisham College Praxis Papers, 4, January, Lewisham: Management Monographs.

Gravatt, J. (1997) *Deepening the Divide: Further Education Franchising and the Diversion of Public Funds*, Lewisham College Praxis Papers, 6, January, Lewisham: Management Monographs.

Gravatt, J. and Sorrell G. (1996) *Equity and Equality: The Impact of Convergence on Colleges and Students*, Lewisham College Praxis Papers, 5, September, Lewisham: Management Monographs.

Grönroos, C. (1997) From marketing mix to relationship marketing: towards a paradigm shift in marketing, *Management Decision*, Vol. 35, no. 4, pp. 322–39.

Harper, H. (1997) *Management in Further Education: Theory and Practice*, London: David Fulton.

Hemsley-Brown, J. (1997) Double disadvantage: the move towards convergent funding in further education, *Management in Education*, Vol. 11, no. 4, pp. 12–13.

Hyland, T. (1992) Reconstruction and reform in further education, *Educational Management and Administration*, Vol. 20, no. 2, pp. 106–10.

Hyland, T. and Turner, M. (1995) Chasing Cinderella: principals' views on FE incorporation, *Educational Change and Development*, Vol. 16, no. 1, pp. 38–44.

Isachsen, A. J., Hamilton, C. B. and Gylfason, T. (1995) *Understanding the Market Economy*, Oxford University Press.

Jephcote, M. with Salisbury, J., Fletcher, J., Graham I. and Mitchell, G. (1996) Principals' responses to incorporation: a window on their culture, *Journal of Further and Higher Education*, Vol. 20, no. 2, Summer, pp. 33–48.

Leonard, M. (1988) *The 1988 Education Act: A Tactical Guide for Schools*, London: Basil Blackwell.

Leonard, P. (1998) Gendering change? Management, masculinity and the dynamics of incorporation, *Gender and Education*, Vol. 10, no. 1, pp. 71–84.

Lumby, J. (1998) Restraining the further education market, closing Pandora's box, *Education and Training*, Vol. 40, no. 2, pp. 57–62.

McClure, R. (1997) How the colleges are financed, *Times Educational Supplement*, 2 June, *TES* Online Archives: http://www.tes.co.uk.

McGinty, J. and Fish, J. (1993) *Further Education in the Market Place: Equality, Opportunity and Individual Learning*, London:, Routledge.

NACETT (National Advisory Council for Education and Training Targets) (1995) *Review of the National Targets for Education and Training, Report on the Outcomes of the Consultation to Update the National Targets*, London: HMSO.

NACETT (National Advisory Council for Education and Training Targets) (1998) *Targets for Our Future*, London: LSO.

NAO (National Audit Office) (1997a) *Further Education Colleges in England: Strategies to Achieve and Manage Growth*, House of Commons Papers, London: The Stationery Office.

NAO (National Audit Office) (1997b) *The Management of Growth in the English Further Education Sector. Report by the Comptroller and Auditor General*, House of Commons Papers, London: The Stationery Office.

NAO (National Audit Office (1997c) *The Further Education Funding Council for England Report by the Comptroller and Auditor General*, London: TSO.

Reeves, F. (1995) *The Modernity of Further Education*, Sandiacre: Bilston Publications.

Russell, B. (1997) Principals to bring budgets in line, *Times Educational Supplement*, March.

Russell, B. and Munro, N. (1998) 13 million pounds failure will not hit private finance, *Times Educational Supplement*, 24 January.

Scott, P. (1996) Markets in post-compulsory education: rhetoric, policy and structure, in N. H. Foskett, (ed.) *Markets in Education, Policy, Process and Practice*, Southampton, CREM Publications.

Seddon, E. (1987) *Advanced Economics*, London: Pan.

Sexton S. (1990) Free market's better values, *Education Guardian*, 14 August, p. 18.

Stanton, G. (1996) *Output Related Funding and the Quality of Education and Training*, International Centre for Research on Assessment, University of London.

TES (Times Educational Supplement) (1997) The professor says the country needs lifelong learning, November, *TES* Online Archives, http://www.tes.co.uk.

THES (Times Higher Education Supplement) (1998) Millennium Magic – Blunkett style? 27 February.

Tuckett, A. (1997) *Lifelong Learning in England and Wales: An Overview and Guide to Issues Arising from the European Year of Lifelong Learning*, Leicester: National Organisation for Adult Learning.

Wills, G., Cleese, J., Kennedy, S. and Rushton, A. (1983) *Introducing Marketing*, Bradford: MCB University Press.

7

WORKING WITH GOVERNORS: A BRIDGE TO THE COMMUNITY?

Peter Earley and Michael Creese

INTRODUCTION

What do we mean when we talk of 'a school'? A school photograph will include the pupils and the teachers, sometimes the non-teaching staff, but where is the governing body? Are the governors seen as part of the school or part of 'external relations' which the school has to manage? This is a difficult question to answer. Some of the governors will be teachers and other members of staff, some will be parents, but others may have only a rather tenuous connection with the school. In a major study of newly-appointed headteachers conducted in the mid-1980s, relations with governors were dealt with under the general heading of 'the management of external relations' (Weindling and Earley, 1987). Governors occupy a unique position – they are members of the community as parents, local residents, employers – and the governing body is on the boundary of the school, partly in the school and partly in the community served by the school. The governing body can act as a bridge between the school and the community and, if operating successfully, can be a two-way conduit for communication between them.

In its widest sense of the word, the 'community' includes both central and local government. The history of the relationship between governors, local education authorities (LEAs) and central government is one of change, particularly over the last 50 years. In 1833 Parliament voted the first grant of public funds to education which was conditional upon schools being open to inspection and being administered under an

approved scheme of management. Public funding thus demanded accountability, locally through boards of managers and centrally through inspection. Local education authorities (LEAs) were established as a result of the
1902 Education Act and their position was reinforced by the 1944
Education Act. The majority of governors and managers were now
appointed by the LEA except in voluntary aided schools.

Sallis (1988) suggests that the greatest weakness of the 1944 Act was
its failure to give any guidance as to the kind of people who were to be
appointed as governors or managers. Disenchantment with the system led
to the establishment of a Committee of Enquiry in 1975 under the chair-
manship of Lord Taylor and their Report, published in 1977, recommended radical changes. The Education (No. 2) Act of 1986 took up the
main recommendations of the Taylor Report and produced further change
in the composition of governing bodies (the term 'manager' disappeared)
which effectively ended political control by the LEA. Governors were now
required to produce an annual report on their work for parents and to
hold a meeting at which that report is discussed.

Hardly had the changes introduced by the 1986 Act been digested than
it was followed by the 1988 Act. Gann (1998) summarises its effect well
when he states: 'While the 1986 Act caused a tremor in schools, the 1988
Education Act brought about an earthquake' (p. 20). The role of the LEA
was diminished in a number of ways. Control of the school's budget (based
upon the number of pupils in the school) was delegated to the governing
body. Central government, in the form of the Department for Education
and Science (DES), would provide some funding directly to schools for
priorities established centrally. Increasingly, LEAs could be by-passed in
the decision-making process. Through the introduction of grant-maintained status, schools were given the opportunity to opt out of LEA control
altogether. Over 1,000 schools chose to become GM and to receive their
funding direct from the centre, via the newly established Funding Agency
for Schools. The governing bodies of these schools had very considerable
powers and it is not always clear to whom they are accountable.
Legislation passed in 1998 enabled these schools to become 'Foundation'
schools with at least some local representation on the governing body.

HOW REPRESENTATIVE ARE THE GOVERNORS OF THE COMMUNITY SERVED BY THEIR SCHOOLS?

Deem (1992) has pointed out that democracy and accountability imply
that those involved in governing schools should include a cross-section
of the population. However, it is by no means certain that the composition of governing bodies reflects accurately the communities served by

their schools. Several surveys (e.g. Keys and Fernandes, 1990; Earley, 1994) have found that the majority of governors come from backgrounds usually referred to as middle class. There are also issues of gender and race in the make-up of governing bodies. Overall, while there are approximately equal numbers of male and female governors (Keys and Fernandes, 1990; Earley, 1994), about 60 per cent of the governors in secondary schools are male and only about one-third of the chairs of governors of all schools are female. Many governing bodies have set up standing committees in order to handle their business more efficiently. Deem and her co-workers (1992) suggest that finance committees, which often wield considerable influence, tend to be dominated by white men. The appointed LEA and elected parent and teacher governors have the power to co-opt further governors up to a specified limit. When considering co-options, the governors are required to ensure that their governing body reflects a balance of interests. However, Streatfield and Jefferies (1989) found that about two-thirds of all co-opted governors are male which suggests that ensuring gender parity on the governing body is not a prime consideration when making co-options. The number of non-white governors across the country is very small – around 2 per cent – and this certainly does not reflect properly the communities served by some schools. Other research has pointed to the limited representation of business and industry on governing bodies (particularly at senior management level) with the largest number serving as parent governors rather than as co-opted governors. Even among those serving in the co-optee category, only just over half were co-opted because of their business or industry associations (Industry in Education, 1995).

ACCOUNTABILITY

Research conducted into the operation of governing bodies showed, however, that the reality – what was happening on the ground – was not necessarily the same as envisaged by the legislation. Several studies showed that the decline in the power and influence of the LEA had not been compensated by a corresponding growth in the influence and role of the governing body. Headteachers, perhaps unsurprisingly, had stepped into the vacuum created and were now in a potentially very powerful position (Levacic, 1995; Shearn *et al.*, 1995). A research team at Sheffield University Management School delineated three types of response to the changing situation brought about by the legislation and local management of schools (LMS). There were governing bodies where:

- the headteacher was clearly in charge and made all the significant decisions, either because the governors wanted it that way, or did not possess the competence or interest, or because of the tactics used by the head

- there was a strong working relationship between heads and governors, with both parties clear about the nature of governance and management and contributing to the direction of the school
- there was disagreement about the boundaries of responsibility and control which often resulted in conflict between the two (Shearn *et al.*, 1995).

The first type of response was found to be the most common and the Sheffield team conclude that the legislation and LMS has resulted in more powerful headteachers and that 'for most schools the governors' role seems to be very limited, sometimes being no more than "supportive" and "advisory"' (Shearn *et al.*, 1995, p. 187). Rarely were governing bodies involved in issues of accountability, in terms of either being accountable to the community served by the school or being able to 'call the school to account'.

Since state schools educate the community's children and are funded by the taxpayer, it seems only right and proper that schools should be held to account by the community for the education provided. A guide to good governance issued to all heads and chairs in the mid-1990s sees the governing body as 'accountable to those who establish and fund the school and also to parents and the wider community for the way it carries out its functions' (DfEE, 1996). The introduction of delegated budgets (LMS) by the Conservative administration in the late 1980s was, in part at least, an attempt to ensure greater accountability and to raise standards. Schools were funded on the number of pupils within them. It was therefore argued that the more popular, that is the more 'successful', schools would attract more pupils and hence more resources which would enable them to improve still further. Less popular schools would have less money and would therefore either raise their educational standards or 'wither on the vine'. However, no matter how popular a school is, it can only take a fixed number of pupils unless it is in a position to build more accommodation. Increased expression of parental preference has led only to increased levels of dissatisfaction as parents are unable to get their child into the school of their choice. Indeed, there is increasing evidence that it is the (successful) schools that are doing the choosing rather than the parents (Whitty, Power and Halpin, 1998).

There is a paradox contained within the changes introduced into the educational system: on the one hand, there was the increased devolvement of power to parents, schools and governors while, at the same time, there was an increased centralisation through, for instance, the introduction of the National Curriculum. The presence of this paradox is not confined to England and Wales. In Sweden during the same period there was increasing freedom of choice of school for parents. Simultaneously there were new proposals for common curricula and the national testing and evaluation of results (Rudvall, 1993). Similarly, in New Zealand, as a result of the Picot Report in 1988, boards of trustees, with a majority of parent representatives, were set up to govern schools. They were expected to play a crucial accountability role between the schools and the national government but were, in fact, the weakest link in that chain (Gordon, 1994). The state had withdrawn from direct control of the schools but the trustees were elected by the parents and therefore were accountable to them rather than the state.

In England and Wales, governing bodies, with their elected parent governors and co-opted representatives of the community, are an important link in the accountability chain. They may be seen as the means through which the producer, the school, is to be made responsive to the consumer, that is the parent, or perhaps more correctly, the child. The governing body can represent (being representative of) the community when it calls the school to account for its actions, but it also provides a mechanism through which the community may have a voice (being representative at) when key policy issues are decided. There are, however, difficulties in this for the lay governors who have no expertise in the field of education. Until very recently, governors have been heavily reliant on the information given to them by the headteacher. As the chair of governors of a school which, following an Ofsted inspection, had been placed on the list of schools in need of special measures said, 'I didn't know what I didn't know!' Thomas and Martin (1996) argue for governors to have access to independent sources of information and performance data, and there have been significant moves in this direction in the late 1990s with the introduction of 'benchmarking' and comparative performance data. There can then be a genuine dialogue of accountability in which governors and staff can deliberate together discussing information on 'how well we are doing', which both bring to the discussion. Thomas and Martin contrast this with situations in which the governors either merely listen to reports prepared by the headteacher and/or staff (accountability by listening) or when governors draw upon their experience or expertise in other fields to question the teachers (accountability by questioning).

Governors, and parents, are now being provided with more and more information about the school's performance, past, present and (via target-setting) future, and the opportunity to compare the achievements of their pupils with those of children in other schools, most importantly, of a similar type. The reports produced by Ofsted inspectors provide governors with an independent 'snap-shot' view of their school. The so-called 'league tables' are now well established and educationalists are becoming increasingly sophisticated in devising means of measuring the 'value-added' by schools. From Spring 1998 schools have had access to 'benchmarking' data (from the Qualifications and Curriculum Authority) and performance and assessment data or PANDAS (from Ofsted). Many LEAs have also produced comparative data or profiles for schools and governors to use for planning and target-setting. From September 1998, governing bodies are charged with the statutory responsibility to ensure that the school sets targets in the National Curriculum core subjects (English and Maths) at Key Stage 2 and in public examinations. These targets will have to be made known to parents and progress reported on them in the annual governors' report to parents (DfEE, 1997).

If the teachers are being made more accountable to the community through the governing body, one has also to consider the governing body's accountability to the community. At present this accountability has some serious limitations. Governors, once elected, are not easily deposed before the end of their four-year term of office. They can be removed through not attending three successive meetings (or six months non-attendance) but generally it is very difficult to remove a 'renegade' or 'maverick' governor. This points to the crucial importance of a proper induction programme for all new governors and the need for the governing body to spell out clearly what is acceptable and unacceptable behaviour.

As noted earlier, the 1986 Education Act requires that the governing body publishes an annual report to parents which explains how the governing body has put into practice its plans for the school during the previous year. It must hold a meeting at least once a year at which parents may discuss the governors' annual report and any other relevant matters such as the progress made on the points covered in the post-Ofsted Action Plan and progress made against the targets set. Anecdotal and research evidence, however, (Arden, 1988; Hinds *et al.*, 1992) suggests that these meetings are generally very poorly attended and are failing to provide an adequate forum in which the governing body can render account.

The report of an Ofsted inspection of the school refers specifically to the work of the governing body particularly under the section on 'Management and Administration'. The report should include an evaluation of the effectiveness of the governing body in fulfilling its legal responsibilities and the leadership provided by the governing body, headteacher and other staff in positions of responsibility (Ofsted, 1994). However, Creese (1997) has shown that inspection reports are rarely overtly critical of the governing body, even when the school is clearly in some difficulties. Interestingly, for the Spring term 1998, inspectors were requested by Ofsted to give governing bodies a grade reflecting their performance, particularly in fulfilling their strategic role. It will be interesting to see the impact this public assessment of governors' performance has on the way in which they fulfil their responsibilities in the future. There is already some evidence that inspection has led to governors becoming both more involved in their schools and more aware of their responsibilities (Earley, 1998).

GOVERNORS AND THE COMMUNITY: SOME PRACTICAL EXAMPLES OF INVOLVEMENT

According to Gann, governors are 'the repository of an enormous amount of information, knowledge and understanding of the community' (1998, p. 159). He suggests that governors can usefully carry out a community audit in which they set out their knowledge under headings such as places of worship, youth activities, transport, voluntary organisations, communications and employment. Governing bodies can be helpful in ensuring that the interests of the community are taken fully into account by the school; for example, when considering community use of the school's facilities. Schools designated as community schools are particularly well-placed to encourage the idea of education as a lifelong activity. Governors, as parents and/or members of the community, can assist the school in transmitting such key messages to parents and the community. Different ways in which governors have used their knowledge and understanding of the community for the benefit of the school and its pupils emerge very clearly in the four examples below.

Example 1

As part of the school's long-term planning, the governors of an 11–16 school were invited to identify their priorities for future development. Amongst other issues they identified the need to develop further pupils' motivation and their sense of social responsibility in order to fit them properly for adult life. The governors were also keen to develop further links with the local community which would include the provision of activities for young people outside normal school hours. This same governing body has a Student, Parents and Community Committee which consists of three governors and three members of staff. It meets three or four times a term and concerns itself with a wide range of issues which over the past few years have included the development of links with parents and the local community.

Example 2

Governors of another 11–16 school serving a community with some social problems have involved themselves even more directly. The governing body has set up a Pupil Services (Welfare) Committee which consists of three governors (including the teacher governor) and two members of staff. Recently, the remit of the group has changed from being a formal stage in the school's disciplinary procedures to having more of an advisory and supportive role for pupils and their parents. Pupils and parents can, and do, ask to see the panel on matters such as the quality of school dinners and bullying. Pupils are also seen in order to congratulate them. 'We give equal status to good as well as bad' (Governor). 'It is good for children to recognise that people want them to do well' (Teacher-governor). As well as addressing more general issues of pupil welfare and behaviour, the group interviews individually pupils whose attendance record gives rise to concern. Pupils who are seriously misbehaving are interviewed together with their parents. In these interviews the governors try to be as supportive and positive as possible though they also make their concerns very clear. 'Children get complacent with the staff. We're an unknown quantity. The children are a little wary – they're not sure just what our powers are' (Governor). 'The fact that they aren't teachers makes a difference – they (the governors) have a street cred' (Deputy Head (Pastoral)). When there was an instance of serious bullying in one form, the governors saw the pupils concerned individually, their parents individually, pupils and their parents together and the pupils as a group. As a result of considerable effort by the staff and governors the difficulties ceased.

Example 3A

A primary school in a northern town serves a stable, tightly knit and supportive community in which the three main languages are Gujerati, Punjabi and Urdu. The governing body, which reflects the ethnic mix of the local community, faces a very different situation from those in the first two examples. English is not spoken in many of the homes and although some written home–school communications are provided in languages other than English, some parents are not used to reading their own language. A very large proportion of the pupils are Muslim and attend the local mosque after school and their religious leaders have considerable influence. One of the issues facing the school, and highlighted in the school's Ofsted report, is the pupils' low attendance rate (the school has almost the worst attendance statistics in the LEA). The problem is due to unauthorised and parentally condoned absence rather than truancy; not only do parents take their children on extended holidays to India or Pakistan but they also allow them to miss school to attend weddings or religious festivals with their families in other towns, meet relatives arriving or departing at the airport or to go shopping, etc.

The head was very anxious to enlist the help of the governors in an attempt to convince the parents of the importance of uninterrupted schooling in the primary phase. Accordingly she met with three governors and an education social worker from the LEA. The governors present felt that the main problem was the attitude of the parents. One of the governors offered to analyse the statistics from the registers in more detail using appropriate computer software. It was hoped that this would give a clearer picture of the nature of the problem and the areas to be targeted. Together, the headteacher and the governors decided upon a range of strategies which they would pursue which included enlisting the help of the Mufti from the local mosque and writing a letter to all parents (in three languages) setting out the governors' concern about pupils' attendance. The target was to achieve a 50 per cent reduction in the present absence rate in nine months. As a result of the combined effort by the governors and the headteacher, attendance improved significantly and appears to be on course to achieve the target set.

Example 3B

School assemblies proved to be another issue in which the governors of this same school were able to act as a link between the school and the community. As noted above, the school had a very high proportion of Muslim children. There are two assemblies for the Muslim children each week, with alternative provision being made for the Christian and Hindu pupils. The headteacher took one assembly each week, another is devoted to presentations devised by the classes in turn and the other to the presentation of certificates, etc. One Muslim parent expressed dissatisfaction with these arrangements to the extent that he visited other parents and persuaded them to withdraw their children from the non-Muslim assemblies. The head was very concerned by this action, wishing to maintain the school as an integrated community. She enlisted the help of the chair of governors and another governor who is a local councillor (both are Muslims). The chair wrote to all parents and the councillor visited those who had stated their intention to withdraw their children from assemblies. The head again enlisted the assistance of the Mufti from the local mosque who was most helpful and supportive. Eventually only two children ended up being withdrawn, one of them being the daughter of the parent who had originally raised the issue.

Issues arising from the practical examples

The first case described above affords an excellent example of governors being representative of the community at the discussions about the school's future priorities for development. Not only did the governors raise issues which had not been previously raised by the teachers but the governors also took what might be seen as a somewhat broader view of the school's role in the community. The governors recognised that it was important that the young people leaving the school should be properly prepared to play an active part in a democratic society. The governors were also keen to see that the school played a full part in addressing the issues facing the community, not only in school hours but outside them as well. Through the operation of their Staff, Students and Community Committee, this governing body has a forum in which these issues can be discussed and appropriate action planned.

In the second and third examples, governors from the two schools came into direct contact with parents and pupils, acting as a bridge and a channel of communication between them and the school. It is worth noting that the governors of the secondary school were at pains to congratulate pupils who had done well in addition to interviewing pupils and/or their parents who were in conflict with the school. The governors were able to reinforce the school's message but were also able to take a slightly more detached stance. It was clear that their intervention was respected and valued by the parents. The governors of the primary school were in a particularly strong position and able to act as mediators because of the nature of the community served by their school. They themselves were part of that community and shared its cultural and religious traditions in a way which the teachers could not. By expressing their views as members of the community and as governors of the school they were able to exert considerable influence and to offer support to the headteacher and the staff.

Governors acting in these ways can have a very considerable impact on their schools. In the case of the primary school, the intervention of the governors eased the tension over assemblies and helped to improve the attendance figures. The governors of the second secondary school also made a significant contribution to the school's efforts to improve the attendance statistics as well as helping to improve the pupils' general behaviour and to reduce bullying. By contrast with these direct interventions, the governors in the first example were in a position to exert a long-term influence upon the nature of their school, its vision and the direction in which it was heading, in other words to be involved in the school's strategic planning.

A NEW MODEL OF PARTNERSHIP?

The degree to which governing bodies can be perceived exclusively in terms of the management of external relations is likely to vary from school to school with some governing bodies perceived as being an integral part of the school and its management. For others there will be a certain distancing with the governing body still seen very much in terms of an adjunct or 'bolt on' rather than being embedded in the structure of the school and its decision-making processes. This chapter, by drawing on specific examples, has shown how some governing bodies are working closely with their schools, acting as a bridge between the school and the community it serves.

The nature of the relationship between the various parties – central government, local government, and schools and their governing bodies – has changed over the years. The role of LEAs has waxed and waned; it will be interesting to see how this continues to change in the light of recent legislation. The need for 'partnership' between the various parties is more important than ever if overall educational standards are to be raised. As the Millennium approaches it may be that the LEA will, once again, play a significant role, particularly in relation to school improvement (Wood, 1998) but very much in conjunction with the other parties.

The governor training organisation AGIT spoke in terms of local partnerships for school improvement as 'a new accountability and a new professionalism' (Martin *et al.*, 1997). A model was suggested which reconceptualises public accountability within an enhanced partnership between schools and the LEAs in which they are situated (see Figure 7.1). It suggests that 'this current refocusing on the relationship between the school and the LEA reflects the maturity of a system of school governance which can be confident in the exercise of accountability by the public for the public' (Martin *et al.*, 1997, p. 4). It draws upon examples of good practice within local school governance which demonstrate 'the importance of vigorous reciprocal accountability in securing and maintaining positive and constructive local partnerships' (p. 4). The model links accountability to professionalism through the governing body. Accountability is the glue binding the partnership together in a spirit of mutual respect and reciprocity. The governing body is seen as playing a key role in raising standards because of its unique position at the interface of the school and the community. It is the link between the headteacher and the professional staff, the LEA, parents and the community, and as such 'a key forum for the mediation and dialogue between all the stakeholders who comprise the local partnership' (p. 5). As such, governors provide that all-important bridge to the community, operating at times externally to the school and at others being an integral part of the school itself.

A new professionalism	A new accountability	
Governors' reports to parents	School Development Plan	
The annual governors' parents meeting	Post-Ofsted action plan	
	Performance review and appraisal	
The LEA Development Plan	Target-setting	
The community	**The governing body**	**The school**

Figure 7.1. New accountability: new professionalism

ACKNOWLEDGEMENTS

The research into the role of governors in school improvement from which the examples above are drawn was funded jointly by the School of Education, Cambridge University and by BT, Royal Mail and Unilever. Their support is gratefully acknowledged. The involvement and encouragement of the headteachers and governors of the three schools was crucial. Without their willing collaboration, the research would not have been possible.

REFERENCES

Arden, J. (1988) A survey of Annual Parents' Meetings by the London Diocesan Board for Schools, in P. Earley (ed.) *Governors' Reports and Annual Parents' Meetings: the 1986 Education Act and Beyond*, Slough: NFER.

Creese, M. J. (1997) *Effective Governance: the Evidence from Ofsted*, Ipswich: School Management and Governance Development.

Deem, R. (1992) Governing by gender? School governing bodies after the Education Reform Act, in P. Abbott, and C. Wallace (eds.) *Gender, Power and Sexuality*, Basingstoke: Macmillan.

DfEE (1996) *Guidance on Good Governance*, London: DfEE.

DfEE (Department for Education and Employment) (1997) *Setting Targets for Pupil Achievement: Guidance for Governors*, London: DfEE.

Earley, P. (1994) *School Governing Bodies: Making Progress?* Slough: NFER.

Earley, P. (1998) Governing bodies and school inspection: potential for empowerment? in P. Earley (ed.) *School Improvement after Inspection? School and LEA Responses*, London: Paul Chapman.

Gann, N. (1998) *Improving School Governance: How Better Governors Make Better Schools*, London: Falmer Press.

Gordon, L. (1994) Who controls New Zealand's schools? Decentralised management and the problem of agency, in G. Wallace (ed.) *Schools, Markets and Management*, Bournemouth: Hyde Publications.

Hinds, T., Martin, J., Ranson, S. and Rutherford, D. (1992) *The Annual Parents' Meeting: Towards a Shared Understanding*, Birmingham: School of Education, University of Birmingham.

Industry in Education (1995) *All Their Tomorrows: the Business of Governing*, London: Industry in Education.

Keys, W. and Fernandes, C. (1990) *A Survey of School Governing Bodies*, Slough: NFER.

Levacic, R. (1995) *Local Management of Schools*, Buckingham: Open University Press.

Martin, J., Earley, P. , Holt, A., Hesketh, J., Pounce, M., Sheriton, J. and White, T. (1997) *School Governing Bodies: From Policy to Practice*. Paper resulting from an invitational seminar, Institute of Education, London, September.

Ofsted (Office for Standards in Education) (1994) *Framework for the Inspection of Schools*, London: Ofsted.

Ofsted (Office for Standards in Education) (1998) *The Annual Report of Her Majesty's Chief Inspector of Schools*, London: The Stationery Office.

Rudvall, G. (1993) Decentralising Swedish schools since 1980, in G. Wallace (ed.) *Local Management, Central Control: Schools in the Market Place*, Bournemouth:

Hyde Publications.

Sallis, J. (1988) *Schools, Parents and Governors: A New Approach to Accountability*, London: Routledge.

Shearn, D., Broadbent, J., Laughlin, R. and Willig-Atherton, H. (1995) The changing face of school governor responsibilities: a mismatch between government intention and actuality? *School Organisation*, Vol. 15, no. 2. pp. 175–188.

Streatfield, D. and Jefferies, G. (1989) *Reconstitution of Governing Bodies: Survey 2*, Slough: NFER.

Thomas, H. and Martin, J. (1996) *Managing Resources for School Improvement: Creating a Cost-Effective School*, London: Routledge.

Weindling, D. and Earley, P. (1987) *Secondary Headship: The First Years*, Windsor: NFER-Nelson.

Whitty, G., Power, S. and Halpin, D. (1998) *Devolution and Choice in Education*, Buckinham: Open University Press.

Wood, M. (1998) Partners in pursuit of quality: LEA support for school improvement after inspection, in P. Earley (ed.) *School Improvement after Inspection? School and LEA Responses*, London: Paul Chapman.

8

MANAGING RELATIONSHIPS BETWEEN SCHOOLS AND PARENTS

David Middlewood

INTRODUCTION

The first education of a child takes place through its parents and family and the early learning of the child before it reaches the age for formal schooling is among the most important of its whole life. The importance of parents as first educators is widely acknowledged and there is widespread recognition that parents have a significant role to play if formal schooling is to be effective. Parental support is seen, for example, as one of the eleven key factors in school effectiveness (Stoll and Mortimore, 1995).

The term 'parents' used in the title of this chapter needs to be clarified. In essence, the words 'parents', 'family' and 'home' are used interchangeably in educational literature, but the word 'family' can be contentious and, indeed, means different things in different countries. When parent representatives are elected to various bodies, 'parent' is usually defined to include absent parents, step parents, foster parents, etc. The use of the word 'parents' in this chapter therefore includes those and does not preclude grandparents, carers and anyone who involves themselves with a school to support a particular child.

If a major trend of the twenty-first century is to be that 'learning is more important than teaching' (Holland, 1998, p. 5), and new technologies will involve more learning from home and learning together in families, the recognition of the importance of parental involvement may need to take on a sharper reality in actual practice. Similarly, if lifelong learning becomes an increasing reality, managers and leaders of schools may need to reconceptualise the contribution of the statutory schooling process in a lifelong process and reconsider the relationship between the formal educators (in schools) and the 'co-educators' in the home. This chapter examines some of the tensions and challenges affecting this relationship, suggests that much is possible and being achieved now, and proposes that it is helpful for leaders and managers to develop a strategic approach to managing an effective relationship between schools and their parents.

CONCEPTUALISING EFFECTIVE PARENT-SCHOOL RELATIONSHIPS

While it is taken for granted that positive relationships between home and school are good for the child's development and learning achievement and for making the school effective, the view of the parents' role in the relationship may depend upon the culture and social tradition within which it operates. In Denmark, for example, the tradition of parental involvement in formal schooling is seen in *democratic* terms, not specifically in educational terms (OECD, 1997). In other words, the question of parents' rights has not had to become an issue because parenthood is one aspect only of democratic citizenship rights. The OECD Report points out that as Denmark's society changes, becoming more pluralistic, the aim is to build up local community cultural centres, based on schools 'so that children, parents and grandparents, as well as other members of the community, can meet on the school premises and carry out activities together' (OECD, 1997, p. 84) Such a development is possible because of the tradition of coherence of home, school and community on which it builds.

Such an outcome has been the aim of certain community education initiatives such as those in Coventry, England, in the 1970s and 1980s. Bull (1989, p. 117) quotes the Director of Education as saying, 'You wouldn't see the join between what the family was doing on the one hand and what the school was doing on the other.'

From one point of view, the actual term 'parental involvement' can be seen as condescending since it assumes the school is the central activity with parents allowed occasional access. The opposite extreme would be to see the family as having embarked on a 'teacher involvement' programme when it sends a child to school! Bull (1989) and Macbeth and Ravn (1994) ask whether teachers or parents are the main educators and which is supplementing the learning of the other.

Certainly some educational programmes, such as the American Head Start programme, assumed that 'parents would benefit from the intervention of the professional, organised the relationship on the professional's terms, and tended to see children as needing to be rescued from inadequate backgrounds' (Ball, 1994, p. 44).

Such models, according to Wolfendale (1996, p. 92), are giving way to ones in which:

- family heritage is valued
- parental expertise is seen as equivalent and complementary to that of professionals
- parents, as primary carers and first educators, are perceived as co-operating *partners* in the educational enterprise. (My emphasis.)

PARTNERSHIPS

'Partnership' is the word widely used in schools in many countries to describe the relationship between parents and schools and it is often in official school brochures and prospectuses, especially those aimed at parents of prospective pupils. The title of the OECD study (1997) of practice in nine countries is *Parents as Partners in Schooling*. However, a relationship has certain elements which make it a partnership and, for effective management, there needs to be a clear definition and understanding of what partnership entails.

Pugh's (1989, p. 80) definition is 'a working relationship that is characterised by a shared sense of purpose, mutual respect and the willingness to negotiate. This implies a sharing of information, responsibility, skills, decision-making and accountability.'

If such a definition is accepted as valid, then the essential point for school managers will concern the processes involved. *How* is sharing ensured? *How* can respect be mutually gained? Some of this will challenge not only accepted practice but also traditional values and will raise important questions. For example, can *all* information be shared? Do teachers see negotiation often as conceding? Do they recognise the skills of parents as complementary to their own professional ones?

In reality, the word 'partnership' can cover a wide range of relationships and links, some of which may be positively disempowering. Kirk (quoted in Macbeth, 1994, p. 30) has suggested the term 'can be used as a kind of professional blackmail' and 'a cover for a whole range of hidden agendas, such as those resorting to institutional or territorial aggrandisement, to institutional insecurity and even to disguise political intent.'

The role of the parent in the partnership varies from country to country depending upon the concept of the parent as envisaged by the country's legislation. While most developed countries have enacted some legislation in recent years which affects parent–school relationships, the emphasis has varied considerably. At one possible extreme is the notion of parent as 'co-educator'; at the other is that of the parent as 'consumer'. In England and Wales since the 1980s, this latter emphasis has been most evident, with all kinds of implications, for example, for assessing the effectiveness of schools. The inspection carried out by the Office of Standards in Education (Ofsted) must involve the views of parents as to their satisfaction with what the school provides. In Spain, parents are involved in addressing any school weaknesses identified by inspectors, in the subsequent development plan. Brown (1997) argues that 'parentocracy' is the third wave in British education history 'where a child's education is increasingly dependent upon the wealth and wishes of parents, rather than the ability and efforts of pupils' (p. 394) and notes similar trends in the USA, Australia and New Zealand.

TENSIONS AND CHALLENGES IN MANAGING PARENT–SCHOOL RELATIONSHIPS

'(Home–school partnership) is a major task that calls for imagination and commitment, initiative and direction; it also needs *management*, understanding and support' (Bastiani, 1993, p. 94, my emphasis).

School managers know that effective parent–school relationships will not just evolve, unaided. They need to recognise the tensions and challenges involved in developing them and consider the implications of these for their particular situation. I wish to identify some of these tensions and challenges and in each case suggest some implications for managers at school level.

Centralist statutory requirements and the individual school's needs

A number of countries have enacted legislation to facilitate parental involvement and these have usually involved statutory bodies (e.g. National Parents Council in Ireland, Parental Advisory Committees in Canada), or entitlement to representation on bodies such as school governors or councils (e.g. governing bodies in England and Wales, councils in Australia). Such involvement at a governance or management level is clearly justified in terms of giving important stakeholders a voice. However, having a voice does not guarantee getting a hearing! The opportunity for parents, via governing bodies, councils and other official groups, to influence policies and processes is significant (e.g. in selecting staff; see, for example, Bush, Coleman and Glover, 1994) but the direct input of parents as partners into the actual educational process in the school is highly questionable through this route. In any case, parents on governing bodies in England and Wales, for example, are only a minority of the stake-holders with legitimised interest and influence.

Legislation in some countries may attempt to 'enforce' parent–school partnership at levels beyond representative levels. In England and Wales, proposals for formal binding 'Home–School Contracts' have, according to Vincent and Tomlinson (1997), become a way of imposing discipline rather than developing a partnership for learning. If parents were compelled to visit schools every six months under a contract, as argued by Barber (1996), the partnership notion can be seen as distinctly one-sided. As Riley (1998, p. 134) says, 'Whether compelling, rather than welcoming, parents to visit the school will improve the relationship is debatable.' For school managers, such examples may be perceived to be actually undermining practice which the school has found to be effective.

Additionally, there is evidence that many parents are not interested in being involved in school governance and management. Martin's (1995) research suggested that the majority of parents do not want to sit on advisory councils, only 12 per cent seek governance roles, and parents were the most reluctant group to serve on advisory committees. Yet 'public policy and legislative trends in several countries and educational juris-dictions in the industrialised world have been to give parents increasingly more power ... in the latter 1980s, Britain, Australia, New Zealand, British Columbia, Alberta, Quebec and Chicago all enacted provisions which gave parents as a group a relatively more powerful role in educa-tional affairs than they had previously' (Martin, 1995, p. 9).

Implications for managers

1. Managers need to make a clear distinction in their thinking and strat-egy between those aspects of the partnership which are *managerial* (governing bodies, councils, parents' associations, fund-raising, etc.) and those which are *educational* (i.e. focused upon the child's devel-opment and learning).
2. A model of practice involving parents in various ways in their child's education needs to be developed. Such a model will almost certainly build on many things that the school already does. Bastiani's (1993) example is shown in Figure 8.1.
   Similarly, Hornby's (1990) model (see Figure 8.2) offers managers an opportunity to analyse a particular school's situation in terms of needs and strengths, so that activity can be focused.
3. School managers need to focus upon how parents can contribute to their child's education by recognising their key role as complementary part-ners, with skills and knowledge different from those of teachers. As

Beare, Coldwell and Millikan (1989, p. 199) point out, 'The parent body of any school constitutes a rich fund of skills and expertise, knowledge and experience, which goes well beyond the capacities of its teaching staff. . . . Where the resource is unused, the school may be sending signals to its public that it sees learning as closeted, esoteric, and bound by teacher possessiveness.'

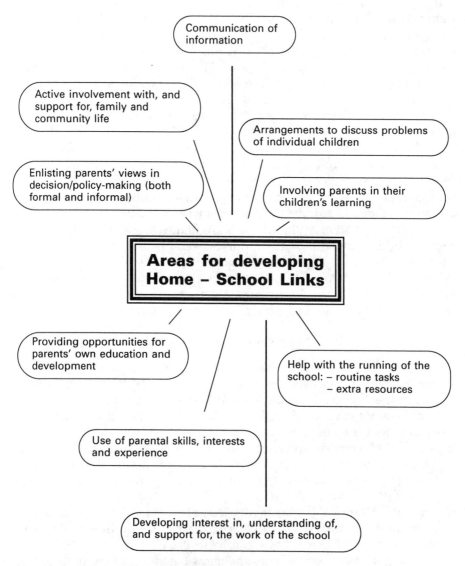

Figure. 8.1 Areas of possible agendas for developing home–school links (Bastiani, 1993)

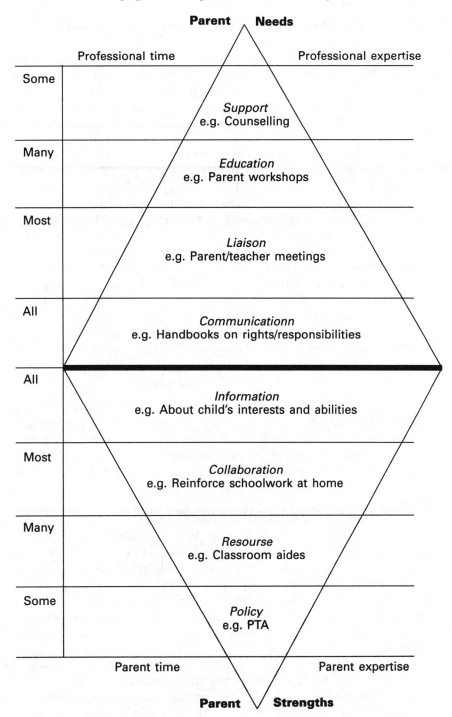

Figure 8.2. Model for parent involvement (Hornby, 1990)

Professional interests versus parental interests

In countries where the parents' role in their child's education is not seen as natural, any development of their involvement may by seen by the teachers as challenging or threatening to their professional status. In France, the OECD Report (1997) suggested that parents and schools were not 'natural' partners (p. 122) but that recognition that supportive parents enabled better performance is forcing change and the challenge was now a social one. In Japan, teachers were seen as controlling the basis on which parental involvement takes place and this was 'only really welcome if it is in support of the status quo' (OECD, 1997, p. 167).

Generally, teachers have a right to have their professionalism respected, as much as doctors and lawyers, and it is not surprising that teachers can become defensive over issues in which they see intrusion. In Germany, 'the teaching staff can block changes when they feel their working conditions will be too strongly affected' (OECD, 1997, p. 136). Teachers today lead very stressful and demanding working lives which are already very exposed to public scrutiny. Many schools have not developed effective strategies for staff supporting each other which do not depend upon presenting a united front against outsiders. Effective leadership and management in the individual school will again be crucial in this.

Implications for managers

1. Managers need to acknowledge that adjusting the relationship between teachers and parents to give parents a greater role in the partnership is not necessarily a concession. The effective partnership needs to be equally demanding of the parent. MacBeath (1994) argues that more effective schools make demands on parents, as well as providing them with opportunities for involvement and ensuring a welcoming atmosphere in the school.

    In their research into effective schools and effective departments in secondary schools in England and Wales, Sammons, Thomas and Mortimore (1997) found that some departments in the same school were better than others at involving parents, while all departments worked under the same broad policies. They use the word 'harness' to describe how effective schools encouraged parents to monitor homework, communicate concerning absence, contribute to newsletters and celebrate positive achievement by the pupil.

2. Managers need to examine current practices to find whether some of them may be based on professional convenience at the expense of genuine parental involvement. Attendance at parents' evenings is, legitimately, seen as one indicator of parental support and interest and Sammons, Thomas and Mortimore (1997) found, as have others, that higher attendance occurs at schools deemed to be more effective.

However, managers need to examine whether that interest is being effectively used and a study (Clark and Power, 1998) of parents evenings found a worrying level of disenchantment and disenfranchisement in that the majority of parents were finding the evenings a very unrewarding experience. Similarly, open days or curriculum evenings which are solely for the purpose of 'selling' the school may be missing an opportunity for advancing genuine partnership.

3. Managers in some schools may need to help staff to rethink the role of parents away from perceptions of those who always need support or who are too intrusive and threatening. Ultimately, life may actually be easier for the teachers. As Riley (1998, p. 135) says, 'If schools start from the assumption that parents and pupils need to be controlled, then they will find that they are always having to look for new and tougher sanctions.'

Needs of disadvantaged versus affluent parents and pupils

One of the features of the trend in many countries towards greater school self-governance is the market-orientation which this brings to the educational world. Glatter (1994, p. 23) argues that 'competition and collaboration are not mutually exclusive' in this context but notes that the environment of heightened competition is now framing all relationships between schools and 'there is a shift in the kinds of partnerships which are likely to succeed and those which may encounter difficulties'. One example he gives of collaboration between schools is of 'helping each other out over transferring pupils where problems have occurred' (ibid.).

However, the competitive frame within which schools operate also offers the risk of relationships between parents and schools being subsumed within one school's perceived desire of the 'right kind' of pupils to achieve measurable success (especially examination and test results) and another school's need to maintain its pupil numbers in a potentially contracting situation. Relationships between parents and school are 'abnormal' in both cases. In schools deemed to be successful, and oversubscribed, the temptation to 'control' the partnership is considerable; in schools threatened by failure, possibly even closure, the temptation may be to 'concede' to parents too easily. Neither scenario is likely to come close to Pugh's definition of a working partnership (see earlier).

In this market-oriented situation, parents from disadvantaged situations often fare worst. In a study of African–American students and school choice, concluding that those perceived to be at the bottom of the social hierarchy were more likely to be excluded from schools, Wells (1997, p. 437) asks, 'What will happen to these children in an educational free market predicated on the existence of both winners and losers?' A study of the consequences of free choice in New Zealand secondary schools led Waslander and Thrupp (1997, p. 454) to conclude that 'Socio-economic segregation between schools has been exacerbated . . .' and that, ironically, those schools with the greatest needs were forced to waste time and resources on marketing to attract parents in order to survive, 'thus further disadvantaging their already disadvantaged students' (ibid.).

In some countries such as Ireland, parents in disadvantaged areas have been especially targeted – with some success (OECD, 1997, p. 150). The OECD Report notes some resistance *'especially in some church circles'* (ibid., p. 151) to giving parents a more powerful voice. Clearly, the idea of co-educating may be only acceptable under the overall control of a still higher authority!

Implications for managers

1. There is need to recognise the importance of managing accessibility for all parents if they are to feel confident about being treated as complementary partners. Examples include:
   - *Language:* not only ensuring the language of communication is for ethnic language minorities too, but also acknowledging that illiteracy may exist in some homes, and that some parents are at ease with the language of the 'tabloids', some with 'broadsheets'.
   - *Reception:* school is an institution, possibly viewed by certain parents as akin to others, such as hospitals, police stations, job centres – and even prisons! Schools have unique advantages over these others in terms of a potential partnership.
2. School managers need to avoid assumptions inherent in practice, which can be either patronising or demanding, that all parents can provide equal resources, whether these be time, computers, transport, etc. Only a genuine partnership will enable schools to offer facilities for learning which go further than remedying a deficiency; for example, by ensuring that a homework club is for *all* students, regardless of home circumstances.
3. Managing effective relationships with parents may also have equal gender opportunities issues for the school. The OECD report (1997, p. 56) pointed out that in all the countries studied the parent most involved is the mother. It goes on to link the possible significance of this with the underachievement of boys. Managers may need, therefore, to consider to what extent male and female adults are involved as parents and perhaps consciously challenge stereotyping, for example in home–school linked reading schemes, by encouraging fathers as well as mothers to read with children. In her study of working class mothers involved in primary schools, Maclachlan (1996) found that, although there were good intentions by the headteachers, and the mothers did become more involved, 'It is to the school's agenda that the mothers

must respond and the agendas of home and school do not always coincide' (Maclachlan, 1996, p. 37).

Sensitive ethical issues may arise in this area. The increasing number of single parent families in England and Wales where the child lives with the mother, for example, may raise the question of the extent to which schools should work with absent fathers, thereby perhaps partially addressing the issue of underachieving boys in particular seeing education as 'feminised'. The critical point for school managers is that their responsibility is to the child and any such work undertaken is for that reason rather than to 'help' the family in any social welfare sense.

Apparent decline in parental interest as child grows older

In countries where there is apparently not a natural tradition of the parent as co-educator, there is a history of much less parental active involvement at secondary level than at nursery and primary level. In England and Wales (Coleman, 1994) and the USA, the perception is marked. 'Partnership activities tend to be concentrated (in the USA) on primary and pre-schools; as children get older, parental involvement in schooling diminishes' (OECD, 1997, p. 195).

Various reasons for this may be proposed, but the issue for managers is that the situation is not allowed to become an assumption such as 'parents don't care because they don't come to parents evenings' or 'adolescents don't need or like their parents involved'. As Coleman (1994) points out, it is not that adolescents don't need their parents but that their needs are expressed in a different way.

Implications for managers

1. Ensuring that assumptions such as those above are not driving practice in the school is crucial. Campion School in Bugbrooke, England, in its strategies to raise achievement in Year 11 (16-year-old) students employed a number of approaches. The evaluation of the strategies (Middlewood, forthcoming) found that the involvement of parents of these 16-year-olds had been one of the key factors in helping the school's students to raise their overall examination pass rate by 15 per cent in one year. While the approach involved inviting parents together to the school to discuss revision, study, etc. and setting up village networks in homes, the research showed that the parents felt a significant benefit of their involvement had been improved relationships with the sons and daughters. There was no one universally 'correct' approach (in some cases, more relaxed, in some more pressured), but the home relationships undoubtedly aided motivation and application. Such

findings can challenge a school view that 'parents won't or don't get involved at that age'.

The extensive work of Coleman (1998) and his research team in Canada with students aged 10–15 centred upon the notion of a 'triad' (teachers, parents and students) as being the most effective component in the development of student learning.

2. There is a need to acknowledge that conflict within a partnership is not necessarily unhealthy and that such conflict is sometimes inevitable (Beresford and Hardie, 1996, p. 51). The skill is in the creative management of conflict rather than its avoidance and on seeing it as a step towards a more productive partnership. Beresford and Hardie (1996) suggest there should be less emphasis on the physical presence of parents and more on a wide range of strategies to develop accessible two-way communication.

3. The focus here and in this whole chapter has been on parents of those of statutory school age. Remarkably little attention appears to be paid, in the literature at least, to the role of parents of children of, say, 16 - 19 years, some of whom may be in schools, some in further education colleges. A literature search of journal articles on 16–19 education management in the United Kingdom over three years (1994–96) found that the only references to parents were to their role as stakeholders or clients for marketing purposes. One investigation by a lecturer at a tertiary college in England found that more than 60 per cent of 17-year-olds rated support from their parents as the most important factors in helping them achieve in their studies (Wright, 1995). Parental contribution may be underestimated by the schools and colleges here.

Individual parents are an ephemeral presence

In developing management programmes for effective relationships with parents, schools are conscious that individual parents and any one group of parents will only be linked with the school for a limited time, that of their child/children's duration. 'Parents do not act monolithically' (Wells, 1997, p. 437). The only effective way for school managers to reconcile an overall approach with the need to manage partnerships with individual parents is, surely, to develop a strategic approach.

WHAT KIND OF RELATIONSHIP, THEN?

Given the issues and challenges described and discussed above, it needs to be emphasised that the responsibility for developing the *management* of the relationship between schools and parents lies firmly with the individual school management. The managers, who are the trained and paid professionals, need to ask first, 'What kind of relationship is needed to facilitate effective education?' If the school has a clear concept of such a relationship, the management of its development will be clearer. To arrive at this concept, the recognition that any professional/lay relationship has within it certain common features will aid the process. Based partly upon the work of Bull (1989), the table in Figure 8.3 may be proposed as a

A   *Information Level*
Process: The professional reports: the parent receives – and can also give own information.
Outcome: Information (e.g. on child's progress at school) is held by both partners.

B   *Explanation Level*
Process: The professional explains: the parent receives.
Outcome: The parent has opportunity to ask (e.g. how and why something is taught in the way it is).

C   *Observation Level*
Process: The professional performs: the parent observes.
Outcome: The parent does not rely on words but sees school and child in action (e.g. open days/evenings, visits, etc.).

D   *Participation Level*
Process: The professional performs: the parent is involved in performance.
Outcome: The parent has opportunity to work in the school, be involved and both parties have some understanding of other's perception (e.g. voluntary support activity, guest speaking, etc. at assemblies or to classes).

E   *Consultation Level*
Process: The professional asks for opinion; the parent gives opinion.
Outcome: The parent is consulted before a decision is made (e.g. over school uniform).

F   *Negotiated Level*
Process: The professional proposes; the parent modifies proposal.
Outcome: A debate occurs so that final decision is more satisfactory to both (e.g. over action to be taken concerning child's behaviour).

G   *Shared Decision-making Level*
Process: The professional shares opinion; the parent shares opinion.
Outcome: Both parties share in decision-making (e.g. over certain curriculum matters, school organisation and policies).

Figure 8.3. Managing the professional/parent working relationship

continuum of the management of professional/parent working relation-ships, from a minimum recognition on the part of the professional through to a genuine attempt at co-educating.

An example of shared decision-making in the curriculum occurred at Pemberton School in Northamptonshire, England. In developing a school policy on residential experience in the curriculum, volunteer parents joined teaching staff on a working group. Since residential experience by its very nature directly involved parents, the joint experience of teachers (during residential visits) and parents (before and after) was essential. A policy and clear statement on practice was agreed. The feedback from parents and teachers following the first experience of the new policy was acted upon in amendments for the subsequent year.

Of course, a number of schools would reasonably claim that they are involved in a number of the levels in Figure 8.3 already and that several of the examples given are occurring at the same time. However, without a strategic view of managing such relationships, such a variety of activity can be confusing for parents and indeed raise expectations, putting pres-sure on staff which cannot be maintained. It is not uncommon, for example, for a new headteacher to offer events such as 'open house', 'cur-riculum evenings', etc. However, unless this rich programme is maintained regularly, parents may even feel cheated.

Equally, there is no suggestion that shared decision-making (G) is always either desirable or appropriate. (E) and (F) levels will be appropriate for a number of areas which both partners feel are more the province of pro-fessionals. The argument for seeing the continuum as helpful is that deci-sions are best made on the basis of the knowledge of both partners involved and that knowledge about the school by the parent and about the child by the parent is gained through processes such as those in (B), (C), (D), (E) and (F).

A STRATEGIC APPROACH TO MANAGING THE RELATIONSHIP

Realistically, school leaders and managers have to manage the situation as it is now and be prepared, in any country, to encompass any new legislation. Such uncertainties provide all the more reason for being proactive rather than reactive, an essential element of strategic manage-ment (Middlewood, 1998). I suggest therefore that developing such a strategic view might involve the following steps for the individual school:

1. Arriving at an unequivocal definition of partnership
Whatever the precise wording, the definition should include reference to:

- common aims, purposes, objectives
- valuing of each partner's knowledge, expertise, etc.
- complementary roles of the partners
- commitment to continuing improvement.

2. **Clarifying the long term aim for role of parent in the home-school relationship**

   Is the role co-educator, or consumer, or consultant, etc? An explicit statement of the role is essential so that the steps taken towards achieving this may be reviewed in this light. Such a process could take several years, given the adjustments on roles and values that may be necessary. The period of time is likely to cover the maximum length of time in which any one individual child and its parent may be involved in an individual school. Houston (1996) describes a *seven year* plan as being appropriate for a home–school partnership in Paisley, Scotland.

3. **Being explicit about the reason for this role**

   If the aim is for the parent to be seen as co-educator, the partnership will assume learning at home being acknowledged in school learning, and parents being closely involved in decisions affecting behaviour at home and at school. If the reason for the parent's role is stated as to raise levels of achievement at school, this will be seen by both partners as underpinning decisions taken and processes followed. As pressures grow on schools to raise achievement for national economic reasons, it is good sense for schools not only to harness parental involvement in a positive relationship but also to have parents in shared advocacy with them.

4. **Developing indicators for monitoring the effectiveness of home–school links**

   In their work with schools in England and Wales, MacBeath *et al.* (1996) developed indicators in a number of areas in which schools could self-evaluate their own progress using both qualitative and quantitative evidence. Some of these are relevant to parents, for example in examining school climate, to determine whether the school was welcoming to parents and other visitors. The most relevant here was that of 'home-school links'. Two of those indicators are shown in Figure 8.4.

CONCLUSION

Some of the possible ways of addressing the issues described in this chapter may require radical changes in the way relationships with parents

Indicator:	**Parents play an active part in their children's learning**
Quantitative evidence:	Numbers of parents involved in home–school initiatives/workshops. Communications from parents about home learning/homework/study. Contacts with home/home visiting. Availability of parents' rooms.
Qualitative evidence:	School understanding of the significance of home learning. Usefulness of information to parents. Staff support/guidance for parents. Parental knowledge of curriculum. Parents know how to help at home.
Methods/instruments:	Examination of records of visits, etc. Home–school diary. Uptake of programmes/information. Review of documentation/language. Surveys and interviews. Home–school video.
Indicator:	**Parents are confident that problems will be dealt with and feedback given**
Quantitative evidence:	Circulation of school policies. Information on, involvement in, policy development. Records of complaints/actions taken. Logs of telephone, correspondence, visits.
Qualitative evidence:	School's understanding of the diversity of the parental group. Parental awareness of school procedures. Attitudes of staff to parental complaints.
Methods/instruments:	Analysis of records and logs. Analysis of parent contacts by category. Case studies/tracking communications. Questionnaire for parents.

Figure 8.4. Indicators of effectiveness in home–school link (MacBeath *et al.*, 1996, p. 122)

are managed in some schools. Davies (quoted in Fine, 1997, p. 460) describes organising parent involvement as 'bringing the ocean to a boil'! Changes in this area will be difficult because 'trying to change power relationships, especially in complicated, traditional institutions, is among the most complex tasks human beings can undertake' (Sarason, 1990, p. 29).

It should be stressed, however, that an abundance of good practice exists. Strategic school managers ask the all-important question, 'What is effective learning in the twenty-first century?' Cultural and social tradition play a significant role in affecting the answers to this question and it is possible that one of the social changes of the future will be a far greater emphasis on the role of the actual learner *of whatever age* than on that of parents specifically. The school that has developed an effective co-learning relationship with parents will be powerfully placed to manage that next stage.

REFERENCES

Ball, C. (1994) *The Importance of Early Learning*, London: Royal Society of Arts.

Barber, M. (1996) *The Learning Game: Arguments for a Learning Revolution*, London: Gollancz.

Bastiani, J. (1993) Parents as partners: genuine progress or empty rhetoric?, in P. Munn (ed.) *Parents and Schools – Customers, Managers or Partners?* London: Routledge.

Beare, H., Caldwell, B. and Millikan, R. (1989) *Creating an Excellent School*, London: Routledge.

Beresford, E. and Hardie, A. (1996) Parents and secondary schools: a different approach, in J. Bastiani and S. Wolfendale (eds.). *Home-School Work in Britain*, London: David Fulton.

Brown, P. (1997) Education and the ideology of parentocracy, in A. Halsey, H. Lauder, P. Brown and A. Wells (eds.) *Education: Culture, Economy, Society*, Oxford University Press.

Bull, T. (1989) Home–school links: family-orientated or business-oriented, *Educational Review*, Vol. 41, No. 2, pp. 113–119.

Bush T., Coleman, M. and Glover, D. (1994) *Managing Autonomous Schools*, London: Paul Chapman.

Clark, A. and Power, S. (1998) *The Right To Know: Parents and School Reports*, University of Bristol.

Coleman, J. (1994) The parenting of teenagers. Talk given to National Children's Bureau Conference, London, September.

Coleman, P. (1998) *Parent, Student and Teacher Collaboration: The Power of 3*, London: Paul Chapman.

Fine, M. (1997) Parent involvement: reflections on parents, power and urban public schools, in A. Halsey, H. Lauder, P. Brown and A. Wells (eds.) *Education: Culture, Economy, Society*, Oxford University Press.

Glatter, R. (1994) What future for school co-operation? *Management in Education*, Vol. 8, no. 3, Autumn, pp. 22–3.

Holland, G. (1998) Learning in the twenty-first century, *New Childhood*, Vol. 13, no. 1, Spring, pp. 4–5.

Hornby, G. (1990) The organisation of parent involvement, *School Organisation*, Vol. 10, nos. 2 and 3, pp. 247–52.

Houston, A. (1996) Home–school projects: influencing long-term change, in J. Bastiani and S. Wolfendale (eds.) *Home-School Work in Britain*, London: David Fulton.

MacBeath, J. (1994) A role for parents, students and teachers in school self-evaluation and development planning, in K. Riley and D. Nuttall (eds.) *Measuring Quality: Education Indicators – UK and International Perspective*, London: Falmer Press.

MacBeath, J., Boyd, B., Rand, J. and Bell, S. (1996) *Schools Speak for Themselves*, London: National Union of Teachers.

Macbeth, A. (1994) Report on the 1993 BEMAS Conference, in *Management in Education*, Vol. 8, no. 1, Spring, pp. 30–1.

Macbeth, A. and Ravn, B. (1994) Expectations about parents in education, in *Expectations about Parents in Education: European Perspectives*, Computing Services Ltd., Glasgow: University of Glasgow.

Maclachlan, K. (1996) Good mothers are women too: the gender implications of parental involvement, in J. Bastiani and S. Wolfendale (eds.) *Home–School Work in Britain*, London: David Fulton.

Martin, Y. (1995) What do parents want? *Management in Education*, Vol. 9, no. 1, February, pp. 8–9.

Middlewood, D. (1998) Strategic management in education: an overview, in D. Middlewood and J. Lumby (eds.) *Strategic Management in Schools and Colleges*, London: Paul Chapman.

OECD (1997) *Parents as Partners in Schooling*, Paris: OECD.

Pugh, G. (1989) Parents and professionals in pre-school services: is partnership possible? in S. Wolfendale (ed.) *Parental Involvement: Developing Networks between Home, School and Community*, London: Cassell.

Riley, K. (1998) *Whose School Is It Anyway?* London: Falmer Press.

Sammons, P., Thomas, S. and Mortimore, P. (1997) *Forging Links: Effective Schools and Effective Departments*, London: Paul Chapman.

Sarason, S. (1990) *The Predictable Failure of Educational Reform*, San Francisco: Jossey-Bass.

Stoll, L. and Mortimore, P. (1995) *School Effectiveness and School Improvement*, Viewpoint 2, Institute of Education, University of London.

Vincent, C. and Tomlinson, S. (1997) Home–school relationships, *British Educational Research Journal*, Vol. 23, no. 3, pp. 361–77.

Waslander, S. and Thrupp, M. (1997) Choice, competition and segregation: an empirical analysis of a New Zealand secondary school market, in A. Halsey, H. Lauder, P. Brown and A. Wells (eds.) *Education: Culture, Economy, Society*, Oxford University Press.

Wells, A. (1997) African-American students' view of school choice, in A. Halsey, H. Lauder, P. Brown and A. Wells (eds.) *Education: Culture, Economy, Society*, Oxford University Press.

Wolfendale, S. (1996) The contribution of parents to children's achievements in school, in J. Bastiani and S. Wolfendale (eds.) *Home–School Work in Britain*, London: David Fulton.

Wright, R. (1995) The role of parents in supporting students in a 16–19 tertiary college. MBA assignment, University of Leicester (unpublished).

9

COLLEGES AND CUSTOMERS

Peter N. Davies

CONTEXT – THE CHANGING NATURE OF THE FE MARKET

The concept of *colleges and customers*, with its connotations of an educational market place where consumers exercise freedom of choice amongst competing providers, first took hold some thirty years ago in the USA as the concepts of marketing came to be seen as relevant to non-profit organisations as well as commercial companies (Kotler and Fox, 1995; Kotler and Andreasen, 1996). Outside the USA, the application of marketing models to the relationships between colleges and those they aim to serve has had most influence in the UK. In most other parts of the developed world, the concepts of marketing are still regarded as inappropriate to the provision of education, which is seen rather as a social service for which central and local government should take the primary responsibility for planning and regulation. These differences in national attitude persist, though the introduction of greater institutional autonomy in the Netherlands, Denmark and other Scandinavian countries, and the effective privatisation of some parts of the further education (FE) sectors of former Eastern-bloc countries in Europe (Svetlik, 1996), presage an extension of marketing's impact on the educational world.

In the UK, colleges have always had more sense of serving customers than have schools or universities. Historically, this country's FE sector has been market-led rather than statutorily defined (Hall, 1994). The *raison d'être* for the original existence of most colleges was vocational, and connected to the provision of non-advanced technical and commercial education. They grew used to adapting what they did in order to survive. They have regularly had to withdraw from those vocational areas that have declined, and move into those that were expanding. Thus, courses for mining and textiles have virtually disappeared, whilst those for the caring professions, travel and tourism, and the performing arts have steadily expanded.

Unlike schools and universities there were also relatively few areas of the UK curriculum for which colleges were monopoly providers. There were always significant overlaps in provision with other colleges, with schools, with universities, with adult education institutions, with private sector training providers, and with companies' in-house training. Colleges have therefore long had a sense of competition.

However, we should not exaggerate the level of customer-centredness present in colleges before the 1990s. At best, they had yet to proceed beyond what Kotler refers to as the sales orientation stage, and most were still firmly product-centred, according to his criteria (Kotler, 1994; Kotler and Fox, 1995). In the early 1980s, the UK government began to express concern about the standards of education and training, especially from the viewpoint of their impact on the country's competitive position internationally (NEDO/MSC, 1984). These developments coincided with dramatic changes in the structure of the economy. Manufacturing employment declined substantially, especially so in traditional heavy industry. Meanwhile, the service sector grew, but with job opportunities insufficient to offset a steady and substantial rise in unemployment.

The impact of these shifts was dramatic. The demand for day-release courses aimed at training young apprentices – the core customer-base for many colleges – rapidly disappeared. In its place the so-called New FE arose – a combination of more general academic and so-called pre-vocational education provision for the increased numbers of young people who now remained in full-time education after the age of 16; training for youth and adult unemployed; reskilling for those in employment or wishing to return to it; and Access provision for adults seeking to take advantage of the expansion in higher education that was now also taking place. In none of these areas did colleges enjoy the same degree of prominence as they had done in apprenticeship training.

Colleges in the UK also reacted by creating a formalised marketing function within their management structures, mirroring changes that had already taken place within the American system of Junior and Community Colleges (Smith, Scott and Lynch, 1995; Kotler and Fox, 1995). A further fillip to focus on the market place came with the Further and Higher Education Act of 1992. Amongst other things, colleges were now required to submit strategic plans, based on evidence of market needs, and a standardised mechanism for funding was introduced that provided direct incentives towards student recruitment, retention and achievement.

The 1992 Act also placed some constraints on colleges' freedom to respond to the changing demands of their customers. Unlike universities, colleges had largely been confined to the delivery of the qualifications of external examining and validating bodies, rather than awarding their own. Schedule 2 of the 1992 Act now restricted government funding almost exclusively to courses leading to these national qualifications. In common with the rest of Europe, the 'product range' UK colleges can offer is influenced considerably by what are, in effect, government-regulated franchises. Many of the decisions that determine curriculum development are hence outside their control.

The 1990s have seen renewed public concern over educational standards, especially in the USA and the UK, the two countries most committed to the model of autonomous institutions operating within a competitive educational market place in which consumers exercise choice. In this country there is now a well-established consensus that participation rates must be increased and levels of achievement raised amongst those who do take part. The current government's Green Paper *The Learning Age* explicitly sets out the leading role that colleges will have to play if these goals are to be met (DfEE, 1998).

WHO ARE FE'S CUSTOMERS?

Typical market segments

Colleges differ in the students for whom they aim to cater, and the range of courses they offer in order to do so. In the USA, the Community College system is founded on a liberal arts tradition, catering for a variety of educational needs, and providing the first part of degree programmes before progression to complete studies at university. In the rest of Europe, the nearest equivalents to the FE-sector colleges of the UK typically provide a broad-based technical and vocational education for young people making the transition from school into employment. The UK is unique in the range of needs for which individual colleges within the further education sector are expected to cater. Many institutions aim to provide a comprehensive range of post-16 education and training, in theory providing for everyone in this age range within their locality; other specialist colleges provide education in areas such as agriculture and horticulture or art and design; and sixth form colleges concentrate primarily on preparing young people for entry to higher education. Typically, however, most UK colleges serve three broad segments which have distinct requirements, namely:

- *young people*, requiring preparation for entry to employment or higher education
- *adults*, requiring vocational training or updating, or wishing to pursue education as a leisure interest

- *employers*, requiring education and training to maintain and improve the skills of their workforce.

In the context of marketing theory, the first two of the categories above are based on segmentation of the mass consumer market by lifestage; the third represents the industrial or business-to-business market. In practice, of course, colleges break each of these broad segments down into more precise groupings, depending on their particular circumstances (see Figure 9.1). Within the scope of this chapter it is not possible to provide specific case studies of effective practice in market segmentation and consequent recruitment strategies, but examples are available from other sources (Pieda, 1996; FEFC, 1998).

The basic concept of market segmentation is well established in the further education sector, though it is not always carried through into

Main Segment	Sub-Group
Young people	Seeking preparation for career entry
	Seeking progression to more advanced education, including university entry
	Unemployed seeking entry to labour market
Adults	Seeking to improve qualifications and/or update skills in order to gain career advancement
	Unemployed seeking to return to labour market
	Women seeking to return to labour market after child rearing
	Retired, seeking new interests
Employers	Seeking study towards national qualifications for members of their workforce
	Seeking tailor-made training courses, consultancy or research services
	(Also typically segmented according to *industrial sector* and *occupational grouping*, which help to determine the specific vocational areas in which training and other services are required)
Other segments with distinctive needs	Ethnic minorities
	Individuals with learning difficulties and disabilities
	Overseas students

Figure 9.1. Typical market segmentation for general FE-sector colleges in the UK

genuine differentiation within the marketing mix to the extent that theory demands (FEFC, 1998). Nonetheless, colleges' understanding of their actual and potential markets has become steadily more sophisticated. Geodemographic techniques, that profile a college's student body against the area it aims to serve based on postcode analysis, are now in widespread use. As a result, colleges have a much better understanding of their relative penetration of markets according to socio-economic factors. The concept of inclusive learning – with its emphasis on tailoring provision to the needs of each student – mirrors trends in the retail trade towards segmentation down to the level of the individual, supported by products capable of high levels of customisation.

At this point, we should note that in itself the term 'customers' provides only a limited guide to the nature of the educational market place. It has long been recognised that colleges serve a complex web of consumers (students), customers (those who pay the fees and other costs, including parents and employers), funders (the government, the funding councils, Training and Enterprise Councils (TECs), payers of taxes and business rates), and influencers (schoolteachers, employers and the media) (Davies and Scribbins, 1985). To ensure success colleges must relate effectively to each of these constituencies, a demanding task since their interests are rarely the same.

Young people

Throughout the developed world colleges are the major providers of education and training for young people between the ages of 16 and 18. In England some 650,000 of this age group currently attend, around 37 per cent of school-leavers enrolling each year (FEFC, 1997a). Though UK colleges are distinctive from schools in their provision of opportunities for study part-time and their wider range of vocational courses, in fact collectively they also enrol more full-time students, and more students who study towards A levels. Traditionally, colleges have seen the education of young people as their primary goal. Though the majority of enrolments in the sector are now adults, young people still represent a substantial proportion of full-time equivalent students (FTEs) – in many colleges, the majority.

Demographic trends mean that the numbers in this age cohort are increasing only marginally over time, if at all. Staying-on rates after the end of compulsory education are now high in most areas of the UK, and offer little scope for improvement. To achieve significant growth in this segment, most colleges therefore have to improve their share of the market. For many this is a formidable prospect, since relative competitive advantage has been slipping away as schools and sixth form colleges have extended their curricula to encompass general vocational education.

When choices are being made of where to study after the end of compulsory education, there exists a well-established pattern of perceptions of the relative attractiveness of the different types of institution (Davies, 1996a; Foskett and Hesketh, 1996; Keys and Maychell, 1998). FE colleges tend to be rated best for factors concerned with choice of courses, vocational relevance, and adult atmosphere; school sixth forms for academic standards, quality of teaching and public reputation. (Sixth form colleges and tertiary colleges sometimes generate favourable perceptions across the board.) In addition, since schools are more numerous than colleges in most areas of the country, they tend to be more convenient to reach.

FE colleges face problems in changing the way they are viewed. Their association in the public mind with vocational qualifications that enjoy less prestige than (supposedly) equivalent academic qualifications conveys a 'down market' image. Elsewhere in Europe, providers of technical and vocational education face similar problems (Stanton and Richardson, 1997). The persistence of this image is reinforced by those who influence the decisions of young people. Schoolteachers understandably wish to encourage their brighter pupils to stay on into the sixth form. A levels, in which schools (and sixth form colleges) are relatively stronger, are still viewed as the best entry route to higher education. The intake to colleges at 16+ contains a relatively higher proportion of students with lower levels of prior attainment (Foskett and Hesketh, 1996). Though colleges often achieve impressive subsequent results in terms of value added, inevitably they tend to compare less favourably with many schools when overall qualification pass rates are displayed in institutional performance tables.

Colleges have implemented a wide range of strategies aimed at maintaining and improving the recruitment of young people, examples of which are displayed in Figure 9.2. These developments have been influenced by research evidence that those who have direct experience of colleges rate them more favourably than those who hear about them second hand (Davies, 1996b), implying that the problem lies more with the promotion element of the marketing mix than with the intrinsic quality of college provision. They have involved expenditures on the design, printing and distribution of leaflets and prospectuses far in excess of most schools (Whitby, 1992; Smith, Scott and Lynch, 1995). The impact of these investments is, however, likely to be greatest on school pupils who are already committed to an active consideration of the alternatives on offer at 16+.

Colleges have turned therefore to other forms of direct communication. Increasingly they have recognised that for many young people the decision-making processes which lead to choices at 16+ start long before their final year of compulsory education (Foskett and Hesketh, 1996). The associated strategies set out in Figure 9.2 build on the established marketing principle that, if the quality of a product is good, the more people who

Aims	Strategies
Improved written communications - to convey positive and reassuring messages that emphasise college strengths and counter perceived weaknesses	Improved design of prospectuses and leaflets Better targeting of publicity materials at young people and parents, including direct mail Emphasis on atmosphere, facilities and opportunities rather than on fine detail of courses Wider use of media to disseminate messages, including computer disks and websites
Increased direct contact with prospective students and parents - to counteract influence of gate keepers and mediators	Establishment of dedicated schools-liaison teams Presentations at schools' careers evenings Cultivation of feeder-schools Mounting of college open days, summer schools, IT workshops and 'taster' courses Establishment of positive links with primary schools and lower years of secondary schools by offering access to college facilities
Ensuring the distinctiveness of the college 'product'	Review of curriculum portfolio Concentration on provision not generally available in school sixth forms, e.g.: – use of economies of scale to provide wide range of subject combinations – offer of wide range of specific vocational and professional qualifications – part-time courses – courses for unemployed young people Investment in leading-edge information and learning technology: establishment of resource-based learning centres offering 'drop-in' service Provision of high levels of technical support for students with learning difficulties and disabilities Promotion of courses to overseas students, and franchising courses delivered in colleges in other countries
Improving opportunities for student progression into employment or higher education	Widespread integration of work placements into vocational curriculum Establishment of recruitment agencies Franchising of university degree courses to allow first year to be undertaken at FE college University–FE college mergers

Figure 9.2. Typical strategies for recruiting young people

come into direct contact with it the more will 'buy'. In particular, they allow young people to meet college staff, and current students, and thereby experience the People element of the mix that is so vital in the marketing of services (Cowell, 1984).

Colleges have not taken product quality for granted, however. Whilst they have been striving to communicate with young people more effectively, they have also been endeavouring to improve the attractiveness of what they offer. As Figure 9.2 indicates, the main means by which they have sought to achieve this has been to ensure distinctiveness in relation to competing providers.

Adults

During 1998/99, over two million students above the age of 19 will have enrolled at colleges in the UK. A further substantial number attend courses in separate adult education institutes, under the responsibility of LEAs – the common pattern of provision for this segment in the rest of Europe. Even though the vast majority of adult students are part-time, together they represent another vital element in colleges' customer-base. So far as Schedule 2 provision for adults is concerned, colleges are significantly the most prominent providers.

Faced with limited scope for expansion in the youth market, colleges have sought to meet targets by expanding their recruitment of adults. Adult participation rates by LEA area vary across England from 3 per cent to 13 per cent, with a median of 6 per cent (FEFC, 1997b). Generally speaking, participation levels drop steadily as age rises. In this segment there is therefore considerable scope for expansion via increased market penetration, rather than as a result of improving market share at the expense of other providers. To achieve this, however, is by no means straightforward. For one thing, the perceptions of many adults of their need for what colleges have to offer are understandably less developed than those of young people conscious that they require preparation for entry to the labour market, or to higher education. For another, they are not usually entitled to the same level of financial support. Moreover, adults are far from being a homogeneous market. In fact, they incorporate a myriad of segments, each with its distinctive requirements. If colleges are not selective, they can easily overstretch themselves and dissipate their efforts to little effect. Figure 9.3 illustrates the range of strategies they have adopted in order to attract a larger proportion of adults.

The realisation of the vision set out in the government Green Paper *The Learning Age* will require colleges to continue their penetration of adult markets with renewed vigour (DfEE, 1998). Though this will present them with major challenges in the absence of significant enhancements in funding, new possibilities are also offered. The launch of the University

Aims	Strategies
Adapting vocational provision to reflect economic and social change	Provision of professional updating and reskilling courses – especially in IT
	Provision of *Access to HE* courses for mature students - especially females
	Adjustment of specialist vocational provision, e.g. diversification of agricultural colleges into tourism, equine studies, golf course management, etc.
	Provision of retraining for unemployed seeking return to labour market
	Provision of *Return to work* courses for women – often delivered by female trainers, and mounted at times and places convenient to mothers of children of school age
	Mounting of training and employment exhibitions and careers days for women seeking to return to the labour market
Broadening the definition of the educational 'product' to include entertainment, leisure and health and social security	Establishment of *Senior citizens* clubs
	Opening up of sports, training, restaurant and hairdressing facilities
	Provision of *Preparation for retirement* courses
	Establishment of advice and guidance centres
Forging stronger community links	Establishment of collaborative arrangements with voluntary organisations, e.g. those representing particular ethnic groups
	Acquisition of outreach centres on housing estates, etc., often employing staff drawn from the communities concerned
	Development of facilities for individuals with learning difficulties and disabilities
Improving communications	Better targeting – including increased use of direct mailing, free newspapers, etc.
	Wider use of dissemination channels, including libraries, community centres, doctors' and dentists' waiting rooms, and family planning clinics
	Co-ordination of outreach workers and ex-students as advocates for the college, spreading positive word-of-mouth

Figure 9.3. Typical strategies for recruiting adults

for Industry will extend the use of commercial marketing techniques to sell learning and link people into new and existing educational opportunities. Pilot projects in Bradford and Sunderland have already involved collaborative partnerships between universities, colleges, TECs and the local authorities, enabling people to learn on their own when it suits them. The Green Paper also announced the intention to introduce individual learning accounts in order to encourage individuals to save to learn, backed by an initial allocation of £150 million to support the involvement of one million people.

Employers

With the exception of some sixth form colleges, virtually all other FE-sector institutions in the UK identify the corporate market of employers as one of the main segments for which they aim to cater. Despite the disappearance of apprenticeships in the UK, the day-release of employees to study at college still persists to provide some institutions with a worthwhile number of enrolments. Colleges remain as major providers of professional qualifications which lie outside the national framework, including those in accounting, personnel management and marketing.

The total take-up of further education provision in the UK by employers is difficult to quantify, as it is impossible to disaggregate the numbers of employees for whom they commission training from the overall statistics for part-time students, which also encompass many who enrol as individuals. Equally, income generated from employers is difficult to disentangle from that arising from other sources. Evidence suggests that around 40 per cent of colleges generate over £250,000 of income per annum from self-financing work for employers, with a further 10 per cent generating in excess of £1 million (FEDA/CBMA, 1996). To these amounts can be added those allocated by the funding council, and other sources of income such as the local TEC, or the European Union, which together also support the college-based training of which employers take advantage. For the large majority of colleges, though, the income that can be attributed directly to employers forms less than 20 per cent of the total.

Corporate expenditure on training is a multi-million pound business. There is a consensus amongst government and employers' organisations that companies need to invest a higher proportion of their budgets in training if they are to sustain competitiveness in the global market place. This is therefore a market in which colleges have the potential to expand recruitment. Moreover, it offers opportunities for colleges to spread their income base and thereby reduce their reliance on government funding. Colleges are well aware that this is also the segment from which there is substantial competition from private sector providers, including companies' own in-house provision.

The range of strategies that colleges have adopted to increase their share of corporate markets is set out in Figure 9.4. In addition to those listed, the larger institutions, in particular, have become more confident in articulating their primary role in economic development, one study indicating a college's beneficial impact on a city's economy at around £20 million per annum (James and Clark, 1997).

Aims	Strategies
Flexible delivery in line with employer needs	Tailor-made delivery of courses, including in - workplace locations
	Collaborative arrangements to support National Vocational Qualification (NVQ) requirements for workplace learning and assessment – including training of company-based assessors
	Franchising of NVQ provision, enabling employers access to FEFC funding
Generation of full-cost recovery provision	Establishment of self-financing *Services* to *business* units, offering a *one-stop-shop* for training and related services – work sub-contracted to non-college staff where appropriate
	Supply of *Training needs analysis (TNA)* service
	Expansion of range of services to include consultancy, research, and hire of premises and equipment
Effective collaboration with agencies involved in supporting employer training needs	Establishment of close links with Training and Enterprise Councils (TECs) in order to obtain labour market intelligence
	Involvement in local and regional Strategic Partnerships, also involving the TEC, local authority and businesses, to assist economic regeneration, etc.
Improving communications	Establishment of *employer-liaison* sales teams
	Better targeted direct mailing – especially to small and medium-size enterprises (SMEs)
	Setting up *Small business* clubs and holding *Business breakfast* briefings
	Seconding lecturing staff to industry

Figure 9.4. Typical strategies for increasing penetration of corporate markets

FROM PROMOTION TO MARKETING

College efforts to meet the changing needs of those whom they aim to serve have been accompanied by a gradual shift from a concentration on advertising and selling, to a more comprehensive vision of the marketing function. In other words, they have come to appreciate that the educational marketing mix contains other elements as well as promotion, a development typical of organisations with growing experience of marketing (Kotler, 1994). Publicity and public relations retain their position as the activities most popularly associated with marketing in the sector, and those most commonly included within the job descriptions of college marketing managers and their staff (Smith, Scott and Lynch, 1995). Nonetheless, there has been a clearly discernible change in the way most colleges discharge the marketing function.

Its first signs became apparent in the increased use of market research to inform decisions about curriculum development and delivery (Pieda, 1995; IES/FEFC, 1997). This development was stimulated by the requirements placed upon incorporated colleges to produce strategic plans and the introduction, in 1994, of the FE Charter which placed a legal obligation on colleges to survey their students and other clients at least annually.

As a consequence, colleges adapted their management information systems (MIS) for the purposes of market intelligence, which had not been a primary consideration in their original design. More sophisticated student record systems began to be developed, capable of tracking an individual through the stages of enquiry, application, enrolment, on-programme, achievement, and even alumni (Donovan, 1996; FEDA, 1997; FEFC, 1997c). More precisely targeted and timely direct mailing has resulted, along with information assisting the maximisation of enquiry–application–enrolment conversion rates. The establishment and use of employer databases has also increased markedly. Via the analysis of the industrial and occupational category data that they typically contain, and the use of other helpful designations such as Key, Active and Casual customers, colleges are able to identify opportunities and plan visits and mailings (Hughes, 1996).

Course teams and Student Services sections, working in conjunction with marketing staff, have become used to reviewing the curriculum and student support services based on empirical evidence. Less apparent as yet is the regular use of rigorous primary research to inform understanding of those segments of the market not represented to any degree amongst existing students. It is still less common for colleges to employ professional market researchers than for them to contract the services of designers, printers and advertising agencies. Here too, though, there is a discernible upswing in activity, particularly as the financial pressures on colleges face them with tough choices about investment and divestment decisions involving whole programme areas (FEFC, 1998). The related use of business models of portfolio analysis (Ansoff, 1987) to help set the future direction of the curriculum has likewise become commonplace.

A further trend has been towards the development of rigorous systems of quality assurance, based on notions of student and client entitlement. Here, the actions of English colleges have been reinforced by the funding council's introduction of formal requirements for self-assessment. As a result they have given more thorough consideration to aspects of students' progress through their life at college. In consequence, a number of institutions have strengthened arrangements for induction, guidance and counselling, health and welfare services, financial assistance and tutorial support. Commercially established concepts of customer-care have also had a marked impact on the fabric and staff of colleges.

Arguably the most pressing incentive to take quality assurance more seriously has transmitted itself through the operation of the funding mechanisms, which have produced potentially crippling financial consequences if rates of student drop-out and unsuccessful completion are not kept in check. Understandably, there has been a dramatic growth in attention to the practical means by which retention and achievement can be improved. Evidence from resulting research indicated that the ability of colleges to make an impact in these areas was more within their control than they imagined. Whilst external factors such as financial and personal problems, and the lures of employment, all played a part, the main differences between the profiles of students who dropped out and those who stayed on and achieved were seen to lie in the lower levels of satisfaction of the former group's experience of college life. Feelings that they were on the wrong course, that it lacked interest, and that the quality of teaching was unsatisfactory, were all more apparent amongst drop-outs (Davies, 1996b; FEDA, 1998; Martinez and Munday, 1998). Acting on this evidence, a number of colleges put in place strategies to improve curriculum delivery, and to bolster tracking and support systems, which demonstrated an immediate positive effect (Martinez, 1997; Martinez, Houghton and Krupska, 1998; Davies, Mullaney and Sparkes, 1998).

The net result of all these developments is that the role of marketing within strategic planning has come to be more widely accepted, at least amongst policy-makers and college managements. The design and delivery of an effective curriculum remains at the centre of college concerns, but marketing is seen as a key element in ensuring that there is a constant focus on the need to adjust to changing customer requirements (Figure 9.5).

ORGANISING AND PLANNING EFFECTIVE MARKETING

By commercial standards, most colleges are large organisations that have to deal with considerable diversity in both the markets they supply, and the product ranges they offer. The establishment of successful external relations requires a degree of formalisation in the planning and organisation of the marketing function (McDonald, 1995). Yet compared to organisations in other sectors, the marketing budgets of most colleges are

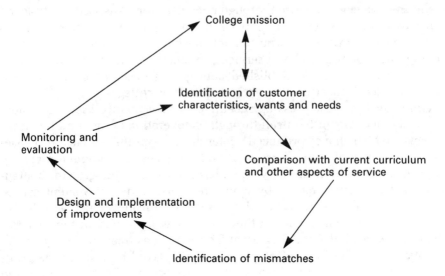

Figure 9.5. The marketing process applied to colleges

modest, in as much as it is possible to identify such expenditure with any precision (Smith, Scott and Lynch, 1995).

There is still enormous variety in the status of the marketing function in colleges. A clear pattern has yet to emerge of its accepted place in organisational structures. Some characteristics, however, do seem to be linked to success, such as the overall responsibility for the function being placed at second-tier level, the achievement of effective co-ordination between activities concerned with market research, admissions, curriculum development, Student Services, quality assurance and publicity, and an emphasis on the techniques of 'relationship marketing' (FEFC, 1998).

CONCLUSION

Marketing models of the relationships between colleges and those they aim to serve have so far had little impact outside the USA and the UK. Even in these nations there has been a reaction against the slavish application of practices derived from the market-place for fast moving consumer goods. But proven applications of marketing concepts in non-profit organisations have come to be widely embedded, and are unlikely to disappear. UK colleges welcome the role allocated to them in lifelong learning, and the emphasis on collaboration between institutions, employers and government agencies in order to achieve the necessary progress. The distance they have travelled in the 1980s and 1990s to develop more effective external relations suggests that they will discharge it resourcefully.

REFERENCES

Ansoff, I. (1987) *Corporate Strategy*, London: Penguin Business.

Cowell, D. W. (1984) *The Marketing of Services*, London: Heinemann.

Davies, P. (1996a) Decisions at 16+. Unpublished conference paper, Bristol: FEDA.

Davies, P. (1996b) Within our control? Improving retention rates in further education. Unpublished conference paper, Bristol: FEDA.

Davies, P. and Scribbins, K. (1985) *Marketing Further and Higher Education*, Harlow: Longman for FEU.

Davies, P. , Mullaney, L. and Sparkes, P. (1998) *Improving GNVQ Retention and Completion*, London: FEDA.

DfEE (1998) *The Learning Age: A Renaissance for a New Britain*, London: DfEE.

Donovan, K. (1996) *Student Tracking*, Bristol: FEDA.

FEDA/CBMA (1996) *College Business Units: Report of Questionnaire Survey*, Bristol: FEDA.

FEDA (1997) *Towards Better Student Tracking Systems*, Bristol: FEDA.

FEDA (1998) *Non-completion of GNVQs: A FEDA Study for the Department for Education and Employmen*, London: FEDA.

FEFC (1997a) *Widening Participation in Further Education: Statistical Evidence*, London: FEFC.

FEFC (1997b) *Student Numbers at Colleges in the Further Education Sector and External Institutions in England in 1996–97*, Coventry: FEFC.

FEFC (1997c) *How to Widen Participation: A Guide to Good Practice*, Coventry: FEFC.

FEFC (1998) *Marketing in Further Education: A Manager's Guide*, Coventry: FEFC.

Foskett, N. H. and Hesketh, A. J. (1996) *Student Decision-Making and the Post-16 Market Place*, Leeds: Heist/Crem.

Hall, V. (1994) *Further Education in the United Kingdom*, London: Collins Educational and The Staff College.

Hughes, M. (1996) Colleges working with Industry, *FE Matters*, Vol. 1, no. 3, Bristol: FEDA.

IES/FEFC (1997) *Identifying and Assessing Needs*, Coventry: FEFC.

James, S. and Clark, G. (1997) *Investing Partners: Further Education, Economic Development and Regional Policy*, Bristol: FEDA.

Keys, W. and Maychell, K. (1998) *Leaving at 16 and Staying On: Studies of Young People's Decisions About School Sixth Forms, Sixth Form Colleges and Colleges of Further Education*, Slough: NFER.

Kotler, P. (1994) *Marketing Management: Analysis, Planning, Implementation and Control*, 8th edition, London: Prentice-Hall.

Kotler, P. and Andreasen, R. (1996) *Strategic Marketing for Nonprofit Organisations*, 5th edition, London: Prentice- Hall.

Kotler, P. and Fox, K. A. (1995) *Strategic Marketing for Educational Institutions*, 2nd edition, London: Prentice Hall.

Martinez, P. (1997) *Improving Student Retention: A Guide to Successful Strategies*, London: FEDA.

Martinez, P. and Murray, F. (1998) *9000 Voices: Completion and Drop-out in Further Education*, London: FEDA.

Martinez, P., Houghton, S. and Krupska, M. (1998) Staff development for student retention in further and adult education, *FE Matters*, Vol. 2, no. 8, London: FEDA.

McDonald, M. (1995) *Marketing Plans: How to Prepare Them, How to Use Them* 3rd edition, London: Butterworth-Heinemann.

NEDO (National Economic Development Office) / MSC (Manpower Services Commission) (1984) *Competence and Competition: Training and Education in the Federal Republic of Germany, The United States and Japan*, London: NEDO.

Pieda (1995) *Labour Market Information for Further Education Colleges*, London: DfEE.

Pieda (1996) *Marketing Case Studies in Further Education Colleges*, London: DfEE.

Smith, D., Scott, P. and Lynch, J. (1995) *The Role of Marketing in the University and College Sector*, Leeds: Heist.

Stanton, G. and Richardson, W. (eds.) (1997) *Qualifications for the Future: a Study of Tripartite and Other Divisions in Post-16 Education and Training*, Bristol: FEDA.

Svetlik, J. (1996) *Marketing Skoly*, Zlin Ekka.

Whitby, Z. (1992) *Promotional Publications*, Leeds: Heist.

10

COLLABORATION BETWEEN SCHOOLS

Margaret Preedy

A number of contextual factors tend to restrict inter-school collaboration. There is no statutory framework to promote such collaboration, and the 1997 White Paper (DfEE, 1997a) makes it clear that schools are viewed by the DfEE as largely autonomous organisations which are held accountable for their own performance in comparison with other schools. They operate in a quasi-market framework, where they are in competition with each other for pupils and resources, on the basis of parental choice of school, coupled with largely delegated budgets and the publication of performance data for each school.

In these circumstances, what scope is there for inter-school collaboration and what are the implications for the management of the school's external relations? Collaboration is here taken to mean a co-operative relationship in which two or more schools work together towards shared purposes to the mutual benefit of the organisations involved. The following issues are explored: the arguments in favour of collaboration; the range of purposes underlying inter-school links; the main contextual factors which facilitate and inhibit such links; and finally the implications of these issues for school managers in establishing and developing inter-school relationships.

THE CASE FOR COLLABORATION

Various arguments have been put forward for the development of collaborative arrangements. From a pragmatic point of view, there can be important *financial* benefits for schools; for example, in terms of economies of scale in joint purchasing of goods and services. There are also important *educational* arguments. Although educational provision for most pupils is organisationally divided into separate sectors – primary, special, secondary, tertiary – it is important that teaching and learning as it is experienced by the individual pupil should form a cohesive and coherent continuum from age 5 to 19. As Lacey and Ranson (1994, p. 79) suggest, 'the advantage of collaboration [between schools] lies in the benefit it brings directly to pupils, particularly that their needs are viewed as a whole'.

A third set of arguments is concerned with the school as a *learning organisation*. Co-operation with others is an important component of learning for individuals, groups and the organisation as a whole. While much valuable development work takes place within schools acting autonomously, working with other schools in a learning network, drawing on external experiences and perspectives, can provide an important stimulus for change and improvement (Goddard and Clinton, 1994). Finally, there is a strong *moral* case for inter-school co-operation. As Bridges and Husbands (1996, p. 6) argue, individual schools are not ends in themselves 'but the means to the provision of the best, most comprehensive public education service that society can afford'. Such provision is not achieved by the self-interested pursuit of their own ends by individual schools but 'by active collaboration . . . between institutions which are in partnership in the education service' (ibid).

As links between schools are voluntary they have developed in an ad hoc and incremental way, sponsored by LEAs or groups of schools in response to particular needs and circumstances. They are characterised therefore by diversity along a number of dimensions: purposes, values, timescale, extent of collaboration, involvement of stake-holder groups, sectors or phases, and size of groupings. Various aspects of these dimensions are explored below.

PURPOSES OF COLLABORATION

Four broad sets of purposes for school co-operation can be identified. While analytically separable, in practice they are overlapping and interrelated, and subject to change over time as external circumstances change and partnerships develop or decline. Just as the goals of individual schools are multiple and complex (Hoyle, 1986), so are the reasons for which schools enter into and pursue partnerships with each other.

Finance

One set of purposes for inter-school collaboration is concerned primarily with the financial benefits of such arrangements. Financial links may vary considerably in timescale and depth, ranging from a one-off purchasing agreement – e.g. to obtain a bulk discount on IT equipment – to a long-term partnership for sharing resources – e.g. where a cluster group of schools uses a pooled budget to employ an SEN teacher or other specialist to work across the partner schools.

Various reasons for financial co-operation have been described by Woods and Levacic (1994). One important purpose is to obtain economies of scale and scope in purchasing physical resources or staff. Thus schools may band together to obtain expensive specialist resources such as CAD/CAM design equipment for technology, making this resource available to pupils and staff from participating schools. Examples of shared staff appointments include bursars, SEN teachers, and caretaking and maintenance staff (Woods and Levacic, 1994; Open University, 1995).

Another purpose for financial co-operation is risk-pooling. Pooling budgets provides a measure of stability since larger budgets are less subject to major fluctuations. There are particular advantages here for small primary schools, which may have considerable differences in pupil numbers from year to year, as the pooled budget can be used to help them over temporary financial problems. Pooling arrangements are also used to redeploy staff within a group of schools thus reducing the costs of managing redundancy.

A further motivation for financial co-operation is using joint action to generate additional funds from central government or LEA grants, or from industry. Education Action Zone funding, which requires a partnership approach between schools as well as other stakeholders, has stimulated a wide range of collaborative initiatives among schools. Other government initiatives, such as beacon schools, specialist schools and independent–maintained school partnerships, have also served to develop inter-school links. The need for schools to develop IT resources has also led to a large number of inter-school bids to gain sponsorship from computer and telecommunications companies, as in the projects piloting networked technology superhighways in education (DfEE, 1997b). Financial co-operation is interrelated with the other purposes discussed below. It helps to promote, and is developed by, broader reasons for collaboration.

Curriculum provision

Another important set of purposes is concerned with curricular issues: ensuring an appropriate range of provision for students, and managing curriculum continuity and progression as pupils move between sectors.

This purpose is evident in various areas of provision, particularly in co-operative arrangements between primary, middle and secondary schools to facilitate KS2–KS3 transition, to ensure that children's educational experiences progress smoothly despite the need to change schools. The National Curriculum (NC) framework and associated assessment arrangements have served to promote greater attention to between-phase continuity and progression. At the same time, the delegation of budgets to schools and greater parental choice has meant that pupil routes between primary, middle and secondary schools have become more diverse, making it harder to plan curriculum continuity for the majority of pupils.

Nonetheless, an NFER study of continuity and progression (Lee, Harris and Dickson, 1995) found considerable evidence of cross-phase links. Over three-quarters of the LEAs surveyed had cross-phase groupings. Cluster groups, often comprising a secondary and its main primary feeder schools, develop links by means of such activities as: teacher working groups on curriculum and assessment, particularly in the core subjects, assessment moderation exercises, team-teaching, joint INSET, pupil projects and agreed work schemes, pupil and teacher visits to each others' schools, and the development of agreed record formats for the transfer of pupil data from primary to secondary school.

Inter-school links to meet curriculum needs are also evident in provision for older students. In some areas, schools have grouped together to form sixth-form consortia, in order to broaden the range of courses available. Minority subjects are offered by one of the schools and pupils from all partner schools are grouped together for these classes. Consortia arrangements sometimes involve cross-phase links between schools and FE colleges, enabling school-based pupils to attend college for part of the week to study vocational courses not available in their schools. Such links are becoming more widespread in the light of government initiatives to encourage work-related learning for under-achieving KS4 students (DfEE, 1997a).

One such scheme is based on a partnership between four secondary schools and North Devon FE College (Whittaker, 1997). The arrangement provides practical training in woodwork and metalwork for 14–15-year-olds from the participating schools. Many of these students go on to attend college full time at 16+. In another school/FE partnership in Cardiff, the tertiary college has been running GNVQ courses at four local secondary schools (Passmore, 1998). Staying-on rates have risen by 10 per cent since the scheme started in 1994.

Another area of inter-school groupings for curricular purposes is in special needs provision. Research by Lunt *et al.* (1994) found examples of within-phase and cross-phase groups. Groupings were usually set up and funded by LEAs, rather than school-initiated. Collaborative activities were of two main types, focusing on aspects of primary/secondary transition and on the sharing of resources. In one example, a pyramid cluster of a secondary and six primary schools had developed a wide range of shared activities for SEN, including funding an SEN teacher who worked with year 6 pupils in the primaries and year 7 in the secondary school.

A final example of inter-school collaboration to meet curriculum needs is concerned with within-phase links to provide appropriate curriculum coverage and staff expertise to support this. Research on the implementation of the NC in small rural schools (Hargreaves, 1996) examined cluster groups which were working on improving the quality and extending the range of the curriculum. The clusters observed in the study evolved gradually, from an initiation stage where schools needed a great deal of outside help and focused largely on their own curriculum priorities rather than common cluster group needs, through a consolidation stage, and finally a reorientation or maturity phase.

School improvement

This purpose for collaboration can be distinguished from (2) above in that while it involves curricular issues, it is also concerned with broader and more ambitious goals relating to school improvement, on-going organisational evaluation and the management of change through working co-operatively with other schools. Groupings pursuing these purposes have often been initiated by LEAs, less frequently by groups of schools themselves. Such arrangements usually involve a relatively long-term and stable partnership, with agreed group aims and objectives, some extent of financial collaboration and a high degree of trust among the partner organisations. These partnerships are also usually informed by a commitment to the moral case for educational co-operation mentioned earlier, i.e. that schools have an ethical duty to the community they serve to work together rather than separately.

One such approach, in Enfield LEA, was based on the belief that improvement in the quality and standards of education requires schools to work collaboratively together and with the LEA to improve educational provision as a whole within a particular area (Goddard and Clinton, 1994). Schools were organised in partnership groups comprising one or more secondary schools, local primary schools and one special school or unit. A major aim of the scheme was to enable schools to manage change more effectively through mutual support and consultancy and to promote co-ordinated planning within individual schools and across the LEA as a whole (Hutchinson and Byard, 1994). Similar school-improvement strategies have been described in other LEAs (Du Quesnay, 1994; McConnell and Stevens, 1994).

The Woodstock School partnership provides an example of a school-initiated cluster, stimulated by an LEA's school self-review programme.

The partnership, comprising nine primaries and one secondary school, began in the 1980s with a range of loosely connected activities relating to curriculum continuity and special needs (McConnell, 1994). It evolved to form a much closer collaborative group, with agreed aims for comprehensive and integrated education provision for 5–19-year-olds and a commitment to progression, equal opportunities, and the evaluation of practice of the partnership as a whole and its member schools, through a process of continuous self-review. Collaborative working by the partner schools, McConnell argues, generated a sense of shared purpose among parents, pupils and teachers, articulated through a common 5–19 curriculum, and a partnership development plan.

Competitive alliance

A final purpose for inter-school collaboration to be examined here can be characterised as 'competitive alliance', i.e. a co-operative relationship based on a coalition of shared political interests, concerned with organisational needs to secure adequate pupil numbers and hence funding to compete effectively, and ultimately to survive in a quasi-market environment. Just as political interest groups within organisations form alliances and coalitions to protect their interests, especially access to resources (Ball, 1987), so inter-organisational political alliances give individual member organisations more power in protecting and extending the resources needed for their continued existence. Such competitive alliances may be more prevalent in areas where there are large numbers of surplus school places, putting the future of smaller and less successful (in terms of recruitment) schools in question.

Competition and collaboration are often perceived as antithetical, as encapsulated in the title of Macbeth, McCreath and Aitchison's (1995) collection of papers *Collaborate or Compete*? However, there is considerable evidence of schools collaborating in order to compete more effectively in the education market place. Research on schools' response to the more competitive environment brought about by the legislative changes of the late 1980s and early 1990s (Glatter, 1995; Woods, Bagley and Glatter, 1998) identifies examples of such instrumental alliances. These include joint marketing activities by groups of maintained schools in areas where there is strong competition from the private sector, and small schools sharing curriculum expertise and resources to ensure their continued survival.

These examples illustrate the complexity and multi-faceted nature of schools' purposes in developing collaborative links. Co-operation may serve pupil needs and school improvement purposes and, at the same time, help to safeguard the existence of member organisations. Thus, for example, while school or school–FE consortia for 16–19 provision broaden the range of curricular choice for students, they may also serve to maintain the viability of small sixth forms. The school–college links providing vocational courses mentioned earlier might be seen in a similar light. It may well be in the colleges' interests to use such provision as a means of attracting potential future clients. Similarly, primary - secondary school links are important to ensure continuity for pupils, but an equally important motivation for many secondary schools in developing such links is to market themselves to local primary schools in order to maintain or increase the numbers of pupils transferring to the secondary school (Woods, Bagley and Glatter, 1998). Thus competitive alliances may co-exist in complex ways with other purposes for collaboration. There may sometimes be tensions between these. Thus, for example, joint marketing arrangements may serve to mask disparities between the schools concerned and hence inhibit purposes concerned with meeting parents' and pupils' curricular needs, just as cartels in industry may work against the interests of consumers.

CONTEXTUAL INFLUENCES

A variety of contextual factors act to inhibit and promote collaboration between schools. Three main sets of factors are considered below.

Values and cultures

Each school has its own distinctive culture or set of values, which shapes how events are perceived and decisions are made. The purposes discussed above are underpinned by differing values about inter-school links. Collaboration is more likely to be successful and enduring where partner schools share similar cultural views on the nature and benefits of school co-operation. Thus, for example, in the Woodstock partnership mentioned above, the member schools have a shared belief in and commitment to collaborative values in the provision of a comprehensive and inclusive education service. Competitive alliances, on the other hand, are based on an acceptance, at least to some degree, of the values of the market place, and the pursuit of their own best interests by individual schools. Such alliances may be short or long-term, but are likely to be inherently unstable, since they are essentially reactive to the demands of the market place, and hence subject to shifts in allegiances as environmental demands change.

The matrix in Figure 10.1 shows a values dimension and, on the other axis, the depth and timescale of inter-school links. On this matrix, the examples of school improvement partnerships discussed above would be likely to be placed towards the top right hand side. Competitive alliances, based on instrumental considerations, would be located on the left hand side, probably towards the bottom, but possibly further up if the alliance continued to be in the interests of member schools.

It is interesting to consider government funding initiatives for Education Action Zones, beacon schools, specialist schools and independent–maintained school partnerships in relation to this matrix. All these initiatives require co-operation between pairs or groups of schools. Thus, for example, beacon and specialist schools are required to share their expertise with other schools as a condition of funding. However, the nature and extent of these inter-school partnerships remains to be seen. On the one hand, they may develop as short-term competitive alliances, located at the bottom left-hand side of the matrix, motivated by instrumental concerns to gain additional funding and resources, and likely to be terminated when the additional funding ceases. On the other hand, involvement in such schemes may provide the basis for participating schools to develop deeper, long-term partnerships based on shared collaborative values, on the upper right-hand side of the matrix.

The cultures and traditions of the various sectors – primary, special, secondary and FE – also exert an important influence on inter-school collaboration. The different attitudes and values of primary and secondary schools tend to act as constraints upon close collaboration relating to pupil continuity and progression between the sectors (Jones, 1989; Weston, Barrett with Jamison, 1992). Similarly the very disparate organisational traditions, cultural norms and values of schools and FE colleges do not

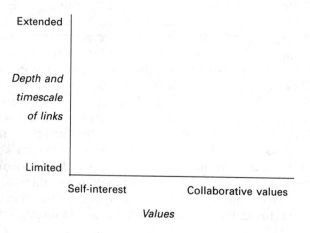

Figure 10.1. Matrix for inter-school links

facilitate co-operation between staff from the two sectors (Preedy, 1997). Subcultural differences and attitudes are perpetuated in separate teacher socialisation in initial and in-service education and training, and separate organisational and administrative frameworks for the various sectors at local and national levels.

Local history and circumstances

The history of the relationship between schools and other local factors, such as demographic and socio-economic circumstances, and the way that these factors are interpreted by participants, also play an important influencing role in promoting or inhibiting inter-school collaboration.

In many areas there has been a tradition of close links between schools, often stimulated by the need to respond to externally initiated change. Thus, for example, TVEI and its extension phase helped to encourage a good deal of inter-school and school–FE co-operative work (Bridgewood, 1996). The implementation of the NC and associated assessment arrangements similarly helped to foster links (Lee, Harris and Dickson, 1995). The history of the structure of the education system in the locality may also be significant. Thus, for example, in areas where there are several post-16 providers there is likely to be competition between them. This means that schools with sixth forms tend to resist giving information access to other providers, and students may not receive full and impartial guidance on the range of post-16 education choices open to them. In those areas where tertiary colleges for all 16–19 provision have been established for many years, school–college co-operation has tended to be closer than in other areas, since there is little or no institutional competition for the post-16 age group (Terry, 1987).

In other areas, existing relations among schools are less cordial, largely as a result of the quasi-market environment brought about by the legislation of the late 1980s and early 1990s. In these circumstances, developing collaborative links is likely to be more difficult. One research study uses vivid imagery to describe the relations between schools in the local competitive arena : 'this arena is the battleground upon which the schools vie with one another for pupil and parental support' (Woods, Bagley and Glatter, 1998, p. 145). Other studies have noted the strengthening of a status hierarchy among schools, accompanied by a 'values drift', with schools moving along a continuum towards market-driven norms and competition, and away from comprehensive values and commitment to co-operative relations with other schools (Whitty, Edwards and Gewirtz, 1993; Gewirtz, Ball and Bowe, 1995;). Demography plays a part in the extent to which relations are competitive rather than co-operative. In densely populated areas where there are several schools available within reasonable travelling distance, the pressures on schools to compete are likely to be greater than in rural areas where there is effectively little choice of school for parents and pupils.

A related factor which has served to weaken inter-school co-operation in many areas in the 1990s has been the diversification of schooling, with the development of City technology colleges, grant maintained schools and specialist colleges. In some cases these developments led to considerable hostility and resentment, dividing schools that had remained loyal to the LEA from those that had opted out, exacerbated by considerable disparities in levels of funding and other resources allocated to different types of school. Despite the changes brought about by the 1998 School Standards and Framework Act, the lack of trust fostered by the diversification of schooling will not disappear easily or quickly. Notwithstanding the DfEE's promotion of partnership models, these will be hard to establish between schools that have a recent history of less than cordial relationships.

LEAs have played an important part in initiating and sustaining collaboration between schools. NFER research on continuity and progression (Lee, Harris and Dickson, 1995) found widespread evidence of within-phase and cross-phase links in the LEAs surveyed. The large majority of LEAs allocated staff time to promote inter-school links, most also had policy statements on continuity and progression, and about a quarter allocated central funds to this. As noted above, many LEAs have also provided support for a culture of collaboration among schools, providing an enabling framework for them to work together on school improvement activities. While there is some evidence to suggest that well-established cluster-groups of schools can become self-sustaining (Hargreaves, 1994), LEAs have fulfilled an important supporting and facilitating function for school partnerships, particularly in the early stages of their development. The provision of this support became more problematic in the light of the diminished role of LEAs and the reduction in the funding centrally retained by them, as a result of the legislation of the late 1980s and early 1990s. As a result of factors such as local management of schools, grant maintained schools and open enrolment, LEAs played a much reduced part in financial and staff support for cluster groups (Lee, Harris and Dickson, 1995).

Structures and policies

Both at national and local levels, structures for the funding, administration and inspection of the education service are based on a separation between sectors and between individual schools. This tends to inhibit rather than promote attention to cross-sectoral issues and groupings. Separate sectoral budgets make the funding of inter-sector liaison more difficult. Similarly there are separate Ofsted inspection teams and frameworks for primary, secondary and special schools. Each school is treated as a discrete unit of analysis; inspection frameworks do not address issues of pupils' continuity between schools/sectors, or cluster group activities in which the school might be involved. Ashton (1998), a parent governor for a linked infants and junior school, argues that these arrangements neglect important issues. The two schools where she is a governor were inspected at different times by separate Ofsted teams, and the management of curricular and pastoral continuity and pupil transfer between the schools – of considerable interest to the schools and parents – were not addressed. Similarly, the FEFC inspection framework, while it includes questions of student guidance on entry to college, does not examine the extent to which colleges collaborate with local schools in managing student guidance and transition. Such factors tend to work against the educational case for collaboration discussed earlier – the need to view school/FE education as a 5–19+ continuum, and the role of each institution in contributing to continuity of experience.

Various recent policy developments are likely to have a significant influence on the nature and extent of inter-school co-operation. Some of these may well make inter-school co-operation more difficult. For example, the reduction in the non-core NC subject requirements for primary schools is likely to complicate the problems of managing KS2–KS3 curricular continuity. Freed from the necessity to follow prescribed programmes of study in the non-core subjects, primary schools are covering them in different ways and to differing degrees, resulting in greater diversity in pupils' knowledge and understanding as they enter KS3.

Despite the rhetoric of partnership in the White Paper (DfEE, 1997a), subsequent policy developments have arguably given greater emphasis to partnerships with other stakeholders – business, the voluntary sector, community groups and parents – than to collaboration between schools. The move to the foundation, community and aided structure for schooling, the bringing together of previously separate administrative and funding arrangements for different types of school, and some rationalisation of admission arrangements may have contributed to blurring the competitive edge of the quasi-market in education. Nonetheless, the market context largely remains, with a continuing status hierarchy of schools, reinforced by the publication of exam and KS test results and the 'naming' of failing and successful schools. As Whitty, Edwards and Gewirtz (1993) and others have pointed out, there has been a trend, not just in the UK but internationally, towards the 'marketisation' of social welfare provision generally, evident in social services, housing, health and community care, as well as education.

On the other hand, a number of policy developments are likely to stimulate greater collaboration between schools. These include the Education Action Zones initiative, which places emphasis on co-operative work by cluster groups of schools, rather than individual institutions, in order to raise performance across the zone area. This may have a wider impact beyond the designated zones. During the bidding process a number of groups noted that they intended to continue to develop their partnerships whether or not they succeeded in obtaining action zone funding.

The government's commitment to, and allocation of resources for, work-related learning within and beyond action zones is also likely to stimulate school–FE links of the kind described on pp. 148–9 above. Study support initiatives (DfEE, 1998), such as homework clubs, study centres and literacy/numeracy summer schools, are helping to promote greater inter-school liaison in managing such schemes. In the current context, the extent to which LEAs will be able in the future to provide supporting frameworks for inter-school collaboration remains unclear. However, the requirements for education development plans and school target-setting are serving to encourage liaison between schools. The availability of detailed comparative pupil performance information for KS1–3 and GCSE, including benchmark data, is enabling LEAs to group schools with similar pupil intakes into 'families' to work together to evaluate performance information, plan and set targets (Laar, 1997). Primary and secondary schools are also working together on target-setting (Gelsthorpe, 1997). This form of co-operation is felt to be an important route to raising standards – pupils are actively involved in target-setting at the primary stage, developing a culture of reviewing and improving their work which is continued and developed in their later school career. Such strategies may provide a useful vehicle for developing collaborative inter-school improvement activities focused on pupil performance.

At a broader level, ICT developments are facilitating cross-school co-operation in various ways: the electronic transfer and analysis of pupil data, exchange of information, joint INSET, sharing of ICT resources and expertise, and curriculum development. At the same time, rapid changes in ICT, coupled with the high costs of equipment and training, provide a strong incentive for schools to collaborate in this field. Thus, for example, one scheme in Bristol links a secondary school and ten primary schools, piloting a national network model that provides schools with a desktop-to-desktop managed network (DfEE, 1997b).

IMPLICATIONS FOR THE MANAGEMENT OF COLLABORATION

Schools, like other organisations, tend to focus on the core internal tasks for which they are held accountable, i.e. the effective and efficient management of teaching and learning. Collaboration with other schools, as a voluntary external activity, might therefore seem a marginal concern, an optional extra, to be undertaken only after the core business of the school has been attended to.

However, as the above analysis of the purposes for collaboration suggests, inter-school partnerships can serve to promote greater efficiency and effectiveness in the management of finance, the curriculum, and school improvement more generally. Co-operation can thus help the school to perform its core tasks better. Such partnerships may also contribute to a broader perspective, concerned with the effectiveness of the community of schools within an area in serving pupil needs throughout the continuum of schooling, based on collaboration among the schools involved.

Moreover, such links also contribute in important ways to organisational needs for support and resources, and help in meeting external accountability demands; for example, meeting government targets for school performance. From an open systems perspective, all organisations are highly dependent on environmental factors, which have a major influence on organisational inputs, processes, outputs and purposes (Scott, 1987). Boundary management – establishing and maintaining links with external stakeholders, including other schools – is therefore a major concern. In the current context, environmental demands on the school are subject to rapid change and uncertainty – as a result of such factors as government initiatives and developing technology. The boundaries between schools and their environments are becoming more permeable – as stakeholders, including central government and business interests, are increasingly involved in the work of schools. In these circumstances the core business of schools is subject to increasing external influence, and the role of the boundary manager in mediating these influences becomes of major importance.

Indeed, according to 'new institutionalist' ideas (Powell and DiMaggio, 1991), the environment has a central rather than merely peripheral impact on organisations such as schools. New institutionalism portrays a deep and embedded relationship between the organisation and its environment. From this perspective, institutional norms (i.e. generally accepted rules, values and patterns of behaviour) define the purposes and legitimacy of organisations and the activities they engage in. Organisations incorporate practices and procedures which are defined by prevailing societal concepts of organisational work, in order to establish and increase their legitimacy and validity, and hence their resources and survival prospects.

The boundary manager needs to take an active stance in ensuring that the school maintains an equilibrium with its environment. This entails balancing the tension between the organisation's need to be autonomous and to resist excessive demands, and, at the same time, to maintain linkages to ensure continuing environmental support, i.e. a balance between independence and interdependence. As Goldring (1997) suggests, an important strategy for boundary managers in addressing these circumstances is an adaptive response, which includes co-operation and joint action with other organisations.

Analysis of the existing evidence on inter-school collaboration suggests a number of key issues in the management of adaptive relationships. These are that successful collaboration is based on:

- a clearly perceived need for joint activities, with benefits for member organisations which outweigh the costs involved in terms of staff time and resources
- analysis of the complex local and national environmental factors which influence the nature and scope of co-operative activities
- recognition that the purposes for collaboration may be complex, including a changing mixture of reasons, concerned with curricular and financial benefits, the promotion of collaborative values, and the school's needs for environmental support
- awareness of the evolutionary nature of such partnerships, which may be initiated to deal with a particular concern and develop to embrace a broader range of issues
- coupled with this, a flexible and adaptive approach to the planning of partnership developments
- the need for a supporting and enabling framework to promote partnership development, provided by either the LEA or the schools themselves.

CONCLUSION

As the above analysis has suggested, there is considerable scope for inter-school collaboration. This issue is an important, though sometimes neglected, one in the management of schools' external relations. In the current context, various contextual factors may help to encourage inter-school co-operation, including the government funding initiatives which promote partnership mentioned earlier. However, the absence of a statutory framework for inter-school co-operation, and the reductions in LEA inspection and advisory services which used to provide an important facilitator for such co-operation, make it likely that collaboration will continue to be piecemeal rather than system-wide, and dependent on initiatives by individual schools or external funding incentives.

It is unclear whether links between schools in the future will conform to the competitive alliance model described above, or whether they will develop deeper links based on collaborative values and parity of esteem between schools. Despite the government's rhetoric of partnership, the quasi-market and 'competitive arenas' continue, suggesting that the

11

WORKING WITH EMPLOYERS AND BUSINESS

Marianne Coleman

INTRODUCTION

This chapter reviews the reasons for links between education and industry, their potential benefits for all parties and the implications that are raised for the management of the links in order to maximise benefits. The relationship between education and industry affects both the management of the curriculum, and the management of finance and other resources in schools and colleges. Although many of the examples used in this chapter are drawn from the context of the UK, the themes which emerge have international relevance in both developing and developed countries.

Schools and colleges have not always related to the community in which they are situated. Sayer (1989, p. 4) refers to the 'monastic tradition' of pre-war education. A countervailing influence has been a tradition of vocationalism, that has identified the need to prepare young people for work and has been one of the major historical influences on the curriculum.

THE INFLUENCE OF VOCATIONALISM

Vocationalism is amongst the many influences that compete for dominance in the curriculum. Lofthouse (1994) refers to the 'pressure groups active in the curriculum field' (p. 143) and names vocationalism amongst them.

In the UK an example of the vocational influence in education is the growth of competence-based qualifications such as National Vocational Qualifications (NVQs) which require that students based in colleges and schools must undertake work-based assessment. Another example is the recognition of the concept of the work-related curriculum. Saunders (1993) identifies the work-related curriculum as having two aspects, one relating to the interface between education and the economy with the attendant need for dynamism and responsiveness between them, while the other is:

> concerned with the process of transition from school to working life for young people, from social and economic dependency to independence.
>
> (Saunders, 1993, p. 76)

Skilbeck *et al.* (1994) claim that the present understanding of vocationalism means that the distinctions between education and training are 'becoming blurred' (p. vii). Indeed education and training are now the responsibility of one government department in England, the Department for Education and Employment, and the concept of partnership between education, training and business is stressed by the new Qualifications and Curriculum Authority (QCA):

> Strengthening the links between the worlds of education, training and employment will be at the forefront of the QCA programme.
>
> (QCA, 1997, p. 8)

The cohesion brought about by linking education and training with business in a partnership is emphasised by the importance that the British government has placed on the work-related curriculum and by the stress on lifelong learning including the proposed University for Industry, the importance of working towards the National Targets for Education and Training, and in the potential involvement of business in managing the new Education Action Zones (Barnard, 1998).

Linking the needs of industry to the provision of training

Skilbeck *et al.* (1994) refer to a 'new vocationalism' which stresses the role played by government, and identifies that :

> There has been a resurgence of interest in the world's industrialised countries in the vocational dimension of education.
>
> (p. 22)

However, an important role can be played by business acting independently of government, and the vocational influence is far from limited to industrialised countries. In relation to St Lucia, Boulogne *et al.* (1994) refer to the importance of links between business and technical and vocational education when:

the growth potential of the economy appears to be constrained by the scarcity of skilled manpower at craft, technician and managerial levels.

(Boulogne *et al.*, 1994, p. 81)

A similar relationship between the needs of industry and the provision of appropriate vocational training may be observed in China, where the increasing demands of the more market-driven economy meant that in Shaanxi Province there was evidence that 'local companies fed in their recruitment needs directly' to the local rural high school (Lumby and Li, 1998, p. 199).

In Brazil, local businessmen responded to the needs for skilled labour by establishing a vocational school themselves, where 'the government and the public agency responsible for training fail(ed) to develop an appropriate programme' (Gomes, 1991, p. 257). In the newly independent Namibia, the 'fragmented and inadequate' technical education system (Turner, 1993, p. 288) was supplemented by training provided by the private sector.

The community colleges that can be found in the USA may provide for the localised and specific needs of industry without government intervention; for example, providing short courses for industry, responsive to market demand and offering the option of college credit to participants:

> The general pattern is to work with industry to develop the course content and the outcome expectations.
>
> (Fulton, 1994, p. 99)

In the UK, the further education (FE) sector is the most important provider of skills updating. Over two-thirds of all FE enrolments are for vocational courses, and many of these are part-time and related to the students' current employment (Department of Employment, undated, p. 35) Despite this important contribution, research undertaken by the Further Education Development Agency (FEDA) has indicated that there are limits in terms of the coherence of the approach of FE to local industry:

> the activities in which colleges are engaged tend to be divergent rather than ones that contribute to a coherent local or regional development plan. . . . Initiatives may compete against each other rather than build a synergy between them.
>
> (Hughes and Kypri, 1998, p. 8)

Inspection reports of colleges tend to confirm these findings (FEFC, 1996). There were areas of criticism which included the facts that labour market information was not always detailed enough to help in planning courses, there was little analysis of student destinations to help with planning, and colleges prioritised the preferences of students rather than those of employers (FEFC, 1996, Summary).

National initiatives related to education–business links: the UK experience

In all economies there appear to be difficulties inherent in providing training that is flexible enough to respond to the changing needs of local industry. Indeed Gomes (1991) refers to the argument for: 'deregulation and a reduced role for the state' (p. 465). However, in recent years there have been a range of initiatives in the UK inspired by central government and designed to encourage the partnership of education and business. Skilbeck *et al.* (1994) comment on the range of influences:

> a complex amalgam of ideas, policies, legal and regulatory structures and practical endeavours whereby the nation's education and training systems have been reformed and restructured through government-led, partnership-type initiatives.
>
> (p. vii)

Government initiatives such as the Technical and Vocational Education Initiative (TVEI) helped to underpin the relationship between business and education. TVEI was possibly the single most important government-led initiative for the promotion of education–business links in the UK, lasting for approximately a decade. At the end of the initiative, Merson (1992) judged that:

> The short-term aim of getting the education sector to be more responsive to the fast-changing vocational needs of society has been achieved in part.
>
> (p. 17)

Brooman (1994) links the growth in education–business links to TVEI, and claims that:

> From the late 1970s, national policy saw school–industry links as one of the few growth areas in education at a time of otherwise substantial cuts.
>
> (Brooman, 1994, p. 221)

However, the promotion of education–business links through government initiatives has not always been effective. The National Curriculum included both Careers Guidance and Economic and Industrial Understanding as two of five cross-curricular themes. Both of these should have led to the encouragement of links with industry and business, but since the themes were non-statutory, and required incorporation into the curriculum by teachers who were non-specialists in these areas, research indicated that: 'the themes had a rather shadowy presence in most of the schools' (Rowe and Whitty, 1993).

The influence of government initiatives has been felt more strongly by the secondary and tertiary sector than by primary schools. For example, the financial support and impetus provided by TVEI was linked to the older age groups. Although the cross-curricular themes were intended to apply to all children from 5 to 16, the perception of primary schools appears to be that education–business links are more important for secondary school (Abbott *et al.*, 1996).

The development of education–business links is now supported in the UK by a national framework provided by the Education Business Partnerships (EBPs) and Training and Enterprise Councils (TECs) (DfEE, 1997, p. 61). The Education Business Partnerships, established in 1990 with funding from the then Department of Employment, are locally based with representatives from business, education, the local councils and the TECs but have the backing of a national network. The mission of the EBPs is to ensure the preparation of young people for adult and working life . The present government places a stress on partnership that looks beyond narrow vocational issues, and has identified that the raising of achievement is more likely to take place where all aspects of society are involved:

> Business, voluntary and public organisations, working in local partnership, can make a major impact in motivating young people and helping raise standards of achievement. We want to support and extend this work, particularly through mentoring and school–business links.
>
> (DfEE, 1997, p. 60)

THE PURPOSES AND BENEFITS OF PARTNERSHIP

Benefits at the macro level

The underlying rationale for business linking with education is outlined by Marsden (1989):

> The fundamental reason for business to work with education is that the future success of all business depends on the vigour and prosperity of the society in which it takes place.
>
> (Marsden, 1989, pp. 88–9)

The benefits of links between education and business are seen here as being related to the health of society and the economy as a whole. There is an underlying presumption of a two-way link between education and the economy and both the tangible and the intangible benefits to be obtained from investment in education:

> Quality education is expensive, but it brings commensurate benefits to individuals, families, business and professional people, and social agencies and institutions.
>
> (Burrup, Brimley and Garfield, 1988, p. 9)

Or alternatively, as a recent Green Paper puts it, 'learning will increase our earning power' (DfEE, 1998, p. 4).

The importance of the relationship between education and industry is recognised throughout a range of countries. Reviewing education business partnerships in the USA, Green (1993) states that:

> It takes an entire community to educate a child, and business, like the other members of the community, must step forward to help make the necessary changes for quality education.
>
> (p. 143)

Benefits to business

Reference has already been made to the implicit benefits to business and industry of their involvement in vocational education. In vocational and other forms of co-operation in the UK, it would appear that for businesses with more than 25 employees, around three in four have some link with educational institutions; overall it is probably about a third of employers who are involved in formal links with education. Of these over 80 per cent had links with an average of six secondary schools, 61 per cent with colleges of further education, 47 per cent with universities and 30 per cent with primary schools (Hillage, Hyndley and Pike, 1995). However, the range and depth of links varies substantially:

> At one extreme, an employer may attend the occasional career evening. . . . At the other some major employers have taken a strategic decision to involve themselves in many aspects of educational life.
>
> (Hillage, Hyndley and Pike, 1995, p. 1)

Marsden (1989) has identified the range of benefits that education and industry may gain through mutual co-operation. He proposes that for industry the 'bottom line' relates to financial results and for schools, the equivalent 'bottom line' is examination results. However, both education and industry have other agendas that also actually affect the two 'bottom lines'. For industry, these include their effect on the environment and a range of human resource issues such as recruitment of workers, equal opportunities, staff development and relationships with the local community. It can be argued that the development of education–industry partnerships and links may be beneficial to human resource issues in industry and may provide positive contributions to both 'bottom lines'.

Benefits for individuals or groups of individuals in business and industry are apparent. In respect of industrialists acting as tutors/mentors to sixth formers, Cummins (1989) identifies:

> without exception the industrial tutors have felt stimulated and encouraged by the fresh and innovative thinking of the young people. It helps the tutors to practise and improve their own skills and they find this to be very useful back in their own working environment.
>
> (p. 119)

Business may obtain 'hard' benefits from education, such as the provision of training services for their staff. However, research would indicate that these objectives are not a high priority in the UK. For business:

> The evidence ... is that employers are primarily driven by motives wider than mere self-interest. Across the whole sample, respondents were more likely to signal their agreement with the statements that indicated some form of benevolent or, in particular, enlightened self-interested motive for their involvement with education.
>
> (Hillage, Hyndley and Pike, 1995, pp. 13–14)

Benefits to education

Benefits to education tend to be of two types: there are the wide range of curricular benefits to be obtained from partnership with industry, and the financial sponsorship that may be vital to the survival of an educational institution.

Benefits relating to finance and resourcing

Reference has already been made to the ways in which industry may subsidise the provision of training, and of the 'hard' benefits to be obtained from industry in the UK in terms of earning income for services such as translation or the letting of accommodation. Financial benefits are generally a feature of the relationship between education and industry, but are inherent in the educational system of China, where schools, colleges and even the educational bureaucracy (Fouts and Chan, 1997) incorporate enterprise activities including factories and farms as well as service industries. The relationship between business and education here is almost symbiotic. The original aim of such activity was to serve an ideological purpose (Fouts and Chan, 1997). However, now:

> virtually every type of school has embraced the idea of school-run enterprises as a source of additional funding.
>
> (Fouts and Chan, 1997, p. 44)

The partnership between education and industry takes many forms, and it is most likely that the vocational aspects of the partnership are concentrated in the secondary and tertiary phase of education. However, the school-run enterprises, referred to above, can be seen in primary schools in China. Two primary schools in Shaanxi Province, questioned about their income, mentioned a peach garden, a little publishing press, a cold drink factory and a small department store (Ryan, Chen and Merry, 1998, p. 181).

Curricular benefits – the primary phase

A recent review of business links in the UK (QPID, 1997) concluded that there has been an increase in activity in recent years. However, it would appear that the majority of contacts between industry and schools are with secondary rather than primary schools. In a UK survey of 451 secondary schools and 432 primary schools in December 1993, 87 per cent of the secondary schools were involved in organising contacts between pupils and business or industry and 54 per cent had undertaken a teacher placement. This compared with figures of 19 per cent and 24 per cent respectively for the primary sector (Abbott *et al.*, 1996).

Nevertheless, knowledge and understanding of the community including business and industry can be acquired at all ages. A topic on local shopping is recommended as a route to gaining economic and industrial understanding for Key Stage 1 (NCC, 1990). A cross-cultural research project with primary school children in England and Germany indicated:

> the complexity, depth and variety of children's knowledge and understanding of the world of work as well as suggesting that there are several key areas deserving of further more detailed investigation.

> (Crawford, 1994, p. 52)

In the USA there has been a particular recognition of the importance of early years education by business, if children are to obtain the most from the educational opportunities offered to them. This has led to collaboration between:

> educators, health care providers, business people and communities to help give children a fighting chance of performing at high levels in school and becoming contributing members of society.

> (Green, 1993, p. 142)

Curricular benefits – the secondary and tertiary phases

In relation to education–business links in the UK, Marsden has identified the 'bottom line' for education as examination results. However, there are also additional desirable outcomes which include:

> communication skills, economic and industrial awareness, technological capability, health education and a whole range of other skills and attitudes.

> (Marsden, 1989, p. 26)

Some of the more obvious contributions to education from partnership with industry include the straightforward imparting of information and experience bringing vocational benefits and enhancing economic awareness. Some of the less obvious contributions may arise from the opportunities that may be offered to students for development of self-esteem and personal skills such as the ability to work independently and in teams. In addition, links with industry provide a range of opportunities for the enhancement of the curriculum.

Warwick (1989) classifies the various aspects of education–business links for education as:

social – extending the students' knowledge of society to include industry and business;

economic – enhancing economic and industrial understanding, perhaps through enterprise education;

vocational – preparation for the world of work including careers education;

affective – learning 'through' industry rather than about it; the development of skills such as communication and team work through simulated activity;

pedagogic – drawing relevant examples to enliven the curriculum from local industry;

instrumental – 'passing on knowledge, experience and practical skills'.
(Warwick, 1989, p. 21).

Examples of partnership activity

Examples of business–education links that are likely to bring curricular benefit include:

- enterprise education
- mentoring of students by industrialists
- placements of teachers and lecturers in industry
- work experience for students.

1. Education for enterprise often includes role play and simulated work activity and may involve the production of goods or services for money. Claims that are made about enterprise education relate strongly to the development of personal qualities valuable in the maturation process of young people. The enterprise education approach is process-driven, student-centred, involves working in small groups, is collaborative, fosters independence and is negotiated (Johnson, 1988, quoted in Harris, 1995, p. 51). The stress on experiential learning in enterprise education places the teacher in the role of facilitator and this in turn has pedagogical implications for schools and colleges. However, Caird (1990) indicates that learning through work experience will be limited unless it takes place within a framework rather than as an isolated incident.

Following research on enterprise education in schools, Harris (1995) concludes that, for a variety of reasons, some linked to their training opportunities, teachers were not able to adopt a truly student-centred approach, and remained in a directive mode. Thus her research findings:

> clearly challenge two fundamental assumptions made about enterprise edu-
> cation in the literature and by the various enterprise projects. Firstly that
> enterprise education necessarily involves student-centred teaching and sec-
> ondly that teaching enterprise education in a student-centred way produces
> enterprising qualities in young people.
>
> (p. 57)

2. Evaluations of mentoring of students by industrialists have found positive outcomes. Although students who are targeted are generally those
that are under-achieving, it is difficult to show that actual educational
achievement is enhanced through mentoring, since there are insufficient
records of value-added collected in a systematic way (Miller, undated).
However, the evaluations are positive in terms of the increased self-esteem
of the students:

> the distinctive factor about mentoring – having an adult other than a family
> member or teacher who is interested in an individual student – had a pos-
> itive impact on the young persons' self-esteem and their awareness of the
> world of work. The most compelling evidence came from the mentees who
> were able to identify benefits to themselves and who felt that there had been
> a positive impact on their school work.
>
> (Golden and Sims, 1997, p. 27)

3. The teacher placement service was set up in England, with the express
intention of helping to bridge the divide between business and education,
and with an initial aim of achieving placements in industry for 10 per
cent of teachers each year (DTI, 1988). Since 1989 almost 250,000 teachers have actually undertaken a placement (Lepkowska, 1998), although the
majority of them have been from the secondary phase. The aims can be
grouped into three classes:

> those aims concerned with enhancing the professional skills of teachers in
> curriculum development, pedagogy and management; those aims concerned
> with improving teachers' industrial and economic awareness . . . finally at a
> level of practicality, encouraging partnerships and links and updating careers
> advice for pupils.
>
> (Abbott *et al.*, 1996, p. 40)

Given the importance of vocational qualifications in further education,
business placements may be of particular relevance to lecturers in ensuring that their skills are updated, in addition to the other aims indicated
above. In a survey of FE and sixth form colleges in 1996 (FEDA, 1998)
it did appear that up-skilling in specified areas was the most common
purpose for a placement. However, the survey also revealed a great vari-
ation in practice regarding placements amongst the colleges, and that
only 15 per cent of those responding related the placement to either
staff appraisal or a development review.

4. The most frequently occurring link is that of work experience which appears to have international applicability. Watts (1991b) gives accounts of work experience in Sweden, Denmark, the Netherlands, Germany, the USSR, Cuba, Australia and the USA. By comparing countries that do offer work experience with those that do not, such as Japan, Watts concludes that:

> work experience is most likely to be introduced where the relationship between education and work is viewed as problematic, but where there is confidence that the problems may be solved or at least alleviated by seeking new forms of interpenetration between the two sectors.
>
> (Watts, 1991b, p. 52)

In England, work experience was offered by 88.2 per cent of the employers who responded to a large-scale survey carried out by the Institute for Employment Studies in 1995. The nature of, and rationale for, the experience may vary considerably. Watts (1991a) gives ten possible aims of work experience. These include a range of *vocationally related aims* such as investigation and sampling of work or preparing for a particular type of work. A further aim might be curricular, such as enhancing concepts learnt in the classroom. Other aims might relate to *personal development*, the affective aspect mentioned by Warwick (1989), such as increasing the motivation of students or facilitating their maturation. A final aim, not mentioned elsewhere, is *'custodial'* (p. 18), although it is unlikely that many educational institutions would use this term even if they were placing recalcitrant pupils in a work setting rather than the classroom. In announcing a plan to place disaffected teenagers in the workplace for one day a week, an education junior minister was keen to point out that:

> work-related learning benefits children of all abilities; this is not an option solely for pupils wanting to follow a vocational training path. Nor is it a soft option to appease the disaffected or truant pupils.
>
> (Pyke, 1998)

American research shows that work experience appears to have a positive impact on students' academic performance – 'despite the fact that the students are out of the classroom for substantial periods of time' (Watts, 1991b, p. 51). There are other potential aims for work experience. In Australia, it was started with radical intentions as:

> a means through which students could be assisted to explore their community and critically to examine various elements of society.
>
> (Watts, 1991b, p. 49)

For students undertaking placements as part of their course – for example, a sandwich course in HE – there may be a different expectation of work experience, given the length of the placement. This may raise its own particular difficulties:

> There has been a great deal of rhetoric about the benefits of sandwich

education. Much work remains to be done, however, on identifying the learning outcomes of periods of supervised work experience, and even more on their assessment and accreditation.

(Thorne, 1995, p. 178)

In addition, Thorne claims that the period of work experience is generally awarded low status in comparison with the more academic part of courses.

Work experience for secondary school and further education students is widespread, and is also present in certain higher education courses. The management of the activity as well as other aspects of working with employers and business raise a number of issues which are considered in the next section.

THE MANAGEMENT OF EDUCATION–BUSINESS LINKS

There is a range of valid reasons for schools, colleges and universities to work with business and industry, and a range of benefits that can be experienced by both parties. However, in order to achieve the maximum benefit, the activities must be managed, in the sense that they should be linked to a strategic plan and take into account the aims and objectives of the school or college. Hughes (1996) emphasises the importance of the part played by senior management in working with business:

A supportive and empowering management is the central 'essential' ingredient to such a strategy.

(p. 18)

Co-ordination and planning is necessary for partners in business and industry too, but this chapter is particularly concerned with the role of the school or college. At present it may be that:

Most schools follow a distinctly 'accidental' approach to industrial links, with activities being arranged upon an ad hoc basis by members of staff who happen to be interested or come across a scheme arranged by the LEA or other body which seems attractive.

(Gorman, 1989, p. 20)

It has already been noted (p. 163) that there is a lack of coherence in relation to the work of FE colleges in meeting the demands of local employers. With regard to the whole range of business education activities, there is agreement on the need for clear objectives, understood by all participants, and linked to both strategic plans and staff development needs.

In reporting on the characteristics of work placements valued by employers, Chivers and Flatten (1996) also comment on the need for support on the work placement and therefore the implicit need to integrate the placement into the wider educational context for the student:

> all parties involved, need to be aware of the importance of relating the practical aspects of placement to theoretical study, the professional and personal development of the student, and the need for high quality supervision by the employers and the university tutors.
>
> (p. 414)

Miller (1991), considering work experience for secondary school students, identifies a range of questions that relate to its management: do all parties share an understanding of the aims and how they are to be achieved? How is work experience linked to the curriculum? Who is responsible for planning and monitoring? How is the programme supported and reviewed?

There is also an issue of training and professional development for teachers and lecturers. Harris (1995) concludes that the objectives of enterprise education are limited by the lack of opportunity for the teachers concerned to consider the way in which they teach and to internalise the new methods required of them. Research on mentoring of pupils clearly identifies the need for the careful training of mentors (Golden and Sims, 1997). Hughes (1996) states that:

> Not all staff are suitable for front-line work with industry. Intensive staff development may be needed to facilitate quality delivery.
>
> (p. 18)

If the education business activity is to be properly integrated into the wider planning mechanisms, the need for careful and appropriate evaluation is essential. Jamieson (1991) refers to the shallow evaluation of work experience through simplistic questionnaires which only test whether the experience has been enjoyable. The lack of in-depth research actually leads him to comment that work experience 'as it stands is a great act of faith' (p. 261). However, there is good practice in the evaluation of some education–industry links. TVEI, in particular, provided 'the most comprehensive evaluation of schools/industry links' (Miller, 1989, p. 259).

Recent research on education–industry links has concluded that the role of the government and resulting national initiatives may be crucial to success. One conclusion of a recent 'stocktake' was that increased activity will only occur if education–business links are given a priority by the government and its agencies, particularly Ofsted (QPID, 1997). In addition, the importance of local co-ordination was stressed by this research, which also identified that the relationship between education–business links and careers education was often a source of confusion and that the disappearance of regional networks such as TVEI and SCIP had reduced the opportunities for dissemination of good practice (QPID, 1997, pp. 5–7).

There are highly practical reasons why education works in partnership with business and employers. There may be financial incentives involved in supplementing income from the government or that from fee-paying students. The needs of local business may feed though, and directly impact on the curriculum. There are also a range of benefits to both business and to schools and colleges that result in the enrichment of the curriculum. In addition, links between education and business may be encouraged at a national level in order to raise the achievement of the workforce and promote economic growth.

However, the optimisation of benefits is likely to depend on a clear understanding of the aims of the activity, and on the quality of management within the institution and co-ordination with business and employers. Success will also depend on the support offered by government and local frameworks which in turn depend on the prioritisation of vocational training and partnership activities on the part of the government. However, most parties, at both a local and national level, do not doubt that it is in the interests of both education and industry to work together in preparing young adults for an increasingly demanding and changing work environment.

Note: The author wishes to thank Gloria Sayer, vice-chair of the national EBP Network for her initial advice.

REFERENCES

Abbott, I., Campbell, R. J., Merson, M. W. and St J. Neill, S. R. (1996) Bridging the historical divide? An analysis of teacher placements in industry, *British Journal of Education and Work*, Vol. 9, no. 1, pp. 31–41.

Barnard, N. (1998) Confusion surrounds the future of local choice, *Times Educational Supplement*, 16 January.

Boulogne, T. with Benett, Y. and McKenzie, P. (1994) Education and business links in St Lucia, *The Vocational Aspect of Education*, Vol. 46, no. 1.

Brooman, L. (1994) School–industry liaison: developing local links, in M. Crawford, L. Kydd and S. Parker, *Educational Management in Action: a Collection of Case Studies*, London: Paul Chapman in association with The Open University.

Burrup, P. E., Brimley, V. and Garfield, R. R. (1988) *Financing Education in a Climate of Change*, Newton, Mass: Allyn and Bacon.

Caird, S. (1990) Enterprise education: the need for differentiation, *British Journal of Education and Work*, Vol. 4, no. 1, pp. 47–57.

Chivers, B. and Flatten, K. (1996) Characteristics of work placements valued by employers, *Journal of Vocational Education and Training*, Vol. 48, no. 4, pp. 405–15.

Crawford, K. (1994) Primary children's perspectives on the world of work: a cross-cultural comparison, *British Journal of Education and Work*, Vol. 7, no. 1, pp. 43–54.

Cummins, R. (1989) Industrial tutors, in D. Warwick (ed.) *Linking Schools and Industry*, Oxford: Blackwell.

Department of Employment (undated) *Labour Market Needs and Further Education*, Sheffield: Department of Employment group.

DfEE (1997) *Excellence in Schools*, London: The Stationery Office.

DfEE (1998) *The Learning Age: A Renaissance for a New Britain*, London: DfEE.

DTI (Department of Trade and Industry) (1988) *DTI – The Department for Enterprise*, Cmnd 278, London: HMSO.

FEDA (1998) Learning with business: the use of business and industrial placements and secondments in FE colleges, *FE Matters*, FEDA paper, Blagdon: FEDA.

FEFC (1996) *College Responsiveness*, report from the inspectorate, Coventry: FEFC.

Fouts, J. and Chan, J. (1997) The development of work-study and school enterprises in China's schools, *Journal of Curriculum Studies*, Vol. 29, no. 1, pp. 31–46.

Fulton, P. (1994) The American community college and its links with industry, in C. Flint, and M. Austin (eds.) *Going Further*, Bristol: The Staff College and The Association for Colleges.

Golden, S. and Sims, D. (1997) *Review of Industrial Mentoring in Schools*, Slough: NFER.

Gomes, C. A. (1991) Vocational education financing: an example of participation by employers in Brazil, *Prospects*, Vol. XXI, no. 3, pp. 457–65.

Gorman, G. (1989) *School-Industry Links*, London: Kogan Page.

Green, R. (1993) Business and education partnerships: a pre-school through higher education perspective in the United States, *Journal of Education Finance*, Vol. 19, no. 4, pp. 138–144.

Harris, A. (1995) Teaching approaches in enterprise education: a classroom observation study, *British Journal of Education and Work*, Vol. 8, no. 1, pp. 49–58.

Hillage, J., Hyndley, K. and Pike, G. (1995) *Employers' Views of Education–Business Links*, Brighton: The Institute for Employment Studies.

Hughes, M. (1996) Colleges working with industry, *FE Matters*, Vol. 1, no. 3, Bristol: FEDA.

Hughes, M. and Kypri, P. (1998) Beyond responsiveness: developing good practice in furthering local economies, *FE Matters*, Bristol: FEDA.

Jamieson, I. (1991) Evaluating work experience, in A. Miller, A. G. Watts and I. Jamieson (eds.) *Rethinking work experience*, London: Falmer Press.

Johnson, C. (1988) Enterprise education and training, *British Journal of Education and Work*, Vol. 2, no. 1. pp. 61–5.

Lepkowska, D. (1998) Industrial placement scheme threatened, *Times Educational Supplement*, 16 January.

Lofthouse, M. (1994) Managing the curriculum, in T. Bush and J. West-Burnham (eds.) *The Principles of Educational Management*, Harlow: Longman.

Lumby, J. and Li, Y. (1998) Managing vocational education in China, *Compare*, Vol. 28, no. 2, pp. 197–206.

Marsden, C. (1989) Bridging the culture gap, in D. Warwick (ed.) *Linking Schools and Industry*, Oxford: Blackwell.

Merson, M. (1992) The four ages of TVEI: a review of policy, *Bristol Journal of Education and Work*, Vol. 5, no. 2.

Miller, A. (undated) *Business and Community Mentoring in Schools*, Warwick: Centre for Education and Industry.

Miller, A. (1989) Evaluation, in D. Warwick (ed.) *Linking Schools and Industry*, Oxford: Blackwell.

Miller, A. (1991) School-based organizations, in A. Miller, A G. Watts and I. Jamieson (eds.) *Rethinking Work Experience*, London: Falmer Press.

National Curriculum Council (1990) *Curriculum Guidance Four: Education for Economic and Industrial Understanding*, York: The National Curriculum Council.

Pyke, N. (1998) Time out plan for unhappy teenagers, *Times Educational*

Supplement, 30 January.

QCA (1997) *Qualifications and Curriculum Authority: An Introduction*, London: QCA.

QPID (1997) *A Stocktake of Education–Business Link Mechanisms*, QPID Study Report, no. 58, Sheffield: DfEE.

Rowe, D. and Whitty, G. (1993) Five themes remain in the shadow, *Times Educational Supplement*, 9 April.

Ryan, P., Chen, X. and Merry, R. (1998) In search of understanding: a qualitative comparison of primary school management in the Shaanxi region of China and England, *Compare*, Vol. 28, no. 2. pp. 171–82.

Saunders, L. (1993) The work-related curriculum: the new entitlement? *British Journal of Education and Work*, Vol. 6, no. 1, pp. 75–89.

Sayer, J. (1989) The public context of change, in J. Sayer and V. Williams (eds.) *Schools and External Relations: Managing the New Partnership*, London: Cassell.

Skilbeck, M., Connell, H., Lowe, N. and Tait, K. (1994) *The Vocational Quest: New Directions in Education and Training*, London: Routledge.

Thorne, P. (1995) Supporting, assessing and accrediting workplace learning, in D. Thomas (ed.) *Flexible Learning Strategies in Higher and Further Education*, London: Cassell.

Turner, J. (1993) Planning technical and vocational education and training: the case of Namibia, *The Vocational Aspect of Education*, Vol. 45, no. 3, pp. 285–97.

Warwick, D. (1989) Interpretation and aims, in D. Warwick (ed.) *Linking Schools and Industry*, Oxford: Blackwell.

Watts, A. G. (1991a) The concept of work experience, in A. Miller, A. G. Watts and I. Jamieson (eds.) *Rethinking Work Experience*, London: Falmer Press.

Watts, A. G. (1991b) Some international comparisons, in A. Miller, A. G. Watts and I. Jamieson (eds.) *Rethinking Work Experience*, London: Falmer Press.

Section III: A Strategic Approach to External Relations

12

FINDING YOUR PLACE: SENSING THE EXTERNAL ENVIRONMENT

Stephen Waring

EXTENDING RESPONSIVENESS

It has been argued by some that educational legislation in the 1980s ushered in a free market, in which 'cut-throat competition' (Ball, 1993, p. 26) for students takes precedence over educational need, and in which a 'culture of self-interest ... obscures and deprecates the egalitarian concerns of the impersonal standpoint' (Ball, 1996, p. 21). In such a situation, it is tempting to see market research in education simply as part of a strategy to gain competitive advantage over rival players in the market.

Even at its most acute, however, education is a 'quasi-market', where choices are made by consumers within the context of policies and regulations determined nationally, regionally and locally. Further, in the most competitive environments of all – 'turbulent fields' (Hoy and Miskel, 1989, p. 42) – it has been argued that 'survival depends on the emergence of values that have overriding significance for all members of the field' (ibid.).

Survival itself is, arguably, a secondary outcome of an approach which stresses responsiveness. Perhaps the most significant of the changes which have been wrought over the last two decades or so is the extent to which the autonomy of the professional, in a whole range of public services, has become limited by increased demands for accountability (Hoyle and John, 1995). Accountability is but one component of responsiveness, which is defined by Scott (Scott, 1989, p. 22) as 'the willingness of an institution – or, indeed, an individual – to respond on its or their own initiative, i.e.

the capacity to be open to outside impulses and ideas'. Educational market research is about extending the 'voice' of the stakeholder (Hirschman, 1970) in decisions which an institution makes.

EXTENDING ANSWERABILITY

It is certainly the case that a naïve interpretation of marketing can lead schools and colleges to neglect the real needs of their stakeholders (James and Phillips, 1995). In post-compulsory education it is undeniable that prior to the demise of so-called 'Super Demand-Led Element' (see Chapter 6) funding, there were instances of an unhealthy preoccupation with discovering 'untapped markets' rather than unsatisfied needs. However, a sophisticated, systematic and community-oriented approach to scanning and interpreting client need and demand (Bagley, Woods and Glatter, 1996; Waring, 1997) can help the organisation to become genuinely responsive.

'The stakeholders' we may define as all those who have a legitimate interest in the continuing effectiveness and success of an institution. Whilst learners themselves will naturally be seen as primary clients, publicly funded organisations in a democratic society need to respond to a diverse range of expectations and demands. Schools and colleges are at the hub of a network of overlapping, sometimes competing, interests, expressed by a whole range of political, business and community groups.

Increasingly, the answerability of educational institutions to wider interests is expressed through a diversification of funding streams. In further education colleges particularly, substantial tranches of income now derive from funds targeted at specific groups, and channelled through bodies other than the Further Education Funding Council, such as Training and Enterprise Councils (TECs), The Employment Service, European sources and local education authorities (LEAs), as well as through contracts to private and public sector clients. Schools, too, increasingly find that not only are funds 'earmarked' for specific purposes, but as capital funding from LEAs becomes increasingly scarce, they must tender for funding streams such as the Lottery Fund, BT Challenge Fund or Education Action Zone funding. All require the bidder to demonstrate market intelligence. Although it is not uncommon in the post-compulsory sector for funds to be allocated to market research activities, it is clearly important for schools also to consider the potential for 'environmental scanning'; the approaches chosen will match their circumstances, and the available resources.

DEVELOPING A CULTURE OF INFORMATION

Schools and colleges, therefore, need an armoury of methods to gather reliable intelligence about their external environments – to include the markets they serve and those they might potentially serve, as well as the social, economic and political contexts in which they operate. In addition, they need to develop management systems which aim to ensure that the knowledge gained is effectively disseminated within the institution, so that the services it provides grow out of a sound understanding of client need.

Because the external environment is constantly changing, it is difficult to conceptualise the process as either linear or cyclical. A straightforward commercial exercise, where a new product or service is subjected to initial market research, product development, further consumer testing and product launch, does not happily translate to an educational setting, where consumers are participants in a continuing process of learning. Instead we might see the strategic planning process as being embedded in a culture of information, whereby it is constantly affected by knowledge of the external environment. The more explicit and the closer the relationship between market intelligence and strategic planning, the more formal the data source is likely to be.

Just as it is difficult to view the relationship between market intelligence and strategic planning as conveniently linear, so it is difficult to identify a management structure ideal for dissemination. In these circumstances, it is perhaps most helpful to view the management of educational institutions as 'ambiguous' (Cohen and March, 1989) where the technology is uncertain, and where solutions are in search of problems. Educational managers might be seen as creators of a culture of information, whose role is to create a climate in which the business of managing learning is seen as embracing an investigation of learners' needs in the widest possible sense. Teachers who would be unlikely to quarrel with the notion that they need to assess learners' needs, perhaps need to see as a necessary component of that assessment an informed knowledge of the external environment in which the learner is located. The teacher then becomes an amalgam of market researcher and product developer, as well as service provider.

The remainder of this chapter describes a range of informal and formal data sources, and indicates ways in which their use might be seen as part and parcel of the ongoing work of the institution. A case study follows which, although drawn from the post-compulsory sector, is nevertheless illustrative of the principles outlined above which transfer well to the compulsory sector.

SOURCES OF MARKET INTELLIGENCE

Informal sources

Much information can be gleaned simply by relying on the networks of informal contacts built up by staff in the school or college. Staff come into regular contact not only with parents but also with other professionals in, say, careers companies and social services. There may be contacts with local businesses, employers' federations, local government agencies and other educational establishments. Often, staff may wear different hats outside school, such as governor or parent of a pupil at another school or local councillor.

The importance of intelligence coming from such sources should not be underestimated. It can lead to direct policy changes to improve customer satisfaction, as in the case of Thurcleigh Hill School where changes to homework policy examination policy, and the introduction of the Duke of Edinburgh Award scheme followed directly from parental feedback (Bagley, Woods and Glatter, 1996).

In addition, such informal intelligence can provide the hunch from which a particular lead is followed through and surveyed in a more rigorous fashion. The headteacher of Wright Robinson High School in Manchester, for example, reports on how the school followed up persistent grapevine rumours about falling standards of behaviour. A programme of interviews and discussions was related to empirical research findings on parental choice of secondary school, and suitable corrective action was taken (Beischer, 1994).

However, there are a number of drawbacks with this kind of information. Firstly, it can provide the illusion of knowing your market: anecdote and hearsay are not necessarily reliable guides for action. Indeed, there is a danger of inaction, resulting from complacency. The head of Thurcleigh School argues that more systematic data collection is not needed:

> That would be silly wouldn't it? From our point of view we don't need it do we? I mean our measurement is based on numbers coming every year ... it's the best measurement we can have.
>
> (quoted in Bagley, Woods and Glatter, 1996, p. 134)

This begs a number of questions, such as how far the school has attempted to predict future numbers and what trends in parental expectations might be identified. Perhaps more important are the thoughts of those clients who do not currently make the school their choice; research into the perceptions of those who do not 'buy' is perhaps most likely to indicate ways in which the school can enhance its provision.

Secondly, there is an inherent bias in such information, a bias which it is not possible to control, since it reaches the institution in an ad hoc fashion. It will reflect the preoccupations of those who convey it. Often, it may be the voice of those who are already well served by the institution, and are well practised in the ways of institutional communications.

Thirdly, and perhaps most importantly, such information doesn't begin to address the question: What *don't* we know? Market intelligence which reveals previously hidden aspects of the external environment allows for strategic planning which is developmental and dynamic. For this to be the case it needs to be collected systematically in relation to a more fundamental question: What do we need to know? Pardey makes the point thus:

> The definition of 'what we need to know' is the hardest to make. Things might be 'useful' to know, frequently 'interesting' to know, but in establishing an effective market information system it is important to identify real priorities.
>
> (Pardey, 1991, p. 93)

If collecting market data is to be about guiding the development of the organisation, the determination of what information is required to realise that objective needs to be undertaken systematically.

Before looking at more systematic data collection, however, it is important to restate that informal sources do have an important role to play. Just because such sources are informal, however, does not mean the dissemination of information so gained needs to be ad hoc. An audit of staff contacts and other links between the institution and its stakeholders can be undertaken, and the results mapped in tabular form. Such a table can provide a useful resource for any staff carrying out development work, and can also reveal gaps in the institution's links with external agencies.

In addition, it can form the basis of a scanning mechanism, whereby key staff are responsible for undertaking more formal research into what may be happening in the locality, which might be of use to the institution. It may be that a colleague has links with a local children's charity which might yield information about demand for special needs provision; a local councillor may have information about changing travel-to-work patterns which can impact on recruitment; another colleague may be a member of an academic society which occasionally provides the school with useful research papers.

Formal sources

The formal collection of market intelligence is an activity for which resources have to be found. As Pardey points out, 'finding out about the market presents a simple example of cost/benefit analysis. There is no possibility of acquiring total knowledge about the market, but a high level of knowledge is feasible – at a cost' (Pardey, 1991, p. 92). It is not a function that can be carried out in one or two free periods a week. The responsive institution will have to make a judgement about how much staff time and other resources can be allocated justifiably in relation to perceived benefits.

It might be expected that in further education colleges where, typically, there are dedicated marketing staff, market research would be a well-developed activity. However, a survey of 777 further and higher education institutions (in which 70 per cent were FE colleges) suggests otherwise. Only a little over a fifth of marketing personnel reported extensive involvement in market research, and institutions spent only a small proportion of their marketing budgets (typically 5 per cent) on research activities (Smith, Scott and Lynch, 1995).

That there is little evidence of a research perspective, even in those sectors where the relationship between financial health and student recruitment is most acute, suggests that the issue is not one of resources but of culture shift. The notion of strategic planning is now well established in education; perhaps the most influential of all educational strategic planning models, Caldwell and Spinks's 'Collaborative School Management Cycle' (Caldwell and Spinks, 1988) clearly includes 'needs identification' as the initial phase of policy-making. Yet it must be questioned how many school strategic plans could claim to be rooted in a client-centred research base – as opposed to a provider-determined assessment. In further education colleges, it is a requirement that a needs analysis be conducted, and this must be attached to the college's strategic plan which, in turn, must be submitted to the local TEC for approval. Yet here, too, the needs analysis may be little more than a paraphrase of the Labour Market Assessment (LMA) carried out by the TEC itself; that is, a summary of general labour market trends.

In such circumstances, strategic planning is actually nothing of the kind; it is, instead, a version of long-term planning. The latter assumes a relatively stable situation, where it can be assumed that the external environment will remain relatively unchanged over a period of years. Strategic planning, by contrast, assumes a turbulent environment, where change is endemic, rapid and often sweeping. Weindling (1997) provides a useful analogy:

> think first about firing an arrow at a target. If the situation is relatively stable, that is, the target is stationary, you are stationary and there is little wind, it is fairly easy to hit the target. If, however, the situation is unpredictable and the target is moving and you are moving, a guided missile is a more useful means of hitting the target. The missile does not fly in a straight line, but uses a feedback system to constantly check on the relative position between the target and the missile and then adjusts its direction accordingly. It is argued that in a situation where the targets are moving and the school is moving, strategic planning is a more useful model. *But this means the school has to monitor its progress and adjust course as the circumstances change.*
>
> (Weindling, 1997, p. 220, my emphasis)

Weindling goes on to argue that the rarity of a true strategic approach in education can be explained in part by a collective delusion on the part of staff, in which they develop a shared stereotypical view of the relationship between the school and the outside world:

> They reinterpret, or ignore, unpleasant information that does not fit in with their preferred way of looking at the world.
>
> (ibid. p. 221)

Objective data has the potential to challenge the taken-for-granted assumptions which might otherwise underpin strategic planning. The DfEE handbook on using labour market information (DfEE, 1995) suggests five main sources of information (although addressed to the FE sector, it is entirely pertinent to the school sector):

- in-house data
- existing local research and information from other organisations
- national/regional research and forecasts
- official statistics
- primary data collection.

In-house data

Existing data already held on the institution's information systems can reveal much about the market, both existing and projected. For example, a simple database of pupils' names, ages, sex, address, feeder school and parental occupation can, if viewed comparatively across years, suggest recruitment patterns and trends. Sorting by postcode can allow for more sophisticated analysis. Well established as a means of direct marketing by commercial concerns, postcode analysis can tell a school a great deal about its catchment.

For colleges, data on course choice and course take-up, and fluctuations over time are important for spotting trends; in schools, trends in option choices are similarly useful. Drop-out rates and destination data provide essential information: as James and Phillips (1995) point out, education is like other services, where there is a need to find physical evidence that customers have received a service appropriate to their needs:

> The proof of sale of a manufactured product is easily obtained and unambiguous. The proof of benefit from a service is less easily obtained.
>
> (James and Phillips, 1995, p. 86)

Hard information about the careers and future educational development of past pupils and students is both a powerful promotional tool and a measure of the institution's longer-term effectiveness.

Local research from other organisations

The Labour Market Assessment published by local Training and Enterprise Councils summarises key labour market trends. Although somewhat general, the information can be a key tool in planning for schools and colleges alike. The Hampshire TEC Local Economic Assessment for 1998 (Hampshire TEC, 1998, p. 3), for example, notes that:

> Trends towards female, part-time and self employment ... are forecast to continue ... As discriminatory barriers in the labour market slowly break down women are also expected to occupy a higher proportion of jobs in management and professional occupations.

Elsewhere, the report notes that the south east of the county has a higher unemployment rate, a lower skills base and a smaller proportion of young people achieving to the level of NVQ3 than elsewhere. All of this information should have a major impact upon the planning of both schools and colleges in the area.

A range of organisations in a locality carry out a variety of research which can be accessed for planning research. Local authority economic strategies and development plans can provide information on patterns of development, population forecasts and business development. Transport surveys may yield information on travel patterns that can impact on school recruitment. The Employment Service produces a labour market review which includes, among other information, details of job vacancies in Standard Occupational Classifications (SOC). The local careers company may produce annual statistics showing destinations of school- and college-leavers.

It can sometimes be the case that research carried out in a locality by higher education (HE) institutions for an initially unrelated purpose can prove useful for planning by educational institutions. A survey of parental and pupil school choice in a sparsely populated rural area carried out by Newcastle University (Hammond and Dennison, 1995), for example, would provide useful information for schools in similar areas in other parts of the country. Access to such information can be fortuitous – a lucky find while browsing through the press.

However, where external links are well mapped in the way suggested earlier, where there are clear channels of communication and dissemination, it is possible to keep the environment well scanned so that leads can be identified and followed up.

National/regional research and official statistics

There is a wealth of census information, research evidence and official statistical information which is in the public domain. This includes research published by industry sector organisations, employers' federations, government departments, private and HE sector research organisations, charities and research foundations such as the Rowntree Trust. The value of such sources depends upon the purpose for which they are being investigated. Large national surveys may be of limited value, yet they can provide useful information when placed in conjunction with more local information. For example, where local census information indicates limited car ownership in a rural area against national trends, there may be possibilities for a school or college to bid for European Union funds to aid access to training. FE colleges may find national market research useful when assessing demand for full-cost training in particular occupational areas. National surveys into educational issues can help guide local curriculum planning in schools.

Primary data collection

Market research that is carried out by the school or college itself has the advantage that it can be tailored uniquely to inform its own planned objectives. There are two ways an institution can go about this: either by assigning staff time and resources to carrying out its own research, or by commissioning an agency to do so. In either case, it is clear that there is a cost to be borne; the justification for such outlay must depend upon how the institution uses the findings to change, develop or, indeed, validate its current practice.

Not all commissioned research has to be expensive. However, commercial agencies are likely to command a higher fee than public sector concerns and, in addition, may not have a well-developed prior understanding of education markets. It is the case, though, that a number of agencies are beginning to specialise in education and training, and see this as a growing market.

TECs and careers services may be keen to work in partnership where there is a demonstrable local need and some mutual benefit to both parties. St Paul's Anglican Grammar School in Warragul, Australia, worked with the geography department at Monash University to provide projected population trends which allowed the school to plan its future provision (Pepper, 1997).

There are clearly benefits in mounting first-hand primary research, carried out by staff in the institution itself, who are intimately acquainted with its aims and objectives. There is, though, an inherent danger of bias, as discussed earlier, and care must be taken to ensure the validity and reliability of results. Many staff may not have research expertise but there has been a growth of postgraduate study in education, and it is likely that many do. In any case, there is a wealth of published practical advice available (Bell *et al.*, 1984; Bell, 1987; Pardey, 1991; Barnes, 1993).

Much research can be ongoing, and built into the institution's regular routine. No open evening should go by without a survey of those attending to find out if the evening met their expectations; letters home where there is a return slip provide opportunities to ask for feedback. The value of qualitative research must not be forgotten, and this can be carried out as part of on-going work. A regular item on a PTA agenda, for example, seeking views on aspects of the school's provision can be tightly minuted and used as customer feedback – much like the focus groups used by commercial marketers. Similarly, regular community liaison meetings or meetings of employer work-placement providers are rich sources of market data.

When there are specific objectives to be met, a separate study needs to be mounted, with an appropriate methodology. Barnes (1998) describes a West Midlands school's initiative to measure public perceptions of the school using familiarity/favourability analysis, image profiling and perceptual mapping. The DfEE report *Marketing Case Studies in Further Education Colleges* (DfEE, 1996) describes the work of a sixth form college in surveying competitors' provision to determine gaps in the market, and follow-up surveys and interviews of parents at a parents' evening, leading to a broadening of the college's adult portfolio.

CASE STUDY: SALISBURY COLLEGE

Although drawn from the post-compulsory sector, this study illustrates many of the principles which transfer to the compulsory sector. For example, although market segments are explicitly defined by further education colleges, schools too have segmented markets (Pardey, 1991). In addition, it is a particular feature of the model described here that all the participants are teachers. Unlike many FE colleges which have a discrete marketing unit, Salisbury College has this work embedded in the curriculum.

Salisbury College is a medium-sized general further education college, offering a wide portfolio of vocational and non-vocational courses, from foundation level through to HND and degree level. In keeping with its view that marketing is about serving client need, and finding ways to encourage learners across the threshold, the college created a Community Services Team which provides a range of services, including outreach provision. The full range of the work of the team has been described elsewhere (Waring, 1997); one part of its responsibility is the gathering of market intelligence and its dissemination throughout the college. It is worth adding that all of the team have a teaching commitment, so that there is no clear split from the academic function.

A Research Co-ordinator has overall responsibility for compiling the annual Needs Analysis. This she does using a variety of primary and secondary sources (see Figure 12.1). The full Needs Analysis is a bulky compilation of these sources, but an executive summary is provided which points to key strategic issues for the coming year. This is presented to a full meeting of academic divisional managers, who have a loose-leaf binder to which updates can be added.

The college recognises four broad market segments:

> *Primary sources:*
> Salisbury College management information systems data
> Employer perceptions survey
> Employer training and business needs survey
> Perceptions, expectations and plans of Year 12 pupils in Salisbury schools in relation to higher education
> Business Network meetings minutes
> Community Focus Group (Organisations) questionnaire
> Community Focus Group (Client) questionnaire
> Community Focus Group meeting minutes
>
> *Secondary sources:*
> Wiltshire TEC Economic Assessment
> Hampshire TEC Labour Market Report
> Dorset TEC Economic Assessment
> *Defence and the Wiltshire Economy* (Wiltshire County Council)
> *Economic Impact on Tourism in Salisbury District* (Southern Tourist Board/Salisbury District Council)
> *Working in Wiltshire* (Lifetime Careers Wiltshire)
> *School Leavers' Destinations* (Lifetime Careers, Wiltshire)
> Wiltshire Rural Development Area Operating Plan (Wiltshire County Council)
> *Poverty Mapping Report, Salisbury and Kennet District* (Oxford University/Wiltshire County Council)
> Citizens' Advice Bureau annual report
> *South West Labour Market Analysis* (Government Office for the South West)
> *Labour Market Briefing for South Wiltshire* (Employment Service)
> South Wiltshire Economic Partnership Survey of Local Employers
> *Employment Prospects for the South West of England*, Institute for Employment Research, University of Warwick
> *Employers' Perceptions of the Adequacy of Further Education Provision in the South West*, Institute for Employment Research, University of Warwick

Figure 12.1. Salisbury College Needs Analysis sources

- 16–19 full-time students
- higher education students
- employer-sponsored students
- independent adult learners

Each of the segments is assigned a co-ordinator whose responsibility it is, amongst other things, to provide market intelligence and disseminate it. In the year referred to in Figure 12.1, primary research into two of the four segments was as follows:

16–19 full-time and higher education

With increasing numbers of students progressing to higher education, and as a higher education provider itself, the college wished to test a number of hypotheses suggested by the prevailing wisdom – in particular, the notion that young people were tending to opt to study nearer home. The college also wanted to discover what the key factors were influencing school-leavers' choices about HEI institutions.

Other stakeholders were expected to be interested in the outcomes. For some years, LMI produced by the TEC had been indicating that employers were finding difficulty recruiting graduates, and discussions were taking place between a number of parties about the possibility of creating a new university in Wiltshire, one of only a small number of counties without one. Employers, schools and the careers company Lifetime Careers were all likely beneficiaries of information gained; with such a broad constituency of interest, it was decided to seek funding for a significant piece of work.

A bid was made to the TEC for funding, and the success of this bid allowed the employment of an independent market researcher. A survey was administered, with the co-operation of local schools, to whole cohorts of Year 12 pupils, and a sample of college students also. The results were analysed, and a random selection of respondents were invited to attend a focus group discussion led by a trained facilitator. The discussion was recorded on video and analysed. A written report was produced, which was disseminated to academic divisions, to an invited audience of local headteachers, and to the local careers company.

Independent adult learners

In many ways this is the most difficult segment to research, because it is the most diverse; much of the market intelligence about this group comes from a well-developed set of community links. Much information is of the informal variety, yet a number of more empirical research instruments have been set up, including regular end-of-course surveys at outreach centres. Twice yearly, a focus group is held, at which representatives of community and voluntary organisations raise issues related to the training needs both of their own staff and of their clients. Membership is diverse, and attendance at meetings can vary considerably. The list of organisations attending one meeting gives a flavour of its composition (see Figure 12.2).

In the year described here, two questionnaires were produced, designed to elicit information about how the organisations and their clients perceived their own training needs, what they believed were the barriers they faced in accessing training, and the criteria they used in choosing between

Salisbury Sight Centre, General Hospital
Durrington Youth Centre
Salisbury Council for Voluntary Service
University of the Third Age
Citizens' Advice Bureau
Salisbury Job Centre
Young Persons Drug Project
Social Services Mental Health Team
Health Promotion Centre
MENCAP
Disability Information Awareness Group
Pre-School Learning Alliance
Probation Service

Figure 12.2. Salisbury College Community Users Focus Group meeting attendance

training providers. Representatives at the focus group were asked to complete the questionnaires and return them prior to the second focus group meeting. The findings were used to prepare an agenda for the second focus group.

CONCLUSION

The systematic collection, analysis and dissemination of market information can lead to the identification of previously unexpressed and unmet needs, as well as providing a basis for continuous improvement in the quality of provision made by a school or college. The strategic planning process needs to be embedded within a culture of information, in which the institution is constantly searching for and reacting to developments in its external environment. Although some aspects of the process may, necessarily, be serendipitous, formal information sources can support and amplify the more ad hoc information derived from informal sources. In this way, the needs of the learner are seen as being rooted in the external environment, and the teaching and learning process informed by an understanding of it.

REFERENCES

Bagley, C., Woods, P. and Glatter, R. (1996) Scanning the market: strategies for discovering parental preferences, *Educational Management and Administration*, Vol. 24, no. 2, pp. 122–34.
Ball, S. (1993) Market forces in education, *Education Review*, Vol. 7, no. 1, pp. 24–35.

Ball, S. (1996) Ethics, self-interest and the market form in education, in N. H. Foskett (ed.) *Markets in Education: Policy, Process and Practice*, Southampton: Centre for Research in Education Marketing, University of Southampton.

Barnes, C. (1993) *Practical Marketing for Schools*, Oxford: Blackwell.

Barnes, C. (1998) How others see us: practical techniques for gauging public perception of your school, *Management in Education*, Vol. 12, no. 1, pp. 7–8.

Beischer, N. (1994) Marketing through the grapevine, *Inside Education Marketing*, Issue 2, pp. 4–5.

Bell, J. (1987) *Doing Your Research Project*, Milton Keynes: Open University Press.

Bell, J., Bush, T., Fox, A., Goodey, J. and Goulding, S. (1984) *Conducting Small-Scale Investigations in Educational Management*, Milton Keynes: Open University Press.

Caldwell, B. J. and Spinks, J. M. (1988) *The Self Managing School*, London: Falmer Press.

Cohen, M. and March, J. G. (1989) Leadership and ambiguity, in T. Bush (ed.) *Managing Education: Theory and Practice*, Milton Keynes: Open University Press.

DfEE (1995) *Labour Market Information for Further Education Colleges: A Handbook for Practitioners*, London: HMSO.

DfEE (1996) *Marketing Case Studies in Further Education Colleges*, London: HMSO.

Hammond, T. and Dennison, B. (1995) School choice in less populated areas, *Educational Management and Administration*, Vol. 23, no. 2, pp. 132–44.

Hampshire Training and Enterprise Council (1998), *Local Economic Assessment*, Fareham: Hampshire.

Hirschman, A. O. (1970) *Exit, Voice and Loyalty: Responses to Decline in Firms, Organisations, and States*, Cambridge, Mass.: Harvard University Press.

Hoy, W. K. and Miskel, C. G. (1989) Schools and their external environments, in R. Glatter (ed.) *Educational Institutions and their Environments: Managing the Boundaries*, Milton Keynes: Open University Press.

Hoyle, E. and John, P. D. (1995) *Professional Knowledge and Professional Practice*, London: Cassell.

James, C. and Phillips, P. (1995) The practice of educational marketing in schools, *Educational Management and Administration*, Vol. 23, no. 2, pp. 12–22.

Pardey, D. (1991) *Marketing for Schools*, London: Kogan Page.

Pepper, L. (1997) Realising the dream: future planning, *Management in Education*, Vol. 11, no. 5, pp. 42–5.

Scott, P. (1989) Accountability, responsiveness and responsibility, in R. Glatter (ed.) *Educational Institutions and their Environments: Managing the Boundaries*, Milton Keynes: Open University Press.

Smith, D., Scott, P. and Lynch, J. (1995) *The Role of Marketing in the University and College Sector*, Leeds: Heist.

Waring, S. (1997) Managing marketing as a community service, *Management in Education*, Vol. 11, no. 4, pp. 32–5.

Weindling, D. (1997) Strategic planning in schools: some useful techniques, in M. Preedy, M. Glatter and R. Levacic (eds.) *Educational Management: Strategy, Quality and Resources*, Buckingham: Open University Press.

13

ACHIEVING RESPONSIVENESS

Jacky Lumby

THE PRESSURES SHAPING RESPONSIVENESS

Despite the fact that 'across the world most teachers still teach alone, behind closed doors in the insulated and isolated environment of their own classroom' (Hargreaves, 1992, p. 220), the pressures of the world beyond that classroom have never been more strongly felt. Many governments have adopted a proactive stance in shaping the curriculum through legislation and through funding. Market forces have increased the force of the claims of students, parents and employers. If it ever was the case that schools and colleges were autonomous institutions, it certainly is not so now. The demands are tumultuous and sometimes felt as intrusive. Despite the fact that the degree of control of educational professionals may have been diminished by the greater control of the state, they nevertheless still face the question of how far to admit or resist those external forces wishing to become involved with education. Goldring and Shapira (1993) argue that the empowerment of the community is of vital importance because the experience of learning is impoverished if there is not a congruence between the values, needs and desires of the community and those of the educational organisation. Consequently, schools and colleges face the challenge of transforming the multitude of pressures into a process of value to all and of crucial importance to education, that of responsiveness.

   This chapter will define responsiveness and explore to whom educational professionals may respond and in what ways. It will consider the barriers to achieving responsiveness and provide examples of the problems and successes experienced by schools and colleges. Finally it will argue that responsiveness underpins a learning society and places a reliance on the sensitivity and skills of educational managers which is of fundamental importance to society and enhances the role of all those who work in education.

DEFINING THE CONCEPT OF RESPONSIVENESS

Michael, Holdaway and Young (1994) offer a broad definition of the concept:

> The ability of an institution to sense and serve the changing needs of its relevant environment.
>
> (Michael, Holdaway and Young, 1994, p. 54)

The general ability to 'sense and serve' begs many questions. Sense what, from whom and respond how? Although many institutions have established vehicles to inform and consult with others, Robinson and Timperley (1996) assert that participation and consultation are not synonymous with responsiveness. In their view, it is the quality of response from the educational organisation, the degree of 'serious engagement' (ibid., p. 70) with the views of interested parties, or as Scott (1989, p. 17) puts it, the ability to be genuinely 'open', which equates to responsiveness. Such a definition has been criticised as:

> a kind of 'half-way house' designed if not to satisfy all interested parties, at least to meet the traditional demand for compromise (some would say fudge).
>
> (Peagram, 1994, p. 48)

The 'half-way house' is the centre point in a spectrum spanning complete abdication of educational decisions to the external community, through to total control of decisions by teachers and school/college managers, overriding the views of all others. Current research would seem to indicate the unacceptability of either extreme, but has not resolved the difficulty of achieving a mechanism to enact the compromise position of the half-way house. Answers are still needed to the questions of responding to whom and in what way?

Goldring and Shapira (1993), writing of schools in Israel, distinguish involvement and empowerment:

> Involvement is without power. Parents are involved in school affairs, for example as volunteers, but this involvement does not carry any influence. The goal of the involvement is to participate in the activities themselves. Empowerment, usually through decision-making forums, is accompanied by sources of power and influence.
>
> (Goldring and Shapira, 1993, p. 398)

Focusing on schools in Tel Aviv, they describe the growing expectation of parents that they should be empowered and the relationship between the schools' willingness to admit such power-sharing and parental satisfaction.

A working definition may then be that responsive schools and colleges are neither those who do as they wish taking no account of others, nor those who do as students, parents, employers ask without question, but rather those who have resolved the issue of to whom they wish to respond with some exactness and commitment, and have moved beyond involving others to empowering them.

RESPONDING TO WHOM?

Despite the state's requirement that schools and colleges are responsive to others, it is clear that responding to the state itself of necessity demands a high priority. Responding to many state-imposed initiatives engrosses much attention and time and may divert staff from a focus on the more local. With the time, energy and resource remaining, schools and colleges respond to the community and may even define that community very exactly in geographical terms. Some institutions do not define their community in terms of their immediate environment, but see the possibility of recruiting students from outside their catchment or indeed internationally. Whether confined to the local area, or situated far distant, each category of stakeholder may include further sub-groupings of interests. Assertions by educational institutions that they wish to respond to the needs of 'their community' conceal the myriad groupings and perspectives which comprise that community, and the realistic need to make choices about to whom to respond. If every group were assumed to be an equal priority, then there is no basis for distinguishing how to act in the face of the potential contradictory requirements of different groups.

Whatever the rhetoric about responding to 'the community', schools are selective in to whom they respond, though such selection may not be made explicit. The Parental and School Choice Interaction Study (PASCI) (Bagley, Woods and Glatter, 1996) found that schools in the UK were more interested in monitoring and reacting to other educational institutions than parents or pupils, and that where they did take account of parents' views, it was those of the middle class which gained most attention, thereby further advantaging an already privileged group (Woods, Bagley and Glatter, 1998). Peagram (1994, p. 48) suggests that responsiveness equals 'adroit' manipulation, balancing different demands. The PASCI data suggest that rather than balancing responses to different groups, schools may not be responding to any, or may be responding with a concealed partiality.

Further education colleges differ. The strategic plans demanded by the Further Education Funding Council (FEFC) offer the opportunity to make the target groups or market niches to whom colleges have chosen to respond explicit and public. For example, one college's strategic plan unequivocally puts the people of a small, particularly disadvantaged estate as their primary target. This, however, does not prevent some colleges describing the local, national and international communities as their target, an inclusiveness which does not discriminate priorities (Lumby, forthcoming). Though colleges may be more habituated to explicit inclusion or exclusion of groups, they are still open to criticism about their choices. For example, the FEFC (1996) suggests the sector is responding less well to employers than to individual students, with the implicit value judgement that the response to each should be equal, even though colleges may see tensions, as schools do, in choosing between the sometimes contradictory needs of different groups.

The first step in a process of responsiveness may therefore be to distinguish explicitly the priority group(s) for response and to be able to justify the choice in educational terms.

RESPONDING HOW?

Responsiveness can demand change in terms of organisational structures able to learn of and respond to external views, and curriculum change as a result of the dialectic of internal and external opinion.

The enforced reform of governing bodies in many countries, though leading to greater sharing of administrative decisions, has not resulted in a much greater involvement of external representatives in the heart of education, the curriculum (MacBeath, 1995). In a study of a high school in New Zealand, Robinson and Timperley (1996, p. 70) found that governors were still, in the words of the Chair, concerned only with 'counting the toilet paper type stuff'. They argue that openness cannot be equated with the existence of structures to promote it. For them it is the culture or attitude of staff which is key. This echoes the distinction made by Goldring and Shapira (1993) between 'involvement' and 'empowerment'. Deem, Brehony and Heath (1995) use Lukes' (1986) theory of three-dimensional power to explain the strategies used by schools to remain in control of their governing body, where the latter may be subject to one-dimensional use of power, simply being overruled by the head, two-dimensional power, where agenda items are not admitted, and three-dimensional power, where the culture of what is an 'acceptable' view or belief is manipulated. The evidence presented by Deem, Brehony and Heath clearly shows governing bodies to be sites of contested power.

Peagram (1994) argues that engagement with a range of opinion will inevitably generate disagreement, and that consequently structures are needed which can resolve conflict. He argues for loose coupling (Weick, 1988) allowing different parts of the organisation to cross boundaries and respond with a good deal of autonomy. A further structural strategy to make connections is to create individual roles to span the perimeter. Clark lists titles given to such roles:

boundary managers

people-linkers

para-intermediaries

(Clark, 1996, p. 101)

There is little evidence that the use of the structural changes above has resulted in a cultural shift to a greater willingness to involve the community in educational decisions in schools, if 'educational decisions' is taken to mean inclusion of teaching and learning issues.

> Basic questions of what constitutes quality education and the values and criteria by which this is judged tend to be a closely guarded area still, from which generally parents, pupils and the wider community are gently deflected. There is not so much debate and openness but dictat and closure; quality remains predominantly a matter for professional and political judgements.
>
> (Woods, Bagley and Glatter, 1998, p. 188)

Figure 13.1 below is drawn from a comparative study of influences on teaching practice, in France, England and Spain (Laffitte, 1993). It provides evidence that parents' influence on teaching and learning in these countries is weak. The differences in the degree of influence suggest a cultural element in how far parents interact with teachers.

In colleges there has been some determination to adapt the curriculum to student needs and wants, driven by the greater power of students to reject what they don't like, and the fierce competition colleges face from schools, other colleges and private trainers. Internally, FEFC inspection of quality systems has driven the development of the systematic collection and response to student views. However, in a study of Canadian and British colleges, Evans (1996) found that lecturers in both countries were often reluctant to change their traditional predilections for an academic or vocational discipline to move the curriculum closer to what students wanted.

The evidence points to limited success in achieving a cultural shift to 'serious engagement' (Robinson and Timperley, 1996) with educational professionals allowing only superficial incursions from students, parents, employers and others who wish to enter into partnership with them.

Some may see this as the appropriate stance, arguing that it is the task of the professional to remain in control because their training and expe-

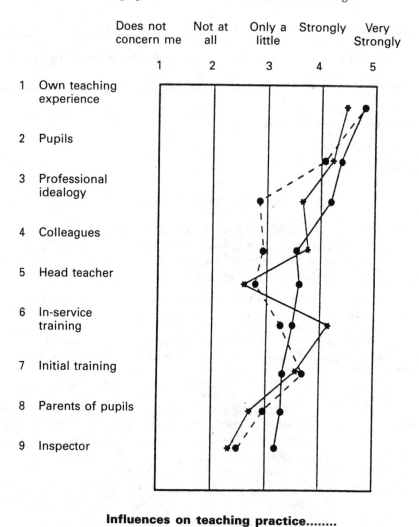

Influences on teaching practice........

(●- -France ●——England ✳——Spain)

Figure 13.1. Influences on teaching practice (Laffitte, 1993, p. 83)

rience best fits them to undertake this role. However, a useful parallel may be the paradigm shift in teaching itself. Just as the emphasis is moving from teaching to learning, and from the teacher as controller to teacher as facilitator, so responsiveness suggests not a diminution of the role of the professional educator, but a change in emphasis. Engaging with others in dialogue about what is to happen in the school or college does not decrease the demands on the role of the professional, but rather increases them. The professional becomes one who does not just support the learning of the groups of young people or adults who come to their classroom or workshop, but also engages with the wider learning of the community, with the teacher/lecturer as a central learner. This is not to deprofessionalise teaching, but to call on the highest levels of skill and commitment to a learning society.

BARRIERS TO ACHIEVING RESPONSIVENESS

If Robinson and Timperley (1996) and Scott (1989) are correct in their assertions that it is not the existence of structures to canvass the views of others which equate to responsiveness, but the attitude of staff, then barriers to achieving responsiveness are likely to be most crucially in the stance of professionals towards non-professional individuals and groups. Robinson and Timperley are forthright in stating the implications:

> Professionals must, in order to be responsive, share power with non-professionals in school decision-making.
>
> (Robinson and Timperley, 1996, p. 66)

Sharing power is not straightforward when the status of those involved differs. Professionals in education accrue power through their professional expertise. Parents and students hold consumer power to choose other schools or colleges, and parents hold the legal authority for the care of their children. Differences in power distort listening. The seriousness with which professionals listen to the views of other groups may relate to the power of those groups, each of the latter having a power base which is dependent on, amongst other things, their expertise and potential financial impact. Power shifts and is persistently contested. Confining the decisions of others reduces uncertainty and increases power. Thus Goldring (1997, p. 292) writes of strategies which headteachers can adopt to 'reduce environmental influence as much as possible'. Colleges enter collaborative arrangements to strengthen their independence and reduce the influence of external forces (Lumby, 1998).

Responsiveness, then, is partly about moves to capture or share power, but this is not an entire explanation. Even where schools are losing power, for example, with falling rolls – there may still persist an unwillingness to respond, which relates to values inherent in the profession.

Evidence (Bagley, Woods and Glatter, 1996; James and Phillips, 1997) suggests that the professional culture of teachers leads them to assume that their views are accurate and desirable.

> At Braelands the headteacher admits that parental viewpoints expressed during the open evening are filtered out according to their congruence with the existing managerial perspectives of senior teachers about the school.
>
> (Bagley, Woods and Glatter, 1996, p. 53)

Ainley and Bailey (1997) document the differences in perspective of lecturers and students in two further education colleges, describing lecturers believing reduction in contact hours had resulted in a worsening of conditions of students, while students saw a lessening of dependence on the lecturer as an improvement. Lecturers assume their perspective is correct. This is the heart of responsiveness, or lack of it. Professionals understandably will not do what they do not believe to be right, but habitually, when confronted with differing views, assume their own beliefs and values to be right. Their dominance over local non-professional individuals and groups is enacted through a culture which often either ignores or demotes the views of others.

> *Deputy Principal:* It comes back to the same problem, what the parents want is not what we think is right.
>
> (Robinson and Timperley, 1996, p. 74)

Woods, Bagley and Glatter (1998, p. 190) describe a changing culture where schools 'are increasingly engaged in the manipulation of images to attract rather than to inform parents'. Headteachers feel impelled to put a positive gloss on events, and fail to share problems openly, even with governors (Deem, Brehony and Heath, 1995). Their role as trainers and teachers may mean, 'We are excellent transmitters but very poor receivers of information' (Sullivan, 1995, p. 90).

The responsibility for this situation lies with those in educational organisations but those outside it also. Governing bodies have sometimes accepted a peripheral role. Employers may undertake their own training rather than work with the local college to move towards a curriculum which better suits their needs. Parents remain silent or uninterested (see Chapter 8). The debate on the management of external relations is therefore often framed in terms of excluding disruptive pressures and shaping others to support the school or college, rather than how the dominance of the professional perspective can be redressed (Goldring, 1997). This is not to argue that any perspective has a monopoly on the best interests of learners. Rather it is to argue that dominance of the largely white, middle class values of educational professionals may disempower particularly those who have less status in society and further privilege the advantaged.

BARRIERS EXEMPLIFIED

The difficulties posed by a clash of values is exemplified by Macbeath (1995). A new female head of a primary school in the middle of a mining, unemployed-male-dominated community used questionnaires to explore views on how the school was improving. An interesting tension emerged between male working class values and perceived female middle class intrusion, where the woman headteacher was in a position which had power to change values and actions. For example, the men of the community believed children should be encouraged to stand up for themselves, physically if need be. The head wished to change this culture to one where differences could be settled through words, or through recourse to a higher authority. There is no easy answer to reconciling or adjudicating between such different beliefs. The headteacher concerned assumed that it was a question of bringing parents round, enrolling them over time in her way of seeing things. In this she may have had little choice. Her obligation was to ensure that children were not physically attacked. However, there was a choice in approaching the situation, in taking seriously the reasons why the parents felt as they did, finding a position which did not discount the values of the parents.

In this case, the headteacher was sure that she was accurate in her perception of the views of parents. In the case of a New Zealand secondary school (Robinson and Timperley, 1996) the school believed that a falling roll was due to the racism of parents, who reacted negatively to the growing numbers of minority ethnic children in the school. Research uncovered that parents did have concerns about the school, but in the area of its performance in helping children learn and become responsible citizens. The school was attributing inaccurate views to parents thereby absolving itself of the responsibility of uncovering and reacting to the community's concerns. Similar beliefs about the racism of parents were held in a secondary school in the UK, where the catchment was largely Bangladeshi (Bagley, Woods and Glatter, 1996). The school believed that white parents were reluctant to send their children to a school which had a majority of Bangladeshi pupils. As a consequence, it felt unable to be responsive because of its commitment to anti-racism. The school had not, as in the New Zealand school, checked the accuracy of its perceptions, but the question arises as to which parents the school wished to respond to. The concern may have been on behalf of white parents, or were the parents of local Bangladeshi families concerned at the number of Bangladeshi pupils? This school's interpretation of being responsive appears to relate to the concern of certain parents and not others. Is the desire to attract white children to a school which has a majority of black students in itself racist rather than responsive?

The barriers explored above relate to differences in values and perceptions. There is no doubt that schools and colleges may be restrained from responsiveness by other factors outside their control. The need to survive financially may limit action severely. There is much evidence that an organisation's ability to respond is contingent on its environment (Foskett, 1998), and that great inequalities result:

> Whilst some schools can be constrained by a range of barriers – bad reputation, inadequate funding, poor location, inappropriate management –

others may experience only one or two, or possibly none at all. Schools' differential experience of these barriers makes it enormously difficult for those facing a range of negative factors influencing responsiveness to compete with schools encountering hardly any.

(Bagley, Woods and Glatter, 1996, p. 57)

Not all of the barriers listed by Bagley are outside the organisation's control. To return to a definition of responsiveness, one element which may need to be included is an ability to distinguish where responsiveness is constrained by barriers genuinely outside the school or college's control and where a professional culture which is resistant to openness is using a mirage of barriers to justify a stance which actually has its basis in staff attitudes.

RESPONDING SUCCESSFULLY

Despite the general evidence of limited progress, there are examples of schools and colleges which have transformed their culture to be responsive. McCreath and Maclachlan (1995) describe the Partnership in Education Project in Strathclyde primary schools in 1983–94 and its determination to move beyond 'parents helping teachers to achieve goals specified by teachers in ways specified by teachers' (p. 71). The project shifted the perspective of teaching professionals to see themselves not at the centre of a child's education but as a part of a complex web. The project:

> set out to develop informal education networks based in the local neighbourhood which would draw upon the whole learning community contained within, and which would ultimately create a cohesive and supportive educational environment to sustain and develop children's learning. To this end it worked with health visitors, pre-five staff, librarians, speech therapists, social workers, educational psychologists, community workers and the voluntary sector.

(McCreath and Maclachlan, 1995, p. 69)

The lessons of the project have profound implications for the redefinition of education itself, seeing the achievement of independence in an holistic experience of learning as the key, and the redefinition of education professionals as enablers, not teachers. The practical challenge was the establishment of processes of working with a wide range of individuals and groups which were founded on a value base of equality. The success celebrated in this project was hard won. Setting up a collaborative network is not a simple solution to achieving responsiveness.

Monck and Husbands (1996) outline the difficulties in achieving the culture change within a group of secondary schools in a project to achieve 'the educative community' (p. 171). Sustaining the resource to drive the project and persuading teachers of the relevance and importance of working more widely within the community were not achieved:

> The wider-community involvement and vision of the educative community has not been sustainable over the years since the project's community co-ordinator returned to his school after a two-year secondment . . . the lesson appears to be that relationships with wider-community groups depend on continuing hard work.
>
> (Monck and Husbands, 1996, p. 60)

Perhaps the lesson is that, as with most projects dependent on additional resources, long-term embedding of changed behaviours must be a top priority if the resource is not to lead to a merely temporary improvement. A more realistic strategy for responsiveness may be to move more slowly if need be, but within existing resource limits. The more successful Strathclyde project actually reframed the use of teachers' time to allow different sorts of work, rather than providing extra time on a limited project basis.

Ainley and Bailey (1997) in their case studies of two further education colleges explore both the progress and the path yet to be travelled in terms of responding to student needs. Many lecturers viewed the years since 1993 incorporation as charting a decline in responding to the needs of individual learners. Students themselves saw the period as one of improvement. They had not been slow to discern the difference in staff attitude when compulsory schooling ends. One described the attitude of staff in the school who wanted the student to enter the sixth form:

> When I said that I was coming back in September they were delighted. Could it be to do with money?
>
> (Ainley and Bailey, 1997, p. 89)

The student concerned decided to go to a further education college. Students also recognised the achievement in colleges in welcoming many of them who would not have had such a chance previously, and in according respect and dignity to those who had not come to expect this as the norm in education:

> It's a massive change, really massive. Definitely the student being the client, it's much more student-oriented, much more to do with helping students. . . . It's definitely much better. One thing they've been keen on here, dealing with clients, actually treating people in a proper manner. I think they do that well.
>
> (ibid., p. 98)

The comments from lecturers show them still reluctant to move from measuring success according to their own professional judgement rather than giving some weight to that of the student, but almost despite themselves, they have achieved a shift of which they could be justifiably proud.

The literature on managing change emphasises the difficulties of achieving cultural shifts. Managers need to plan long term and to persist, recognising that culture cannot be controlled, but may be influenced (Morgan, 1986). Success is likely to be partial and related to the degree of commitment with which managers attempt to achieve change (Lumby, 1998). If responsiveness is to be more than rhetoric, then making it a reality will need to be sufficiently important to those with the most power in any organisation. The conviction that it is indeed important may relate to the growing strength of connection between the satisfaction of stakeholders and their degree of empowerment, but equally, to the underlying motivation of educators, their wish to support learning.

CONCLUSION

Scott (1989, p. 17) concludes that 'a totally satisfactory definition of responsiveness, is, of course, impossible'. However, it may be possible to outline some elements of responsiveness which could be of use to educational managers. Practice is inevitably an art, not a science, and as such deeply dependent on individual beliefs and the context within which the individual works. First to be resolved is the relationship of responsiveness to the concept of marketing. Most schools and colleges interpret marketing as being essentially about promotion. While this is so, responsiveness will inevitably be hampered, in that the need to present the glossy and positive image will preclude honest engagement between stakeholders with the issues that confront the organisation. If marketing is understood as an overriding philosophy, as outlined by Foskett in this book, then responsiveness is the cultural stance underpinning the practical planning and structures of a complete marketing strategy.

Secondly, the issue of to whom to respond cannot be fudged. Responsiveness relates not only to external individuals and groups but also to pupils and students. In both compulsory and post-compulsory education there is much to be done in relation to internal responsiveness:

> To explode the secondary school and establish a society-wide context for learning requires that pupils themselves be treated in a very different way. Many young people of secondary age are still subject to a form of direction and control which will hugely reduce the potential of education in the twenty-first century.
>
> (Clark, 1996, p. 145)

It may be that all pupils, from the youngest pupil in a nursery school, have the potential to make a valuable contribution to shaping the way their education takes place and the right to have their perspective accorded serious consideration.

Robinson and Timperley (1996) offer a set of skills which may be needed to achieve responsiveness:

- The first set of skills concerns openness: that is, the ability to say what one thinks or wants in a way that increases the chance that others can do the same.
- The second set of skills is concerned with testing; the point of openness is not just to hear a range of views, but to express them in ways that increase the chance that errors can be detected and corrected.
- The third set of skills concerns the way power and control are exercised by participants in dialogue. The value of enquiry is served by bilateral (or multilateral) rather than unilateral control of the content and process of the interaction.

(adapted from Robinson and Timperley, 1996, pp. 73–74)

The emphasis on interaction is worth stressing for responsiveness is not being customer-driven. It is not simply doing what others demand. Neither is it an assault on the professionalism of those in education, or a devaluing of their role. Rather it makes great demands on their capacity to empower others and to harness the full range of resources for learning. From a responsiveness perspective, the role of the professional who assumes an automatic control of education is an impoverished one, with a hidden agenda of adopting superiority, in contradiction to genuine education, which is founded on a bedrock of mutual respect and equality.

In summary, educational managers may wish to consider the following possible approaches to encompassing responsiveness:

- To which internal and external individuals and groups will the organisation respond and what are the criteria for assigning priority?
- Is the possible connection between the priorities assigned and the power of the relevant groups understood, acknowledged and resolved?
- What is the attitude of staff to those with whom they have professional relations? Is the community seen as school/college centric or is the educational organisation an equal player?
- Do individual staff assume a superiority of view, or is there a genuine willingness to engage in dialectic?
- Where there is conflict in values, beliefs and preferences for action, what criteria will be brought to bear to arrive at a resolution?
- Are sufficient resources given to allow responsiveness to happen, going beyond a promotional or marketing budget to reframing staff's time to allow them to work in different ways?
- Are organisational structures in place which will complement cultural change and support genuine interaction?

This chapter has argued for responsiveness as reducing the dominance of professionals and increasing the sharing of power. However, such action is underpinned by paradox. The relinquishing of power does not necessarily result in its diminution. The willingness to listen, to interact, to assume an equality of status, to move from the central position to one of support, both places limitations on the role of the educational professional and considerably enhances it. The enabling role, leading from behind, is leadership exactly corresponding to a vision of education in the twenty-first century, where learning is enacted through a range of means in a variety of locations, with education professionals valued for their ability to support independence and confidence.

REFERENCES

Ainley, P. and Bailey, B. (1997) *The Business of Learning*, London: Cassell.

Bagley, C., Woods, P. and Glatter, R. (1996) Scanning the market: school strategies for discovering parental preferences, in M. Preedy, R. Glatter and R. Levacic (eds.) *Educational Management: Strategy Quality and Resources*, Buckingham: Open University Press.

Clark, D. (1996) *Schools as Learning Communities*, London: Cassell.

Deem, R., Brehony, K. and Heath, S. (1995) *Active Citizenship and the Governing of Schools*, Buckingham: Open University Press.

Evans, K. (1996) Reshaping colleges for the community in Canada and Britain, *Research in Post-Compulsory Education*, Vol. 1, no. 2, pp. 199–218.

FEFC (1996) *College Responsiveness*, Coventry: FEFC.

Foskett, N. (1998) Schools and Marketisation: cultural challenges and responses, *Educational Management and Administration*, Vol. 26, pp. 197–210.

Goldring, E. (1997) Educational leadership: schools, environments and boundary spanning, in M. Preedy, R. Glatter and R. Levacic (eds.) *Educational Management: Strategy, Quality and Resources*, Buckingham: Open University Press.

Goldring, E. and Shapira, R. (1993) Choice, empowerment and involvement: what satisfies parents? *Educational Evaluation and Policy Analysis*, Vol. 15, no. 4, pp. 396–409.

Hargreaves, A. (1992) Cultures of teaching: a focus for change, in A. Hargreaves and M. Fullan (eds.) *Understanding Teacher Development*, London: Cassell.

James, C. and Phillips, P. (1997) The practice of educational marketing in schools, in M. Preedy, R. Glatter and R. Levacic (eds.) *Educational Management: Strategy, Quality and Resources*, Buckingham: Open University Press.

Laffitte, R. (1993) Teachers' professional responsibility and development, in C. Day, J. Calderhead and P. Denicolo (eds.) *Research on Teacher Thinking: Understanding Professional Development*, London: Falmer Press.

Lukes, S. (ed.) (1986) *Power*, Oxford: Blackwell.

Lumby, J. (1998) Restraining the further education market: closing Pandora's box, *Education and Training*, Issue no. 2, March–April, pp. 57–62.

Lumby, J. (1999) Strategic planning in further education: the business of values, *Educational Management and Administration*, vol. 27, No1, pp. 71–83.

MacBeath, J. (1995) Clients evaluating the school, in A. Macbeth, D. McCreath and J. Aitchison, J. (eds.) *Collaborate or Compete? Educational Partnerships in a Market Economy*, London: Falmer Press.

McCreath, D. and Maclachlan, K. (1995) Realising the virtual: new alliances in the market model education game, in A. Macbeth, D. McCreath and J. Aitchison (eds.) *Collaborate or Compete? Educational Partnerships in a Market Economy*, London: Falmer Press.

Michael, S., Holdaway, E. and Young, C. (1994) Institutional responsiveness: a study of administrators' perceptions, *Educational Management and Administration*, Vol. 22, no.1, pp. 54–62.

Monck, L. and Husbands, C. (1996) Education 2000: collaboration and co-operation as a model of change management, in D. Bridges and C. Husbands (eds.) *Consorting and Collaborating in the Education Marketplace*, London: Falmer Press.

Morgan, G. (1986) *Images of Organization*, London: Sage.

Peagram, E. (1994) Now you see it – now you don't! Illusion and reality in the rhetoric of the responsive school, *Education Today*, Vol. 44, no. 1, pp. 47–51.

Robinson, V. and Timperley, H. (1996) Learning to be responsive: the impact of school choice and decentralization, *Educational Management and Administration*, Vol. 24, no. 1, pp. 65–78.

Scott, P. (1989) Accountability, responsiveness and responsibility, in R. Glatter (ed.) *Educational Institutions and their Environments: Managing the Boundaries*, Milton Keynes: Open University Press.

Sullivan, M. (1995) The perspective from an urban primary school, in A. Macbeth, D. McCreath and J. Aitchison (eds.) *Collaborate or Compete? Educational Partnerships in a Market Economy*, London: Falmer Press.

Weick, A. (1988) Educational organisations as loosely coupled systems, in A. Westoby (ed.) *Culture and Power in Educational Organisations*, Milton Keynes: Open University Press.

Woods, P., Bagley, C. and Glatter, R. (1998) *School Choice and Competition: Markets in the Public Interest?* London: Routledge.

14

COMMUNICATING THE ORGANISATION

Nick Foskett and Jane Hemsley-Brown

The growth of a market-driven culture in education has focused institutions on issues relating to the external communications of the organisation. Chapter 3 has identified a wide range of perspectives on the ways educational institutions perceive their interaction with external stakeholders, emphasising the importance of issues such as quality assurance and community relations, as well as recruitment, in shaping a school or college's marketing stance. This chapter focuses on the communication process in external relations, and in particular the management of communications about the organisation to audiences beyond the school or college boundaries. This is an important arena of operational management, representing what Middlewood (1998) terms 'on-the-ground' activities, often with a short-term dimension. However, it is also essentially strategic management since all such operations need to be set into the wider strategy of the institution and linked to its vision and mission. In this context this chapter will consider:

- strategic planning and external relations strategy
- making strategic choices
- planning and managing communications processes

STRATEGIC PLANNING AND EXTERNAL RELATIONS STRATEGY

Strategic planning is essentially a process linking the institution's vision with its day-to-day operational activities. West-Burnham (1994) shows how vision and mission are the starting points for strategy, but these are mediated by an analysis of the external environment (Hanson and Henry, 1992), before medium-term and short-term operational tactics can be selected. The link between strategic planning and planning for external relations has been explored in Chapter 3, where three broad groups of external relations were identified:

1. transactional-based external relations
2. relationship-based external relations
3. public accountability external relations.

Within any organisation each will have distinctive planning requirements, although the interaction of the three areas will mean that an overall, integrating approach is needed to planning. It is possible to identify a common rational planning model that can be applied to each of these strands of external relations management, comprising seven key steps. While the validity of rational planning models has been questioned (e.g. Levacic, 1995), and it is recognised that the rapidity of change of the external environment means long-term precision is difficult to achieve, this is not an argument for avoiding planning since some planning is better than none! What Levacic (1995) terms 'fuzzy planning' may be more appropriate as a concept, with the broad direction set by the planning process integrating continuous environmental monitoring so that fine touches of steering can be made in terms of tactics in response to external changes. The seven stages are:

1. Identify the strategic position of the organisation.
2. Identify the principal target audiences.
3. For each, identify the aims of the relationships in the context of the organisation's mission.
4. Plan the organisational systems to 'manage' the specific relationships and communications in the context of the organisation's strategic position, and identify the resources (human and financial) that can be applied to this component of external relations management.
5. Plan the specific communication tactics to achieve the aims.
6. Implement the tactics.
7. Monitor, evaluate and review the implementation.

Key components of this model will be examined in the sections that follow.

MAKING STRATEGIC CHOICES

Strategy is the process of identifying what an organisation wishes to be and to achieve (its strategic position), and how it will progress towards those aims in the context of the external environment. Kotler and Fox (1995) have identified three broad aspects of strategic positioning that relate to an organisation's interaction with its external environment, and these provide a background to the detailed development of strategy and tactics in transactional, relationship and accountability-based external relations arenas. They are:

1. target market strategy
2. competitive positioning strategy
3. marketing mix strategy.

Perhaps the most important transactional relationship any school or college has is through its role as a provider of education or training to pupils and students and the resulting need to persuade 'customers' (be they *proxy customers*, i.e parents or organisations buying on behalf of a third party such as children or employees, or *actual customers*, i.e. the students themselves) to choose the institution's provision. *Target market strategy* is choosing which combination of markets the school or college wishes to operate in, and requires some consideration of the structure and nature of the markets available. An important step in choosing a target market strategy is *market segmentation*. This is the process of identifying sub-parts of the overall market with distinctive common characteristics, and can be undertaken in relation to geographical, demographic or psychographic (e.g. lifestyle, social class) variables. For example, the post-compulsory education market would include broad segments such as 16–19-year-olds, or adult returners, and the 16–19-year-old market could be subdivided into those demanding academic pre-HE programmes, vocational programmes, or restitution programmes (e.g. GCSE resits). Market segmentation requires detailed understanding of the nature of the market and can be taken to considerable lengths. Readers are referred to Kotler and Fox (1995) for further development of these ideas.

In the context of market segmentation, organisations can identify the market(s) they wish to operate in. Three broad target market strategies can be identified (Kotler, 1991) for an organisation:

1. An *undifferentiated strategy*, in which the school or college will seek to satisfy the needs of all consumers in all segments of the market.
2. A *differentiated strategy*, in which the school or college identifies a number of specific segments of the market that it wishes to operate in. This might involve specialisation in specific programmes (e.g. business studies), specific markets (e.g. 16–19-year-olds) or specialist niches (e.g. furniture restoration).
3. A *concentrated strategy*, in which a single segment of the market is chosen for focus.

In post-compulsory education, colleges have substantial freedom to choose the markets they wish to target, although funding policies from central government agencies (e.g. FEFC) may steer choice of markets. For example, colleges in England and Wales are encouraged to target markets with programmes providing vocational qualifications in support of the government's National Education and Training Targets (NACETT, 1990) by a funding policy which provides higher levels of funding for such programmes. Pieda (1996) provide a number of examples of target market strategy in this phase, including:

- a sixth form college (Pieda, 1996, p. 21), competing in its borough with two traditional FE colleges, which has targeted 16–19-year-olds seeking two-year academic courses (A-levels) or one-year courses (GCSE resits, intermediate GNVQs), and adult learners seeking to join such programmes alongside 16–19-year-olds
- a general FE college (Pieda, 1996, p. 17), in a highly competitive urban market, targeting all 16–19-year-old provision, both academic and vocational, on its side of the city, a specialism in science programmes, for which it has a regional target market, and a specialism in printing for which it has a national target market.

In schools, the choice of strategy is more constrained, for most state schools must deliver commonly-agreed or statutorily imposed curricula. However, where this does not dictate 100 per cent of the curriculum there is some potential for differentiation, and hence the development of target market strategy. Murgatroyd and Morgan (1993) have identified four generic marketing strategies that schools might adopt:

1. a *broad, open strategy*, where the school seeks to satisfy the educational needs of all the pupils in its locality (in Kotler's terms this is an undifferentiated strategy)
2. an *enhanced open strategy*, in which there is additional peripheral provision which is distinctive to the school, such as the provision of a third foreign language or overseas field trips in geography
3. a *basic niche strategy*, in which the school emphasises a particular area of expertise within the broad curriculum, such as a strong IT emphasis, or excellence in art
4. an *enhanced niche strategy*, in which the school makes these strengths a primary focus of the school; for example, in designation as a technology college, or sport-focused school.

A number of patterns of strategic choice can be identified in the research on school external relations. The notion of serving a small local community is a characteristic of most primary schools (Hardie, 1991) and a focus on a broad open strategy predominates. Grove Primary School (see Chapter 3) illustrates this approach with a clear view from the headteacher that the school serves the whole of the local community. Most secondary schools, however, have always possessed some degree of differentiation (Gewirtz, Ball and Bowe, 1995), with many choosing to stress the comprehensiveness of their provision, while adopting an enhanced open strategy or a basic niche strategy. In such circumstances the emphasis on the 'non-standard' component of the strategy is highly variable, with some schools emphasising particular strengths in their promotional activities, while others see excellence in some areas detracting from the comprehensive philosophy of the school. Foskett (1995) shows how, for example, Castle School, an 11–16 mixed comprehensive school in central southern England, promotes its distinctiveness in terms of excellence in languages, while neighbouring Downsview School emphasises its achievements across the ability range, despite its excellence in science and mathematics.

Competitive positioning strategy involves identifying the distinctive features of the school or college which distinguish it from competitors operating in the same market. Diversity between providers is present even in strongly centrally planned education systems, and each school or college can identify a *diversity profile* against each of the factors identified below, choosing a negative or positive stance on each, to provide its competitive position:

- structural diversity (e.g. state or independent institution)
- curricular diversity (e.g. with specific enhancements or specialisms within the curriculum)
- style diversity (e.g. emphasising particular approaches to learning or discipline)
- religious/philosophical diversity (e.g. faith-based schools or colleges)
- gender
- age range diversity (e.g. 11–16, 11–18)
- ability range diversity (e.g. selection by ability, or internal setting or streaming)
- quality diversity (e.g. either a focus on absolute achievement, or on 'value added', or on quality related to the operation of the school as a community)
- price diversity (e.g. expressed in direct costs such as course fees, indirect associated costs such as transport costs, or non-monetary costs such as entry grades).

Most schools emphasise the virtues of their inherited diversity characteristics such as structure, gender and age range, then adopt a competitive position based on quality diversity (James and Phillips, 1995; Glatter, Woods and Bagley, 1996; Foskett, 1998). Independent schools also emphasise style diversity or ability range diversity, together with price diversity, whether monetary or non-monetary price based. In further education, particular emphasis is placed on curriculum, style and quality diversity, as illustrated by contrasts between, for example, a grammar school sixth form, a sixth form college and a general FE College, all providing A level programmes. Greenstreet Community School (see Chapter 3) has chosen to emphasise its curricular diversity, with a focus on sport, music, literacy and vocational programmes for 14–16-year-olds, and its achievement diversity with an emphasis on value added for traditionally under-performing groups of pupils. Lowlands College (see Chapter 3) emphasises its style diversity (as an 'adult' community) and its curricular diversity with its focus on engineering programmes and IT.

Marketing mix strategy represents the specific combination of characteristics that the institution presents to potential customers. It is characterised in business settings by the notion of the four Ps:

- *Product* – the particular features of the product or service that is being offered, both in relation to specific course or programme content and the wider components of the education or training experience and its long-term benefits
- *Place* – the location of delivery of the service
- *Price* – the 'price' (in monetary or other terms) demanded for the product or service
- *Promotion* – the promotional strategies selected to present the product or service (e.g. advertising, or direct mail).

This has been extended to five Ps in relation to service sector marketing (Cowell, 1984) by the addition of:

- *People* – the staff delivering the service, e.g. teachers and support staff.

Kotler and Fox (1995) have further extended this idea to seven Ps in the context of education marketing by adding:

- *Process* – the manner and style in which operational processes such as teaching, administration and pupil/student support are conducted
- *Physical facilities* – the nature of the facilities for teaching (e.g. classrooms), student support (e.g. IT facilities) and extra-curricular activities (e.g. common rooms, sports facilities).

While it is rare to find schools and colleges explicitly conceptualising their marketing mix (James and Phillips, 1995; Foskett and Hesketh, 1997), except in FE colleges in highly competitive markets, analysis of case studies shows its implicit presence. Figure 14.1 shows the key features of the marketing mix in relation to the three case study institutions examined in Chapter 3.

The development and conceptualisation of the three components of strategy outlined here represents the creation of a framework for managing all external relations, for it delimits and describes the nature of the organisation. Although relationship-based external relations and public

Element of Marketing Mix	Grove Primary School	Greenstreet Community School	Lowlands College
Product	Quality general primary education Excellent results	Quality general secondary education. Emphasis on literacy, special needs and value added	Vocational focus especially engineering and business links
Place	Compact village school, new classroom	Attractive campus, heart of the community	Convenient location for city centre access
Price	Low transport costs No school fees	Low transport costs	Low entry grades
Promotion	Word-of-mouth Proactive head Media coverage	Word-of-mouth, use of facilities by primary schools. Proactive head	Prospectus, open days Business links Media coverage
People	Head's welcoming personality	Quality of teaching and support staff. Staff expertise	Professional experience and staff expertise
Process	Quality of teaching and learning demonstrated by Ofsted report and word-of-mouth	Quality of teaching and learning demonstrated by Ofsted report and media coverage	Quality of teaching and learning as shown by FEFC Inspection Report
Physical Facilities	Spacious classrooms, attractive village location	Excellent IT, attractive campus, good sports, drama and music facilities	State of the art IT, engineering and conference facilities

Figure 14.1. Marketing mix of three case study schools/colleges

accountability external relations have a secondary rather than primary focus on 'recruitment', the institutional character defined in the three strategic steps underpins those external relations too. In relation to external inspection for quality assurance purposes, for example, each of the components of the marketing mix and the diversity profile will be an area of focus for inspectors. Similarly, the clarity of the institution's market position will be important in framing its role as a political player or as a community partner (see Figure 3.1). The design and development of a successful media relations programme for a school or college must be driven by what the institution seeks to gain from press and radio coverage. If the strategic position of the institution has been established, the messages in media coverage can be designed to reinforce that position.

An important extension of such market strategisation is the centrality of *institutional identity* in providing a tangible expression of the school or college. Olins (1989) describes the nature and importance of institutional identity:

> In order to be effective every organisation needs a clear sense of purpose that people within it understand. They also need a strong sense of belong-

ing. Purpose and belonging are the two facets of identity. Every organisation is unique, and its identity must spring from the organisation's own roots, its personality, its strengths and weaknesses. . . . The identity of the organisation must be so clear that it becomes the yardstick against which its products, behaviour and actions are measured. This means that the identity cannot simply be a slogan, a collection of phrases; it must be visible, tangible and all-embracing.

(Olins, 1989, p. 7)

Institutional identity is reflected for a school or college, therefore, in the educational service it provides, the nature of the school/college environment, its visual identity expressed through communication technology (letterheads, logos, letter styles) and in its internal and external behaviour and relationships. It is the 'image the institution would like to have and to present to its various internal and external audiences (and) will be the creative product of a planning process . . . designed to support and facilitate the achievement of the organisation's goals' (Foskett, 1992, p. 161). Its creation is intimately linked to market strategisation, and the identity must reflect and reinforce the institution's market position and marketing mix (Kotler and Fox, 1995). Foskett (1992) has suggested a process model for the development of an institutional identity comprising:

1. an identity audit
2. comparative identity analysis to examine the identity of competitors and of institutions that the school or college might wish to emulate
3. internal consultation with the school or college's key stakeholders
4. design
5. proposal, presentation and consultation
6. implementation
7. monitoring and evaluation.

The model of strategic planning and positioning considered here represents the first stage of the rational planning model outlined earlier. It provides a 'driver' for the day-to-day management of communications processes. It is these operational processes which are considered in the following section, and which constitute stages 2–7 in the planning model.

PLANNING AND MANAGING COMMUNICATIONS PROCESSES

Much of marketing activity is centred around planning and managing communications processes. Educators have extensive experience of communication as a key 'tool of the trade', yet two issues can be identified in the delivery and management of marketing communications. Firstly, until recently relatively little attention has been paid to considering the *total* communication process (Cannon, 1988) as educational managers have concentrated their operational activities on single specific areas of activity such as advertising, media relations and selling, rather than developing an integrated communication process that relates to the institution's aims and mission. Communications management has been piecemeal, ad hoc and 'bolt-on' to other activities. Secondly, an effective communication programme requires strong management and professional skills and cannot be left to the chance availability of appropriate skills within the staff. The development of communication skills has not featured strongly in in-service training even for headteachers and deputies, and the integration of effective practice from marketing communication professional expertise is still not common. Prejudices about the motives, values and expertise from either side of the business/education divide have signally prevented both professional educational managers and business communication professionals learning from each other.

Channels of communication between organisations and their markets, or what might be termed 'marketing communications', can be divided broadly into two areas, although each works synergistically with the other:

1. *Sales communications* including advertising, promotional literature, prospectuses, web sites, events, visits and exhibitions.
2. *Relationship communications* including personal professional communications, media relations (relationships with local media and long-term media relations), the establishment of alumni associations, newsletters and 'front-of-house' communications.

Sales communications

In an educational context the primary purpose of *sales communications* is the recruitment of pupils or students. The choice of communication methods will be designed to lead choosers through the four stages of information need described by the acronym AIDA:

- Gaining **A**ttention, perhaps through advertising or through the development of positive media coverage over a period of time. For primary schools serving a well-established and discrete community such communications are less important than for an FE college seeking to break into new market segments.
- Creating **I**nterest amongst potential consumers in what the school or college can offer. This might involve the use of brief 'flyers' which can provide more information about the institution and its distinctive characteristics, or be developed by the continuing use of media coverage.
- Creating **D**esire to enrol in the school or college, through the use of

effective prospectuses, open days, visits to 'feeder institutions' by staff, or guided tours of the school for parents.
- Stimulating Action to enrol by providing enrolment support, following up enquiries and mailed information, and timing events, media coverage or further advertising to coincide with enrolment deadlines.

The range of sales communications methods available is extensive (Cannon, 1988; Devlin and Knight, 1992), and the technology and processes involved in each are well-documented elsewhere in a wide range of guides on the practice of marketing, both in generic terms (e.g. Lancaster and Massingham, 1988) and specifically in the context of education (for schools, for example, see Devlin and Knight, 1992; Evans, 1995; for FE/HE see Davies and Scribbins, 1985; FEFC/NAO, 1997). In developing the use of such approaches, a number of important strategic and tactical management issues should be considered:

- The communications should represent and reflect the vision and mission of the institution, its ethos and its competitive positioning strategy.
- The communications should be designed to reach the target audiences in the chosen market segments.
- The 'form' of the communication should ensure that, firstly, it takes the customer's view, secondly, that it delivers sales messages, and thirdly, that the emphasis is on benefits not characteristics (Evans, 1995).
- The communications should be developed on the basis of a detailed understanding of the decision-making processes of those involved in choosing. Research on decision-making in education and training markets has focused strongly on the issue of parental choice of schools at age 11 (e.g. Coldron and Boulton, 1991; Carroll and Walford, 1997), and to a lesser extent on choice at 16 (e.g. Foskett and Hesketh, 1996, 1997; Keys and Maychell, 1998), and 18 (Roberts and Allen, 1996). This research has shown the complexity and extended timescale of the choice process, the contrasts in engagement with the choice process between parents and young people in different cultural, economic and social settings, and the relative influence of alternative sales media (e.g. whether the prospectus is more influential than the open day) and messages (e.g. emphasising examination results or attitudes to pupil behaviour) in the choice process. Figure 14.2 summarises some of the key findings of research into pupil and student choice.
- The communication process should be planned with careful attention to timing throughout the school and college annual cycle, so that messages reach choosers at key times in their decision-making with the sort of information they need. The importance of using annual sales communication planners is stressed by Keen and Greenall (1987) and Devlin and Knight (1992).

When are choices made? The choice process is long term, with the gradual emergence of choice aspirations over many years. Choice at 16 or 18 of FE or HE begins to emerge in primary school, and can be influenced substantially by early contact with FE and HE institutions. Choice ambitions at 11 often shape choice of primary school for 4/5-year-olds.

How does the choice process work? The choice is made by 'parent + pupil', with the balance of influence between them changing with age. Arriving at a 'choice' is a long process of working and re-working ideas, absorbing new information, interacting with friends, family, teachers and others, and responding to 'the unpredictable pattern of turning points and routines that make up the life course' (Hodkinson and Sparkes, 1997, p. 33).

Who engages with choice? 'Active choosers' can be distinguished from 'passive choosers'. Active choosers (5–30 per cent of parents) seek out information on a range of choices, passive choosers make 'choices' by default. While active choosers are more likely to be middle class parents/young people with 'cultural capital', there is no simple relationship between class, ethnicity and 'active choice'.

Which sales communications have most impact? 'Word-of-mouth' is the most important influence on choice at all ages and stages of the AIDA process. For schools the community grapevine supported by a high positive profile in the media and the school's engagement with the community, raises awareness and cultivates interest. This is fed substantially by present and past students and their parents. Advertising, whether through direct mail, poster campaigns or media adverts, only influences this for post-16 colleges, which have less presence in 'local communities'. The conversion of 'interest' to 'desire' and 'action' is most influenced by the direct communication with choosers that occurs through open days, personal attention to visiting parents, and visits by teachers to feeder schools. Prospectuses have a supportive role, in that the existence of a well-presented prospectus is essential before choosers will consider a school or college, but their content serves only to confirm the availability of courses or facilities. They do not persuade choosers.

Who has most impact on choice? At all stages, parents, teachers and careers teachers have most influence. The explicit influence of parents is large in choice at 5 and 11 – by 16 and 18 it is implicit, and often denied by students. Careers teachers are a major influence in choice at 16 and 18. Other teachers are very important in forming perceptions and opinions over long periods. The influence of media personalities on general perceptions of particular education or training pathways is very significant.

What factors are important in choice? In the choice of primary and secondary schools, of superordinate importance are 'security' factors – a caring ethos, safety in travelling to school, and the school's reputation for 'bullying'. Linked strongly to this is the manner of teachers and the headteacher, with an emphasis on a welcoming, child-friendly but highly professional approach. Second come 'achievement' and 'output' factors, dominated by 'results' and performance in entry to the subsequent stage of education. Next in importance are organisational factors, such as religious affiliation, or single sex character, and facilities factors, such as the quality of buildings, environment and equipment. In choice of FE, the most important factors are 'achievement reputation'; the availability of specific courses or course combinations; the 'inertia' factors of a desire to stay in the same institution post-16 as pre-16 and, where this is not possible, proximity and 'security' factors; and the impression gained from visits, either to the institution or by staff from the college or school.

Figure 14.2. School and college choice – a summary of research evidence

- Choice of sales communication methods should be developed in the context of financial planning linked to the school or college development plan. Foskett (1998) has shown how most schools finance their sales communications through a process of 'remainder budgeting' or 'opportunity budgeting' (i.e. allocating what is left after all other commitments, or drawing funds from other budget headings if a sales need arises) rather than through 'planned budgeting'.
- Measuring the impact of sales communications is important to support future planning and development (Kotler and Fox, 1995). Identifying how and why enquirers and enrollers have come to the institution is a key, yet relatively simple, data collection exercise.

Developing and managing effective sales communications raises a range of resource management and ethical issues for schools and colleges. While in 'for-profit' organisations marketing may take up to 25 per cent of the total organisational budget, in colleges this is more typically 1–5 per cent, and in schools is usually less than 1 per cent. While good sales communications can be achieved with low expenditure but large inputs of time resource (for example, with the headteacher showing visiting parents round the school), of importance is the measurement of cost-benefit and an awareness of value for money. Both require the monitoring of impact against objectives for each sales communication activity.

In both schools and FE the early 1990s saw the rapid growth of the use of sales communication techniques. A concern about ethical issues relating to marketing practice (Chonko, 1995) was a dominant theme in professional debate (e.g. NAHT, 1990; Gray, 1991), particularly in relation to:

- *Advertising standards* – a concern that communications should be legal, decent, honest and truthful. A key ethical issue facing marketing professionals is how far to go in attempting to be persuasive, since pressure and persuasion can lead to deceptive practices. The importance of a truthful and honest approach to advertising has been demonstrated by Hemsley-Brown (1996) where new entrants to a post-16 college quoted the college's advertising messages as post hoc justification of their choice, even where the message was patently untrue. The potential for creating consumer dissatisfaction through misleading information is clearly very large! Figure 14.3 shows the truth/deception continuum showing degrees of truth and untruth in sales communication.
- *Comparative promotion* – a concern about schools or colleges denigrating competitors.
- *Professional objectivity* – a concern that the key priority in advice to parents and pupils should be *their* needs, not the organisation's recruitment need.
- *Resource misdirection* – a concern that expenditure on promotion

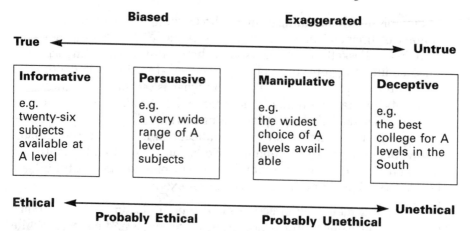

Figure 14.3. Truth and deception in sales communications

would divert valuable resources from the education process.

- *Declining collegiality* – a concern that competition would reduce opportunities for sharing professional educational practice between schools and colleges.

The development of codes of marketing practice by many professional bodies in education (e.g. NAHT, 1990) has helped to reduce concerns about some of these issues. In addition, in some localities shared approaches to marketing have been established (Evans, 1995), where the focus is on promoting local education rather than individual schools, or agreements between schools and colleges on the way in which examination results are released to the media (Foskett, 1995) have been operated by headteachers and principals. Nevertheless, concerns about ethical issues remain in some highly competitive markets – Gewirtz, Ball and Bowe (1995) and Woods, Glatter and Bagley (1998) provide examples of schools concerned about the loss of local collegiality and the marketing practices of competitors, while Nicholls (1994) raises concerns about the practice of schools with sixth forms limiting access for their pupils to information from other post-16 institutions.

Relationship communications

Kotler and Fox (1995) indicate that sales communications are not only about attracting new 'customers', but are also about gaining support for current activities, keeping people who already know the institution up-to-date, and helping to present an overall professional image in a local, national or even international arena. There is, therefore, substantial overlap with the aims of relationship communications, which have emerged as a focus during the last decade. From this perspective marketing is viewed as developing relationships, networks and interaction and provides a framework for managing long-term relationships with external audiences – what has been labelled 'relationship marketing' (Grönroos, 1997). Paradoxically, just as schools and other public services were being urged to copy private sector marketing approaches, some of the basic concepts of marketing were being challenged. Grönroos (1997) maintains that establishing relationships with customers can be divided into two parts: attracting the customers and building relationships with customers, in both of which a key element is trust. Establishing such long-term relationships with stakeholders has been discussed in greater detail by Payne and Ballantyne (1991) and can be related to education in the following ways:

- *Customer markets.* This means building links with feeder institutions by, for example, applying consistent entry procedures and sustaining delivery of quality educational programmes over a long period (Kinnell and MacDougall, 1997).
- *Referral markets.* Market-orientated organisations pay close attention to recent customers – with very good reason (Keen and Greenall, 1987). Advocates and alumni have often proved themselves to be good allies who help to promote the institution.
- *Supplier markets.* Building trust between the institution and its suppliers, including the local business community. The need to communicate with other sections of the local community and develop relations with other stakeholders requires some external marketing activities. In a primary school, for example, these may be integrated into internal relationships by involving parents (Stokes, 1996).
- *Employee markets.* It is also helpful to build relationships with staff in the institution, including ancillary and teaching staff. Together with alumni and current students, staff make a considerable contribution towards 'word-of-mouth' promotion. Relationship marketing, therefore, normally pays great attention to human resource management.
- *Influencer markets.* Institutions may benefit from developing relationships with government through the DfEE, the LEA, TECs, the FEFC and HEFC and other funding bodies, in order to influence policy (Kinnell and MacDougall, 1997).
- *Press and media markets.* A well-managed and systematic approach to media relations can promote a school or college, and an image of education generally, to a very wide audience. This relies on developing and building good relationships with local and national newspapers, radio and television (Davies and Scribbins, 1985).

At the heart of developing these effective relationships for schools and colleges lie three key issues – the pursuit and monitoring of quality in all aspects of the delivery of the education and training experience of pupils/students; the management of the interface between the institution and its stakeholders; and the management of relationships with the media.

Building quality management into the heart of the school or college is central to relationship communications. Quality Assurance (QA) systems such as the Ofsted Framework for Inspection of Schools, or external examination requirements, contribute to perceptions of quality, but in-house QA in relation to the establishment of, for example, behaviour management policies, ability grouping or reporting procedures is also important. In relation to internal audiences, too, the establishment of, for example, *Investors in People* accreditation provides a QA system that contributes to a key relationship for the organisation.

The second issue, that of the interface with external bodies, relates to 'front-of-house' activities and communications by all members of the institution with the community. Consistency, clarity, concern, co-operation and confidence (the five Cs) are key components of this interface, and provide direct communication of the school or college's aims and ethos. Managing their development within staff may be an issue of staff development and training – however, managing their development in pupils and students is an issue of managing the delivery of a quality education and training experience over long periods of time.

The third issue is that of media relations, which provide an important component in the development of image and perception in the community but which are less controllable for any organisation. Reader (1992) indicates the importance of establishing relationships with all the local media to ensure a high profile for the school or college and a more sympathetic response when 'bad news' emerges. Reader (1997) suggests that such a media relations strategy should comprise:

- clarifying the message the school or college wishes media relations to convey, linked tightly to the institution's mission
- developing a two-way relationship between the media and the institution to meet the needs of both sides
- ensuring that relevant individuals within the school or college are apprised of their role in the event of media attention (for example, the chair of governors, or the head/principal)
- establishing a clear structure for managing both proactive and reactive media relations
- evaluating the impact of media attention, to learn the lessons and adapt policy accordingly.

Managing relationship communications raises resource and ethical issues in the same way that managing sales communications does. However, since relationships are more firmly rooted in the educational processes of schools and colleges, the challenges for managers may be seen to have clear educational benefits rather than simply financial benefits emanating from increased recruitment.

CONCLUSION

This chapter has discussed how schools and colleges can communicate with their external environments in support of the aims of the institution, and has highlighted the importance of strategic planning, management and evaluation in communicating the organisation effectively. Within any organisation the external communications strategy needs to be driven by the institution's relationship with external and internal markets. In the education system the choice of communications strategy may be limited by resources, especially in the compulsory sector, but there is, nonetheless, considerable potential for developing a relationship marketing approach to communication with markets based on one of the generic marketing strategies outlined in this chapter. In this way external communications can be rooted in the educational aims and ethos of the school or college, as it seeks to play a significant, formative and essential role as a service to the community it serves. Against such a model, the perspective of Keen and Greenall (1987) is more acceptable than it might have appeared when first written:

> Public relations activity is in no sense hostile to the (college or school) ideal, but an ethical endeavour wholly compatible with the pursuit and dissemination of truth.
>
> (Keen and Greenall, 1987, p. 5)

REFERENCES

Cannon, T. (1988) *Basic Marketing: Principles and Practice*, 2nd edition, London: Holt, Rinehart and Winston.

Carroll, S. and Walford, G. (1997) Parents' response to the school quasi-market, *Research Papers in Education*, Vol. 12, no. 1, pp. 3–26.

Chonko, L. B. (1995) *Ethical Decision Making in Marketing*, London: Sage Publications.

Coldron, J. and Boulton, P. (1991) Happiness as a criterion of parents' choice of school, *Journal of Education Policy*, Vol. 6, no. 2, pp. 169–78.

Cowell, D. (1984) *The Marketing of Services*, Oxford: Butterworth-Heinemann.

Davies, P. and Scribbins, K. (1985) *Marketing Further and Higher Education*, York: Longman for FEU (Further Education Unit).

Devlin, T. and Knight, B. (1992) *Public Relations and Marketing for Schools*, London: Longman School Management Resources.

Evans, I. (1995) *Marketing for Schools*, London: Cassell.

FEFC (Further Education Funding Council)/NAO) (1997) *Marketing in Further Education – A Good Practice Guide*, Coventry: FEFC.

Foskett, N. H. (1992) Institutional identity in the school context, in N. H. Foskett (ed.) *Managing External Relations in Schools: A Practical Guide*, London: Routledge.

Foskett, N. H. (1995) Marketing, management and schools: a study of a developing marketing culture in schools. Unpublished PhD thesis, University of Southampton.

Foskett, N. H. (1998) Linking marketing to strategy, in D. Middlewood and J. Lumby (eds.) *Strategic Management in Schools and Colleges*, London: Paul Chapman.

Foskett, N. H. and Hesketh, A. J. (1996) *Student Decision-making and the Post-16 Market Place*, Leeds: Heist/CREM Publications.

Foskett, N. H. and Hesketh, A. J. (1997) Constructing choice in contiguous and parallel markets: institutional and school-leavers' responses to the new post-16 marketplace, *Oxford Review of Education*, Vol. 23, no. 2, pp. 299–330.

Gewirtz, S., Ball, S. J. and Bowe, R. (1995) *Markets, Choice and Equity in Education*, Buckingham: Open University Press.

Glatter, R., Woods, P. and Bagley, C. (eds.) (1996) *Choice and Diversity in Schooling: Perspectives and Prospects*, London: Routledge.

Gray, L. (1991) *Marketing Education*, Buckingham: Open University Press.

Grönroos, C. (1997) From marketing mix to relationship marketing – towards a paradigm shift in marketing, *Management Decision*, Vol. 35, no. 4, pp. 322–339.

Hanson, E. M. and Henry, W. (1992) Strategic marketing for educational systems, *School Organisation*, Vol. 12, no. 3, pp. 255–67.

Hardie, B. (1991) *Marketing the Primary School*, Plymouth: Northcote House.

Hemsley-Brown, J. V. (1996) Marketing post-16 colleges: a qualitative and quantitative study of pupils' choice of post-sixteen institution. Unpublished PhD thesis, University of Southampton.

Hodkinson, P. and Sparkes, A. (1997) Careership: a sociological theory of career decision-making, *British Journal of Sociology of Education*, Vol. 10, no. 2, pp. 30–49.

James, C. and Phillips, P. (1995) The practice of educational marketing in schools, *Educational Management and Administration*, Vol. 23, no. 2, pp. 75–88.

Keen, C. and Greenall, J. (1987) *Public Relations Management in Colleges, Polytechnics and Universities*, Banbury: Heist Publications.

Keys, W. and Maychell, K. (1998) *Leaving at 16 and Staying On: Studies of Young People's Decisions about School Sixth Forms, Sixth Form Colleges and Colleges of Further Education*, Slough: NFER.

Kinnell, M. and MacDougall, J. (1997) *Marketing in the Not-for-Profit Sector*, Oxford: Butterworth-Heinemann.

Kotler, P. (1991) *The Principles of Marketing*, 4th edition, Englewood Cliffs: Prentice-Hall.

Kotler, P. and Fox, K. F. A. (1995) *Strategic Marketing for Educational Institutions*, 2nd edition, London: Prentice-Hall.

Lancaster, G. and Massingham, L. (1992) *Essentials of Marketing*, London: McGraw-Hill.

Levacic, R. (1995) *Financial Management in Schools*, Buckingham: Open University Press.

Middlewood, D. (1998) Strategic management in education: an overview, in D. Middlewood and J. Lumby (eds.) *Strategic Management in Schools and Colleges*, London: Paul Chapman.

Murgatroyd, S. and Morgan, C. (1993) *Total Quality Management and the School*, Buckingham: Open University Press.

NACETT (National Advisory Council for Education and Training Targets) (1990)

National Targets for Education and Training, London: HMSO.

NAHT (National Association of Head Teachers) (1990) *The Marketing of Schools*, Haywards Heath: NAHT.

Nicholls, A. (1994) *Schools and Colleges: Collaborators or Competitors in Education?* Report for LASER Further Education Council.

Olins, W. (1989) *Corporate Identity: Making a Business Strategy Visible Through Design*, London: Thames Hudson.

Payne, C. M. and Ballantyne, D. (1991) *Relationship Marketing*, Oxford: Butterworth-Heinemann.

Pieda (1996) *Marketing Case Studies in Further Education Colleges*, Manchester: Pieda, for DfEE.

Reader, P. (1992) Liaising with the media, in N. H. Foskett (ed.) *Managing External Relations in Schools*, London: Routledge.

Reader, P. (1997) Dealing with the media: developing a strategy. Unpublished briefing paper, Public Affairs Department, University of Southampton.

Roberts, D. and Allen, A. (1996) *Year 12 Students' Perceptions of Higher Education*, Leeds: Heist.

Stokes, D. (1996) Relationship marketing in primary schools, in N. H. Foskett (ed.) *Markets in Education: Policy, Process and Practice*, Vol. 1, Southampton: CREM.

West-Burnham, J. (1994) Strategy, policy and planning, in T. Bush and J. West-Burnham (eds.) *The Principles of Educational Management*, Harlow: Longman.

Woods, P., Glatter, R. and Bagley, C. (1998) *School Choice and Competition: Markets in the Public Interest?* London: Routledge.

INDEX